Hidden Chicano Cinema

For the Center
of the Southwest
Students and
community -

Regards,

[signature]

Sept. 9, 2016

LATINIDAD
Transnational Cultures in the United States

This series publishes books that deepen and expand our knowledge and understanding of the various Latina/o populations in the United States in the context of their transnational relationships with cultures of the broader Americas. The focus is on the history and analysis of Latino cultural systems and practices in national and transnational spheres of influence from the nineteenth century to the present. The series is open to scholarship in political science, economics, anthropology, linguistics, history, cinema and television, literary and cultural studies, and popular culture and encourages interdisciplinary approaches, methods, and theories. The series grew out of discussions with faculty at the School of Transborder Studies at Arizona State University, where an interdisciplinary emphasis is being placed on transborder and transnational dynamics.

Carlos Velez-Ibañez, Series Editor, School of Transborder Studies

Rodolfo F. Acuña, *In the Trenches of Academe: The Making of Chicana/o Studies*

Adriana Cruz-Manjarrez, *Zapotecs on the Move: Cultural, Social, and Political Processes in Transnational Perspective*

Marivel T. Danielson, *Homecoming Queers: Desire and Difference in Chicana Latina Cultural Production*

Rudy P. Guevarra Jr., *Becoming Mexipino: Multiethnic Identities and Communities in San Diego*

Lisa Jarvinen, *The Rise of Spanish-Language Filmmaking: Out from Hollywood's Shadow, 1929–1939*

Regina M. Marchi, *Day of the Dead in the USA: The Migration and Transformation of a Cultural Phenomenon*

Marci R. McMahon, *Domestic Negotiations: Gender, Nation, and Self-Fashioning in U.S. Mexicana and Chicana Literature and Art*

A. Gabriel Meléndez, *Hidden Chicano Cinema: Film Dramas in the Borderlands*

Priscilla Peña Ovalle, *Dance and the Hollywood Latina: Race, Sex, and Stardom*

Luis F. B. Plascencia, *Disenchanting Citizenship: Mexican Migrants and the Boundaries of Belonging*

Maya Socolovsky, *Troubling Nationhood in U.S. Latina Literature: Explorations of Place and Belonging*

Hidden Chicano Cinema

Film Dramas in the Borderlands

A. GABRIEL MELÉNDEZ

RUTGERS UNIVERSITY PRESS

NEW BRUNSWICK, NEW JERSEY, AND LONDON

LIBRARY OF CONGRESS CATALOGING-IN-PUBLICATION DATA

Meléndez, A. Gabriel (Anthony Gabriel).
    Hidden Chicano cinema : film dramas in the borderlands / A. Gabriel
Meléndez.
        pages cm. — (Latinidad: transnational cultures in the United States)
    Includes bibliographical references and index.
    ISBN 978–0–8135–6107–3 (hardcover : alk. paper) — ISBN 978–0–8135–6106–6
(pbk. : alk. paper) — ISBN 978–0–8135–6108–0 (e-book) (print)
    1. Mexican Americans in motion pictures. 2. Mexican-American Border
Region—In motion pictures. I. Title.
    PN1995.9.M49M46 2013
    791.43'65296872073—dc23   2012038528

A British Cataloging-in-Publication record for this book is available
from the British Library.

Visit our website: http://rutgerspress.rutgers.edu

Manufactured in the United States of America

CONTENTS

PREFACE AND ACKNOWLEDGMENTS

Hidden Chicano Cinema addresses a series of "film moments" that are at once a set of cultural encounters between filmmakers, film as a technology, and the people of the communities that became the subjects for various film depictions. Thus, the "film drama" I reference in the subtitle also refers to "the drama of filmmaking," something which is as much about what happens onscreen and as what happens offscreen. Like first impressions, these film encounters often found Borderlands residents and filmmakers eyeing each other from opposite sides of the camera lens. Vexed by mutual scrutiny and laden with the distrust and tension, these moments surged with dramatic intensity kindled by the politics and poetics of "shooting" the Southwest.

The book is composed of eight chapters. The first three concern themselves with the advent of still photography and early film in New Mexico during a period when the most impermeable lines of misunderstanding mark the earliest encounters of Borderlands residents with the camera. The inverse is also true, as these chapters also account for the awe photographers and filmmakers experienced in their determination to film what they considered a "foreign locale" within the boundaries of the United States. Chapters 4 and 5 center on representations of Chicanos in the United States during the Cold War period, a time when older representations gave way to images invested with a greater degree of sociological realism. In chapters 6, 7, and 8, I look at several film encounters produced after the filmic turn in which Chicano/as took hold of the camera and returned their own gaze, giving expression to their creative voices as documentarians and filmmakers. As I argue in the final chapters, in doing so, emergent filmmakers have changed the nature of the more recent film moments and encounters.

I have come to learn that it is far easier to start a book on film than it is to bring it to a close—starting one might be as simple as going to the movies. As I write this, I have just become aware that the highest-selling and most widely known Chicano novel, *Bless Me, Ultima*, written by New Mexico native Rudolfo Anaya, has been turned into a film. I have seen the YouTube trailer, and premieres of the film are being planned for El Paso and Santa Fe. Without a doubt, if there ever were a film to include in my study, this would be the one. Following from my assertions about the nature of Borderlands film encounters, the screen version of *Bless Me, Ultima* is ripe for analysis. I can only hope that readers of my book will screen the film with eyes more fully attuned to the history that precedes it. For now, it must stand as the stellar example of just how difficult it is to close a book on film. But knowing that *Bless Me, Ultima* is now a film is a reward of its own, as I am assured that Borderlands narratives will continue to show up on the radar of filmmakers and film audiences, many of whom will want to know more about the "distant locale" depicted by recent and older films.

At times it's clear to me that this book really began with my earliest visits to the movies. It was a time when as far as I knew everyone referred to motion pictures as movies, never "films." I have a distant and vague recall of my parents taking me to see whatever new blockbusters made it to the Serf Theatre in Las Vegas, New Mexico, in the early 1960s. I remember seeing *The Ten Commandments, Ben Hur, Giant*, and a huge number of *charro* movies featuring Antonio Aguilar and Flor Sylvester, the Roy Rogers and Dale Evans of the Mexican screen. Despite this exposure to the blockbuster, I didn't choose to write a book about biblical Hollywood or about life in México—though surely these subjects made an impression on me. I find it a matter of continuing interest that I did take up the subject of Chicano/a portrayals on film, a point that turns me back to George Stevens's widescreen epic *Giant* (1956). What I remember about *Giant* is stepping out of a stuffy movie theater, walking down the sidewalk beside my parents, and having the vague feeling that I had just witnessed seeing some part of us—my parents, my neighbors, and my relatives—up on the screen. I wasn't connecting with Leslie Lynnton (Elizabeth Taylor), Bick Benedict (Rock Hudson), or Jett Rink (James Dean). The sensation I felt was rather from some yet unclear identification with the brown-skinned ranch people, the hired folk and the Mexican American neighbors that populated key scenes of the Texas ranch country in *Giant*. As best I recall, their speech and attitude reminded me of family and neighbors. Lacking the ability to analyze in any meaningful way what I had just seen, I carried out small bits of emotion onto the streets of our little one-theater town. In some sense, I have continued to search for other "third eye" film moments (to use Fatimah Rony's term) and to probe this question: What do the representations of Mexican Americans onscreen have to do with me and my community? In keeping with this starting point, my list of acknowledgments would have to begin with my parents, Santos and Adela V. Meléndez (both deceased), who both liked and distrusted the movies and gave me a healthy skepticism of popular culture. In addition, the actual writing of *Hidden Chicano Cinema* requires mention of a number of friends, colleagues, and family members who, knowingly or not, have helped this book take shape.

A good portion of the research for this book happened over the course of my most recent sabbatical leave. I am thankful to the Department of American Studies and the College of Arts and Sciences at the University of New Mexico for allowing me to take time away from the classroom for this project. Much of the credit for the book is owed to the Center for Regional Studies and its director, Dr. Tobías Durán. CRS provided me with a major research grant that made it possible for me to take an extended sabbatical in the first place. It was during this phase of research that I identified most of the early films and encounter stories that helped me to develop the methodological foundations of the study. I also was fortunate to have been able to attend the *Memoria, Voz y Patrimonio* conference on Latino/Hispanic Film, Print, and Sound Archives at UCLA, where I received enormous encouragement from the Chicano Studies Research Center and from its director, Chon A. Noriega. The late Yolanda Ritter (1947–2007), archivist and chief research librarian at CSRC, was a consummate professional who steered me straightaway to some of the most difficult-to-locate film sources. Over a period of several months I conducted interviews with numerous filmmakers and with participants in some of the films I discuss here. I wish to thank Gabriel Chávez, Moctesuma Esparza, Danny Lyon,

Paul Espinosa, and Federico Reade for their openness and the generosity of their remarks and insights.

In the years since my sabbatical, *Hidden Chicano Cinema* competed for my attention with other book projects (*Recovering the U.S. Hispanic Literary Heritage: Volume 6* [Arte Público, 2006], *Santa Fe Nativa* [University of New Mexico Press, 2010], and *The Writings of Eusebio Chacón* [University of New Mexico Press, 2012]) and with my administrative duties as chair of American Studies. My UNM colleagues Phillip Gonzales and Enrique Lamadrid read some early drafts of my manuscript and offered encouragement and ideas that enriched the process of writing. In continuing my search for archival material and lost footage, I had the help of a group of relentless archivists who handled my requests with patience; and to my delight and astonishment managed to retrieve the most elusive of items from their collections. I want to thank Marva Felchlin and Marylin Kim at the Autry National Center (Southwest Museum of the American Indian) in Los Angeles; Joseph Shemtov of the Rare Book Department of the Free Library of Philadelphia; and Jen Peck, archivist at the Center for Southwest Studies at Fort Lewis College in Durango, Colorado. In Santa Fe, archivists Al Regensberg, Samuel Cisneros, Felicia Luján, and Brian Graney at the New Mexico State Records Center and Archives increased the reach of my sources with their extensive knowledge of the state's early film archives. I thank Alberto Pulido at the University of San Diego for his counsel, help, and insight along the way and my colleague Miguel Gandert, a distinguished documentary photographer and director of the Interdisciplinary Film and Digital Media Program at UNM, for his assistance in helping to format the images used in the book.

I am indebted to Paul Espinosa and Marta Sánchez at the University of Arizona, whose intervention was decisive in getting the manuscript to Rutgers University Press, which has published a notable list of titles in film studies. I thank the editorial board of Rutgers University Press's Latinidad Series for adding my book to a series that is highly regarded for its excellent contributions to Latino/Chicano studies. I especially want to thank Leslie Mitchner, editor-in-chief at Rutgers, for her early support of the manuscript. Not only did Leslie move to get the project reviewed promptly, but her remarks have been among the most rewarding for me. Giving up a part of the Thanksgiving weekend in 2010 to read a full draft of the book, she wrote, "I do not know New Mexico well, but I did spend nearly a week there after the American Studies meeting in Albuquerque in 2008, mainly in the north. I was puzzled by much of what I saw and astonished by the poverty/beauty combination in places like Truchas. I wish I had read your manuscript *before* going." Even if the manuscript had not been accepted for publication, I would still retain the immense satisfaction of her comments, since putting readers in touch with northern New Mexico and the awe it has inspired in filmmakers is a major reason that I wrote the book. Leslie's co-workers, Lisa Boyajian and others whom I am just getting to know, have not missed a note regarding the details of publication and I thank them for their careful handling of the manuscript. In June 2012, I spent two weeks finishing the final version of the book on the Costa Blanca in Spain. This getaway was only possible with the help of Jaume Buigues i Vila, a good friend, a marvelous *dulziana* player, and one of the most knowledgeable historians of the *el levante español* (Valencia). Jaume located the perfect living quarters for me, a place where I could work unencumbered by the regime of the mundane.

Though the following individuals are named last, they are first in the order of helping to make this book a reality. First among them is my wife, Cristina Durán-Meléndez, who deserves special thanks for her unshakable honesty and for the wise way in which she has removed from me the guilt of the long hours I have spent away from her, writing in solitude. Our son, Camilo, a budding tenth-grade film buff, recently floored me by asking if he could read my chapter on *The Milagro Beanfield War*, a film to which he gave a thumbs up when he watched the DVD a few evenings ago. I shall, in the parlance of the young, "turn him on" to the chapter, even as it means I will certainly face my toughest critic. Finally, thanks to Alejandro, who is always looking out to make sure I don't burn out and who in Camilo's words is a cool brother because he works as an editing production manager at Industrial Light and Magic. Here's fair warning, Ale: we are coming out to visit you in San Francisco.

Hidden Chicano Cinema

1

Borderlands Cinema and the Proxemics of Hidden and Manifest Film Encounters

More than once I have recalled an exchange among graduate students in my seminar "Critical Regionalism: Discourses on the Southwest." Early one semester students brought forth their ideas regarding the ethnic and cultural make-up of the Southwest. From the discussion that ensued I learned that some newcomers to the region were working from the assumption that the American Southwest was a region populated by whites and American Indians, as in the notion of "playing cowboys and Indians." Indeed, this view seems to follow what recently has become the strongest projection of the region in the American cultural imagination. Other students held to a different view. One student in particular, a well-read, well-traveled white woman, asserted: "I've always thought of Mexicans when I think of the Southwest." As I came to learn, this student's view had not been colored by what she had read (she was forthcoming about having enrolled in the seminar to read and study the region's history and literature) but rather from what she had seen and learned from movies. Until then the idea had never dawned on me that segmented and mutually exclusive images of the Southwest lived in the public imagination. This differentiation of the region by race, ethnicity, and culture challenges the notion of "triculturalism" so often invoked by scholars of the Southwest Borderlands. For some it seems the Southwest is almost always "Indian Country," a land of desert cliff dwellers and mobile Apaches, a place renowned today for the "Indian Market" held each summer in Santa Fe. For others, the Southwest is a tableau upon which white cowboys yodeling over happy trails are ever threatened by desperados, bandidos, or "bad hombres" and are driven by their heated desire for hacienda maidens or loosely corseted cantina girls.

The discussion with my graduate students, and now this work, circles me back to an early piece of Chicano film scholarship by Carlos Cortes. In "Who Is María? What Is Juan? Dilemmas of Analyzing the Chicano Image in U.S. Feature Films," Cortes asserts that schools and formal learning are not uniformly synonymous with education (1992, 75). Cortes argues that we are constantly receiving information from a "societal curriculum" (the informal curriculum of family, peers, and the media) that has as much if not more to do with the formation of hegemonic knowledge than do schools and universities: "Movies teach. The celluloid curriculum teaches about myriad topics, including race, ethnicity, culture, and nationality" (1992, 75). Cortes arrives at several considerations that are pertinent to my study. He makes the case that movies provide information about race, ethnicity, culture, and foreignness, they organize information about these very notions, they influence values and attitudes, they help shape expectations of viewers, and they provide models for action (80–85). Equally useful are Cortes's observations on the role of moviemakers as textbook writers. Cortes notes that the intention and purpose of filmmakers varies widely and, he maintains, there is a tendency in films to employ ethnicity as a social signpost to mark difference and, in the worst of cases, to perform deviance. According to Cortes, some image-makers intentionally set out to create celluloid portraits of ethnic groups while others do so incidentally by inclusion or exclusion, or by adding ethnic traits to their film characters. Cortes divides U.S. feature films with racial and ethnic content into three categories: (1) films that use ethnic images to examine national character; (2) films that attempt to influence societal attitudes toward ethnic groups; and (3) films that simply take advantage of existing audience predispositions about ethnic groups (often ideas fueled by earlier movies) (86–87).

The Proxemics of Mexicans in Front of the Camera

The filming of the Borderlands has been a vast proposition, one that over the decades has involved the crafting of images of Indians, Mexicans, and Anglos, with representatives of each group casting about in a mix of inter-ethnic relationships set against the backdrop of the Southwest as either a mythic landscape or a foreign and wild place. From time to time some representations have been redeemed, though most remain dated fixtures of a multiethic regionalism that has come to be known as triculturalism in New Mexico or, as José Limón (1994) notes, as wars of maneuver and position in South Texas.

In legend, it was none other than Thomas Alva Edison himself who cranked out *Indian Day School* at the Isleta Pueblo in 1898, the first film shot in the Southwest Borderlands. In reality, it was Edison's underlings who shot several minutes of footage of Indian children marching around and around the old schoolhouse at Isleta Pueblo. Amazingly, the Edison Company and other pioneering film companies (Biograph, Lubin, Selig Polyscope) were filming the Southwest a mere two years after the first public screenings of the flickers in New York and Paris ("100 Years," 9), and these companies filmed many subjects. Thus, it can be said that filming the ethnic other is braided into the history of film itself, a process that began much earlier in the border states and can be dated to the arrival of photography in the West.

In this book, I wish to consider the image of Mexicans in U.S. films and photography. I write as a member of a particular social group that in the latter half of the nineteenth century became the object of a neo-colonial gaze magnified on celluloid by that handmaiden of modernity: cinema. To the adage "Know thyself" I append the cautionary question: how do film and photographic images reveal, trouble, or otherwise disturb what I or others are able to know about the self or about the people who share a cultural experience distinct from mainstream American society? One thing is clear: once caught in the colonial gaze of early image making, subalterns remain the victims of that past, for, as Cortes reminds us, "Celluloid images go on for decades as television reruns and on videocassette" (Cortes 1992, 88).

My forebears were cast onto film in ways they as subjects could not have imagined when, according to the New Mexico Film Office, "movie-makers fell prey to the intoxicating charms of New Mexico [at] the dawn of film history . . . cranking their cameras at the heart-thumping natural splendors, framing in their viewfinders the dazzling array of exotic native cultures" ("100 Years," 9). Like other scholars of color, I, too, cannot move away from the nagging sense of dislocation that comes from the kind of encounter described above, nor from the lingering effect of such encounters into the present.

Fatimah Tobing Rony calls the phenomenon of discovering that one's cultural inheritance has been the object of the filmic gaze an "experience of the third eye." For Rony the experience of the third eye comes as a momentary realization when one is seated in a darkened movie theater or standing before a certain photograph. These moments are about becoming conscious, sometimes painfully so, that one hails from a cultural community that has been under some kind of quasi-anthropological surveillance and scrutiny for quite some time. Ancestors and forebears, one discovers, have been spied upon for purposes not solely filmic and not solely incidental. It is the sense of having been studied that is particularly disconcerting to members of historically excluded populations; they are forced to confront visual representations which they recognize as themselves but which they also understand are not of their own making. "Most everybody has had this experience of the third eye," observes Rony. "But for a person of color growing up in the United States, the experience of viewing oneself as an object is profoundly formative" (1996, 4). Expanding on her point, Rony brings forth W.E.B. Du Bois's concept of "double-consciousness" to suggest that such moments are not only intimate, but powerful ruptures that rend the veil between the object of the filmic gaze and the intention that gets locked into the imagination of the consumer of the image. In Rony's words:

> The experience of the third eye suggests that Dubois's [sic] insight can be taken one step further—the racially charged glance can also induce one to see the very process which creates the internal splitting, to witness the conditions which give rise to the double consciousness described by Dubois. The veil allows for clarity of vision even as it marks the site of socially mediated self-alienation.
>
> The movie screen is another veil. We turn to the movies to find images of ourselves and find ourselves reflected in the eyes of others. The intended audience for dominant Hollywood cinema was, of course, the "American," white and middle-class. Not Hopi, Sumatran, or Dahomeyan or even African American, but "American." (4)

In her book *The Third Eye*, Rony convincingly demonstrates that "understanding how the 'native' is represented in film" requires a broad critical examination of the various "scientific" and popular forms of visual representation that have given form to "ethnographic cinema." For Rony, "ethnographic cinema" involves "the pervasive racialization of indigenous people in both popular and traditional scientific cinema" (1996, 8). She points out that "ethnographic film, at least in the popular imagination, is still by and large *racially* defined" (7). Rony calls attention to the ways in which early filmmaking has been complicit in representing the Other as savage, exotic, hypersexual, or quaint, that is, anything but real. I agree with Rony's assertion that "cinema is not only a technology, it is a social practice with conventions that profoundly shape its forms" (9). Like her, I find it necessary to broadly investigate the whole notion of "ethnographic cinema" and its constituent parts, as Rony suggests, accounting for "the broad and variegated field of cinema which situates indigenous people in a displaced temporal realm" (8). As in other parts of the globe, it is critical to investigate the broad spectrum of film genres and formats that constitute the early film archive of the Southwest. Such an undertaking must properly account for the gamut of film products made about the Borderlands, including scientific research films, educational films, colonial propaganda films, and commercial entertainment films (8). Rony notes that film studies have only recently begun to examine the construction of race in classic Hollywood cinema, and she alerts us to how fundamental to critical scholarship is the need to examine the links between ethnographic representations, popular media, and Hollywood's penchant for presenting the culture of non-Westerners as entertainment, spectacle, and pseudo-history.

Traveling among the Mexicans and Indians

The Southwest, a region acquired from Mexico in the nineteenth century and inhabited by widely different Native American groups and distinct castes of *mexicanos*, is perhaps the only part of the United States that was subjected to the visual scrutiny typical of Western imperial penetration in other parts of the world. Much of this scrutiny can be credited to the tribe Eliot Weinberger winsomely labels "the Camera People." Weinberger's description is parodic:

> There is a tribe, known as the ethnographic film-makers, who
> believe they are invisible. They enter a room where a feast is being

celebrated, or the sick cured, or the dead mourned, and though
weighted down with odd machines, entangled with wires, imagine
they are unnoticed—or at most, merely glanced at, quickly ignored,
later forgotten. Outsiders know little of them, for their homes are
hidden in the partially uncharted rainforests of the Documentary.
Like other documentarians they survive by hunting and gathering
information. Unlike others of their filmic group, most prefer to con-
sume it raw. (qtd. in Grimshaw 2001, 1)

Sardonic wit aside, we are still left with a group of power and relationship
brokers who by virtue of accidents of history were exclusively in possession of the technology of photographic reproduction and, no less important, of the means to distribute their products to a consuming public that
anxiously awaited them. It was almost always the case that the camera
people who entered the Borderlands came with varying degrees of professional standing in the emerging field of visual ethnography. Some were
self-directed, start-up impresarios in the burgeoning field of tourist exploration. The film and photography this tribe turned out in its drive toward
"scopic possession"—the obsession of Westerners "to prospect the world
as tourist-explorers"—follows the logic of imperialist expansionism, a chief
goal being the creation of an "entertaining narrative of evolution . . . by
juxtaposing the white tourist with the peoples filmed." For Rony, the juxtaposition of the "enlightened white tourist" exploring the margins of civilization ensured that the dichotomies of "the Native versus the Civilized,
the Ethnographic versus the Historical, the Colonized versus the Colonist"
would become indelibly inscribed in the West's apprehension of non-
Western peoples (1996, 82).

Ellen Strain calls this drive to possess the margins of the world "touristic viewing." The tourist gaze along with the dominance of the West at
the end of the nineteenth century and its multiple consequences have
been amply documented in cultural studies and American studies scholarship.[1] Still, what Strain and others have deemed to be the scopic form
of an imperial-pursuit travelogue reminds us that the visual objectifica-
tion of the cultural other in foreign and distant lands for both "scientific
research" and "entertainment" was replicated in the U.S.-Mexico Borderlands. It bears noting that for historically specific reasons, New Mexico,

even more so than other border states, remained "a distant locale" for most white Americans. While the Southwest was geographically inscribed in the boundaries of the United States in the mid-nineteenth century, for all intents and purposes it remained a region on the periphery of U.S. modernity, a distinct place, vast and removed from the technological developments that could be found in the urban areas of the eastern United States. To most urban Americans, New Mexico and what José Limón calls "Greater Mexico" were as exotic and as dark a place as any that could be found on the world map. Its people, too, the majority mexicanos and American Indians, were viewed as a part of the archive of human variation (Rony 1996, 85) to be photographed, filmed, catalogued, scrutinized, and ultimately possessed by legions of amateur and quasi-scientific adventure-seekers.

Of course, the era of the adventure-tourist sauntering into the Southwest came at the end of a long interval of nefarious military and political conquests over its native inhabitants. Not until several tumultuous decades had passed and reports to the eastern United States signaled that the Borderlands were firmly in the political control of the United States, its inhabitants having been formally detached from the Republic of Mexico, did more ordinary adventure-seekers deem it time to film the people of the region. As if taking a step back in time, a fledgling movie industry seized on the spectacle of conquest and quickly began the work of reifying Manifest Destiny in the American imaginary. War, conquest, and battlefield heroics made good drama, and thus entertainment film gorged itself on the self-justifying logic of American imperialism. Charles Ramírez Berg calls the movie industry of this period "a sort of Monroe Doctrine and Manifest Destiny Illustrated." "On the whole," he explains, "Hollywood endorsed North American dominance of the hemisphere, and as often as it depicted the hegemony uncritically, movies helped to perpetuate it" (2002, 4–5). The earliest of these historical film dramas were long on heroics and short on accuracy; in a word, they were partial to the winners.

Nowhere in the history of film is the concept of Manifest Destiny more celebrated than in the popular culture that surrounds the Alamo. In fact, were it not for the emergence of dramatic motion pictures, the now iconic 1836 battle at the mission of San Antonio de Bexar fought at the outset of the Texas War of Independence might be just one among many military confrontations dead and forgotten in the American imaginary. But as

Richard Flores astutely notes, "It is the emergence of motion pictures, with their visual texture and iconic density, that best exemplifies the linkage between the Alamo as a historical event and its emerging cultural memory, made real by the project of modernity" (2002, 95). In pointing to an early treatment of the Alamo story, Flores makes this point: "Once the West was firmly established and secure from the threat of outsiders (i.e., after the Mexicans had been defeated at the Alamo), a Utopic elsewhere could be imagined as the material place of future colonizations. Mélies's Alamo film, then, anticipates and explores his later cinematic motifs where the Mexican Other serves as both a threat to the West and an aggressive savage in need of rule" (2002, 98).

Although a spate of entertainment films on the Alamo were made between 1911 and 1915 (Flores 2002), it is William Christy Cabanne's *Martyrs of the Alamo or the Birth of Texas* (1915) that installed the Alamo tropes that would come to be the cornerstones of Texas-U.S. nation building. These tropes would stretch from the famous "line drawn in the sand" to "death before disgrace," items immediately ascribable to a "heroic" defense of the Alamo by Anglo American frontiersmen. In doing so, *Martyrs* effectively recasts history into myth and becomes one of the most powerful magnifications of Manifest Destiny set before audiences in 1915.[2] Released in major American cities within months of D. W. Griffith's infamous racist film *The Birth of a Nation*, *Martyrs* is a knockoff of *Birth* that utilizes all the stylistic and narrative conventions pioneered by Griffith (who supervised Cabanne). In the logic of American filmmakers of the silent era, historical drama was fodder for ideological and propagandistic enterprise. History, especially if it dealt with the "vanquished other," was meant to raise the stock of white Americans, making them out to be the triumphant victors. *Martyrs* and *The Birth of a Nation* are so much of a piece that it is now necessary for scholars to examine both films side by side. Rooted in notions of white superiority, they provide evidence that Griffith was an equal opportunity racist whose ideological basis for filmmaking went beyond a black-white binary. His aims, stated or not, were to devalue non-whites and reify white supremacist logic through the power of film.

These historical dramas of conquest and white triumph present the unique circumstance of bringing into view the circumspect qualities of individual or residual encounters with the Other. They emerge as public diatribes on nationhood and nationalism. It is in this sense that they are only minimally about Reconstruction and the Texas War of Independence and resolutely about the fear of ethnic others. This fear was relegated to the past but was called up at the very moment the films were being made. Reminding us that "*Martyrs* is more concerned with 1915 than with 1836," Flores assails this apparent paradox by underscoring how the myth of the Alamo is merely an expansion of the nationalistic discourse of the United States:

> I contend that in this film we have a series of cinematic projections that mediate local, national, and international concerns. At the local level, the cinematic collapsing of the historical relationship between the United States and Mexico, in which the Battle of the Alamo plays a key role, into one of social and cultural difference serves to render the Mexicans as radically Other. The projection places the burden and responsibility of socio-economic displacement of Mexicans on Mexicans themselves and posits their "uncivilized, inhuman, and socially threatening behavior" as the cause. But this rendering of Mexicans, and by default, Mexico, as radically Other serves a second purpose. It provides visual code for the advancement of modernity whereby the need to control what is culturally foreign and socially different legitimates the imperial project itself. The production of Mexicans as uncivilized serves, as Trouillot reminds us, as an imaginary effort through which the West, by means of the trope of the West, constitutes its legitimacy. (Flores 2002, 107)

In works such as *Birth* and *Martyrs*, entertainment passes for history. Both films are set on the scale of social and epic proxemics where ideologies of nation and citizenship—specifically, what it means to be a citizen of the United States—are rehearsed for public consideration. Anna Grimshaw's work on ethnographic film turns out to be very instructive, for it allows us to see how the proxemics of group or social encounters is observable in Griffith's work. Indeed, the distancing and disfigurement of ethnic others in Griffith-led films is at the very core of his cinematic narratology.

Grimshaw argues that as photography became available to anthropologists in the field, it also quickly became a structuring mechanism that determined the proxemics of encounters between groups. In her view, the preponderance of montage or of mise-en-scène in Griffith's films acts as a distancing mechanism that filmically segregates subjects as effectively as any Jim Crow measure. It allows the filmmaker to create differentially based spatial treatments in scripting the film's storyline. In this sense, Grimshaw contends, *montage* is about rearrangement and redrawing the proxemics of any preexisting, preconditioned relationships as these might have actually been found in the world. She suggests as much when defining the first of these two processes: "At its simplest, montage indeed means juxtaposition, and as such, it foregrounds relationships rather than discrete entities, it emphasizes processes rather than static states of being; and it draws attention to the generation of meaning through processes of contrast rather than of continuity or development" (Grimshaw 2001, 26). The effect of this racial montage is as much at work in *Birth* as in *Martyrs*. In the latter, Griffith purposefully avoids examining the historical context of the Alamo conflict; rather, Griffith's aesthetic is exclusively built from the reordering and alternative juxtaposition of chronological actions so as to produce a dramatic, conflict-order narrative. Grimshaw explains: "The basic unit of Griffith's new cinematic language was the shot, rather than the scene with its origin in older theatrical form; and action was no longer conveyed as whole and continuous, unfolding within a single, extended, and unchanging shot. Action was broken down into a series of fragments, and movement generated through their manipulation during editing. But just as the single action can be broken down into parts, so too can the overall narrative itself" (27).

With the film version of the Alamo standing as the conquest myth of the Southwest, modernity and, in particular, tourism made New Mexico a kind of sub-regional pocket of culture, an especially well suited destination for the tourist-spectator intent on bringing back dazzling tales with which to regale urban audiences. It was habitual that these chronicles of the unusual would be illustrated with images of the bizarre and the "alien," made all the more intriguing by the realization that such rare phenomena could be found within the political boundaries of the United States. As with any foreign locale, New Mexico's difference was brokered to consuming audiences through an entire cultural industry, which, as Strain explains, operated at full throttle in Europe and the United States:

The ascendancy of touristic viewing took place against a backdrop of unprecedented Western contact with the so-called margins of the earth. In the decades before the close of the nineteenth century, missionaries, surveyors, explorers, anthropologists, and colonists vowed to fill in the few remaining blank spots on world maps and to close the larger gaps in the knowledge of the globe's various inhabitants. Traveling merchants negotiated the purchase of physical types previously unseen in Europe and the United States, and showmen, gaining possession of these human display items, collected profits from audiences eager to look into the dark eyes of the world's jungles and deserts. Natural history museums sprouted in U.S. cities as expeditions and world fairs created the need for permanent warehouses to store and display the West's increasing collection of exotic booty. And magazines followed the cross-cultural adventures of fieldworkers, helping to establish the traveling anthropologist as cultural hero. (1996, 73)

Here, too, we are engaged in a kind of social proxemics that laminates local relationships in the Borderlands over and onto the larger scale of a new political reality forced onto the region by the annexation of the Southwest and U.S. modernity.

The motives of the tourist could not, of course, always be observed on the surface of things and often moved over a range of undeclared interests. The "tourist-explorer" could easily morph into the "speculator" or the "civic booster" whose reasons to visit a marginal region might include encouraging investment, pushing for white-settler immigration, or making business contacts.

A telling example of this convergence of interests can be found in *Adventures in Kit Carson Land*, a 1917 film tour of New Mexico sponsored by the once-active New Mexico Publicity Bureau. The commission for the film went to the El Toro Film Company based in Santa Fe, which produced twelve thousand feet of film touting the wonders of northern New Mexico. So sure were boosters in state government of the importance of film to sell the region to tourists that the Publicity Bureau allotted $6,800 to the project, a full 42 percent of its yearly operating budget.

Made to tout the wonders of New Mexico to uninitiated Americans, *Adventures in Kit Carson Land* lays out its program of interest in the

Southwest. One intertitle aptly links the region's natural beauty to the bygone era of American frontierism: "Motor travel through the scenic wonderland of northern New Mexico where the greatest of scouts and Indian fighters blazed the trail for the tourist and home builder of today." Automated maps appear, as a cursor traces the route this adventure-tour will take in following the Santa Fe Trail from St. Louis, Missouri, across the Texas Panhandle (a region labeled "No Man's Land"), to La Junta, Colorado, and down into Santa Fe. In Santa Fe, the tourist group meets with the governor of New Mexico, Washington E. Lindsey, who, as we are told, "welcomes our party and outlines directions for the journey to Kit Carson Land."

The travelers cut a circular path around Santa Fe as they motor to historic points of interest and to scenic and economic sites along the way in an effort to show that New Mexico is endowed with great natural and physical wonders important to the state's future economic development. The tourists, a party of a dozen or so men and women, travel to the Ruins of the Pecos Mission, the Mora Valley, Tres Ritos Canyon, Taos Valley, the Pueblo of Taos, Eagle Nest Dam, the Questa Valley, Cliff Dwellings at Frijoles Canyon (now Bandelier National Monument), and back to Santa Fe. Ostensibly, the primary aim of the film is to tally up the region's quality-of-life index as exhibited by its natural beauty and its potential for economic development, but viewers along the way are also served up great helpings of the exotic. By highlighting the region's ancient beginnings, its diverse peoples, and wholly foreign displays of culture, the film also indulges in the kind of "touristic viewing" Strain finds to be the staple of filmic forays into other parts of the globe.

The longest segment of this six-reel travelogue presents a number of events associated with the San Gerónimo Fiesta, which takes place annually at Taos Pueblo and in the Hispanic Plaza at Taos. Another intertitle informs viewers, "The unique celebration occurs on September 30 each year, in it the Taos Indians pay tribute not only to their patron saint of the Christian religion, San Gerónimo, but also to the ceremonials of their worship of the sun." The film pays special attention to capturing those aspects of life in Taos that appear as odd, different, or unusual to white audiences. Intertitles for this segment give some idea of the filmmakers' interest in ethnic and cultural difference: "Taos Indians in white ceremonial blankets"; "Governor of Taos and members of his council consent to go to the

horse races in our big car"; "The Real Thing: Mauricio Martínez, Oldest living Taos Indian (looks the part)"; and "The Real Thing in Indian Dancing:
Four braves of Taos Pueblo rehearse in the security of La Glorieta Canyon,
their parts in the festivities on San Geronimo Day."

Adventures in Kit Carson Land is, of course, an important film record of
an otherwise uninspiring motorcade. It stands out for the fact that in it we
find a precursor to the famous Indian Detours initiated by the Fred Harvey
Company in 1926. The Indian Detours, a set of promotional tours, ushered
in the era of organized automobile tourism to north-central New Mexico,
which brought hundreds of sightseers to the region over the course of the
next decades.[3] Thus, the rare footage in Adventures in Kit Carson Land is significant, a point not lost on the research librarians at the New Mexico State
Library who in 1996 asked Taos resident Helen Blumenschein, the daughter of Ernest Blumenschein, a founding member of the Taos Art Colony, to
add her narration to the footage and to identify the places and people in
the film.

By and large, Blumenschein's oral history illuminates significant points
on the early history of Taos and northern New Mexico, and it is only when
the cinematic veil of Adventures in Kit Carson Land is torn momentarily by
the appearance of Blumenschein's father that one of those uncanny "experiences of the third eye" results. In this instance, it comes to envelop not
the spectator but the raconteur as she presents an oral history of Anglo
artists living and painting in Taos. The impact of the moment weighs on
our contemporary sensibilities, for it is a "racially charged glance" cast
back in time that unexpectedly splits the film tour internally and exter-
nally. In contemporary audiences it produces a clarity of vision at a place
Rony calls "the site of socially mediated self-alienation" (1996, 4). The split
lasts only for the few frames that constitute the segment, "The Real Thing
in Indian Dancing." An intertitle announces: "But in Taos Village Indians,
Natives, Cowboys, Artists, Tourists, a cosmopolitan group, gather to take
part in the festivities." Helen Blumenschein interjects, "Well, we're back
in Taos plaza again." Her comments are followed by frontal shots of several Taos Colony artists costumed as Apaches, Plains Indians, and Moroc-
can tribesmen. Amid the nods to local exotica we are surprised to find
a cosmopolitan group of Taos newcomers adding to the festivities with
their antics and parodies by, in a phrase, "playing Indian." Blumenschein

identifies people she remembers knowing as a child: Victor Higgins, Mr. Rosen (in a turban), Mr. Ruford (in black face), Mr. Ufer, and Mr. Couse. She adds, "This is my father . . . with the American flag and Apache hat and a cigar." We then are privy to how the cosmopolitan group entertained themselves and others at fiesta time as they whoop and holler in a circle imitating the dance of their Indian neighbors, the same people they consign to canvas as portraits of the idyllic and noble representatives of a vanishing race.[4] Blumenschein's narration falters, betraying some discomfort: "Whenever you see that Apache hat, that is my father dancing," she pauses nervously. "Mr. Couse, I think . . . probably, he was the funniest. He used to imitate . . . and the Indians just loved it. He used to make believe he was talking to them on the plaza when he'd walk around."[5]

What I find compelling about this segment of *Adventures* is its unguarded, devil-may-care, candid view of the native residents of north-central New Mexico. It is a rare instance when, unwittingly, the hidden transcript of what was the prerogative of white immigrant settlers to play Indian emerges as a painful illustration of interethnic relationships built on asymmetrical grids of social and cultural power. It is an example that goes to the concerns Sylvia Rodríguez registers in her work on the Taos Art Colony in which she describes the "differential awareness of ethnic boundaries among dominant and subdominant groups" (1989, 90). Caught in their antics, these Taos artists seem immune, seemingly without a clue that their actions are offensive to their Taos neighbors. That this was commonplace, Rodríguez explains, resulted from the dominant social privilege of these artists:

> Members of a racially or ethno-politically dominant group do not think of themselves as part of an ethnic group at all. They tend to be less directly aware than are the subordinates of the complex rules and markers, which govern face-to-face interethnic relations. Thus members of different ethnic groups or strata actually tend to perceive and interpret interethnic interaction differently. Moreover, in mixed and in-group company, they are differentially candid about what they do, see and feel. (90)

As an "experience of the third eye," it is also intriguing to think that such a moment in film can provide a means to undo the effects of an earlier period of white social and racial privilege.

It is important to remember that racial and cultural difference at this early moment in film history is channeled through both scientific and popular mediums. Thus, as Ellen Strain insists, it was a time when the "spectorial pleasures of the touristic" were passed off as surrogate knowledge about the marginal peoples of the world through various film mediums. For Strain, "a two-way path of causality links the two realms with popular culture and anthropology influencing one another and with political and technological changes affecting both academia and entertainment" (1996, 80). In a real sense, the door was open to any enterprising traveler to become an authority on the life and habits of the foreign Other. As Strain points out, "Late nineteenth-century anthropologists were thus not professional travelers financed by the academy but more commonly xenophiles with the education, economic means, and leisure time to take their hobby more seriously than other visitors to the same exotic attractions" (82). Thus, to the figure of the "tourist-explorer" can be added his/her adventuresome kin: the vagabond reporter/photographer, the "artist-explorer," and the intrepid film director of the adventure-saga movie. According to Strain:

> With the popularization of science during this period, tourism—
> perhaps the first form of 'edutainment'—cannot be divorced from
> the pedagogical discourses of science and its view of a structured
> universe. In fact, the concept of the "world as picture" with the cen-
> tral role it assigns to science could be extended to include the phe-
> nomenon of the "world as postcard," a form of mastery available
> to the layperson outside scientific communities. This individual as
> actual or "virtual" tourist not only views familiarity with the world
> as an educational goal but employs learned touristic strategies to
> derive pleasure from the spectacle of cultural difference. (77)

Scientific research and interest in ethnic performance and spectacle grew out of a broad fascination in the United States with indigenous peoples as subjects. Rony asserts, "Early cinema showed a fascination for the subject of indigenous, non-European peoples in its proliferation of travelogues, scientific research films, safari films, scripted narrative films, and colonial propaganda films" (Rony 1996, 43).

In this sense, the Southwest Borderlands drew a high number of visitors whose goal was to discover the region's unique difference. Among them came the leading anthropologists, filmmakers, photographers, and travelers of the day. Their part in the drama of touristic viewing was to deliver the pleasure that came from the spectacle of cultural viewing to their co-citizens in urban centers. Quite naturally, these observers lost no opportunity to enhance their stature as authorities empowered to make pronouncements on the peoples and cultures of distant corners of the globe. They constantly reminded their audiences that they knew of what they spoke because they had lived and resided among the foreign and the different. In Strain's words, they accrued a "mystical form of authority gained from simply 'being there'" (1996, 90).

The best-known popularizer of the Southwest was the journalist and photographer Charles F. Lummis (1859–1928). In his own time Lummis was hailed as the "first and greatest Southwesterner" and he played a decisive role in molding early public perceptions of the Southwest and of Southern California. Lummis's diaries, letters, and in particular his most famous series of photographic plates, those he made of the Penitente processions and ceremonies at San Mateo, New Mexico, in March 1888, conditioned the American public to anticipate exotica, foreignness, and spectacle as an essential part of New Mexico and the territory's populations.

Others would follow suit, feeding the public's taste for spectacle and drama by playing up the ethnic difference of Mexican Americans in commercial and ethnographic films produced in the 1920s and 1930s. In the 1920s, Burton Holmes, the foremost traveler/lecturer after John L. Stoddard, canvassed the Southwest in search of ethnographic material to add to his travelogues and lectures. Regrettably, research has yet to produce any extant footage of Holmes's travels in the Southwest and Mexico. His biographers credit Holmes with having invented the term "travelogue" to describe the manner of his stage lectures. His appellations, the "travelogue man," "everybody's tourist," and "the rover boy," heightened his stature as a legendary vagabond. Before his death, Holmes was billed as having spent fifty-five summers abroad in which he crossed the Atlantic thirty times, the Pacific another twenty, and recorded a half million feet of film during his travels. In 1953, Holmes published his autobiography, aptly titled *The World Is Mine.*

But before entering into a discussion of the role Lummis, Holmes, and others played in the dramas of the Other in the Southwest, I first wish

to examine commercial filmmaking and its role in popularizing misper-
ceptions of the Mexican Americans in the Southwest. I do this at Ellen
Strain's urging when she remarks, "The historical intertwining of popular anthropology and toursitic academics should continue to inform our
understanding of early cinema. Contemporary film historians have unbur-
ied the numerous connections between early filmic experiments and other
entertainment forms of the same period" (1996, 97).

Strain's assertion is amply illustrated in the work of the Lubin Film Company and by the films made by its most famous explorer-director, Romaine
Fielding, while the company toured the U.S.-Mexico border region.

Proxemics and the Camera People

As both Strain and Rony astutely note, by the end of the nineteenth century
it was impossible to sort out what part of early photography and cinema
representing native others was entertainment and what part was science,
the tribe of documentarians swooping down over the Southwest in search
of exotic prey having so blurred these distinctions. Once commercial film
factored in the entertainment value of exotic encounter, it would not be
long before proffering the exotica as performance would become a cliché
in Hollywood travel-adventure films. Now American audiences could be
further entertained by depictions of hunter-gatherer anthropologists consuming their game raw on screen. As I have pointed out, one aim of my
book is to understand how "the Camera People" brokered the vision of
the Other and made it a part of American mass consumption, but I do not
mean to neglect how their very instruments, cameras themselves, determined the spatial orientation, the proxemics of the encounters between
those in possession of photographic technology, and those who could
never be more than their subjects. Thus, I turn to Edward Hall's enor-
mously persuasive theory of proxemics, the study of human space in a
cultural context, as a useful way to measure the role of both "the Camera
People" and their instruments in the photographic and cinematic encounters that I wish to discuss here. Applying Hall's proxemics to photography
and cinema is complicated work, not least of all because I am extrapolat-
ing ideas Hall first applied to matters of the unconscious demarcation of
personal space and social space in ordinary and routine encounters, such

as conversations, seating, and so forth as prescribed by the sociocultural conventions of one's culture of origin. Like others who have seized on the enormous fecundity in Hall's theory to illumine any number of cross-cultural encounters, I also seek to tap the theory's considerable plasticity to illustrate how the roving eye of the camera zooms away the proxemics of offscreen encounters while at the same time consigning these spaces to the onscreen story.

The Proxemics of Expansion and Conquest

The Rattlesnake, A Psychical Species (1913) is among the earliest two-reel features shot in the Southwest to concern itself with Anglos and Mexicans interacting upon a Borderlands landscape. *The Rattlesnake* is the work of Romaine Fielding, an actor turned movie director who was put at the head of Siegmund Lubin's Southwest Film Company in 1912 (Eckhardt 1997, 129). Born William Grant Blandin in Iowa, Fielding took his acting seriously. For example, he claimed to be the son of wealthy Spanish and Italian-French parents from Corsica, and he often passed himself off as having extensive medical training from prestigious medical schools (Eckhardt 1997, 129).

With Fielding at the helm, the Lubin Southwest Film Company zig-zagged around Arizona, Texas, and New Mexico doing novel and interesting work in the Borderlands. Fielding scholars agree that he was the first commercial filmmaker to shoot extensively on location in the American Southwest (Eckhardt 1997; Woal 1995). Linda and Michael Woal found that Fielding shot over 107 films in the Borderlands but that only 8 survive, some in partial form (Woal and Woal 1995, 28). The Woals offer a generous critique of Fielding's work and suggest that he "provided film patrons with many of their first authentic views of the real West and earned for himself the title, 'the man who put *real* in *realism*'" (28). Fielding shot his first film, *A Romance on the Border*, in Tucson in 1912. In *Romance*, Fielding is credited with "challenging standard racist assumptions about Mexicans and American Indians" (28). According to one source, in *Romance on the Border* Fielding has a Mexican hero kill an American soldier to save a señorita from being raped. This kind of role reversal, in which a Mexican hero is pitted against an American villain, is unusual for this period or, indeed, for any period of U.S. commercial film, something that arguably would not be seen again until Orson Welles's *Touch of Evil* in 1958. Fielding's audacity on this

FIG. I. Romaine Fielding (upper right, holding U.S. flag) and film crew on the U.S.-Mexico border, 1912. New Mexico Historical Film Collection, image number 39474. Courtesy of the New Mexico State Records Center and Archives.

point has led scholars to declare that as a filmmaker he moved away from producing negative portrayals of Mexicans in the silent period.

In early 1913 while in Nogales on the U.S.-Mexico border, Fielding managed to film an attack on the town by Mexican constitutionalist forces and then supplemented the footage with his own staged battles to create the impression that he had filmed the action on both sides of the international border (Eckhardt 1997, 128). That same year, Fielding released a documentary on the Mexican Revolution under the title *Mexican War Pictures.* The length of this film is unknown. What is known of its content has been pieced together from the plot synopsis provided in copyright records. *Mexican War Pictures* is reported to have contained the following scenes:

> Fighting between the Federals and Constitutionalists during the Mexican War is documented. Among the sequences included are pictures of Colonel Alvaro Abrogon [*sic*] commanding the Constitutionalists and of Colonel Juan Cabrol commanding their advance guard at his camp. In front of federal headquarters, Romaine Fielding consults with Red Cross surgeons. Scenes of day-to-day activities

of the soldiers are presented. Fielding advises Abrogon on the care of
the wounded. Fighting along the American border and the guarding
of the border by American troops is included. The Constitutionalists
are successful in the day's battle. (Hanson and Gevinson 1998, 606)

The civil strife in Mexico that erupted with the Mexican Revolution (1910–
1920) became a favorite subject of several other commercial filmmakers
whose work shaped a view of Mexico in American audiences as a violent
and unstable society.

Leaving Nogales, Fielding had two extended stays in New Mexico,
first setting up shop in Silver City, where he would spend the next several
months, in April 1913. It seems Fielding created close relatives to match
his alias, or so area newspapers reported in auguring the reasons Fielding
chose Silver City as a film locale. Silver City newspapers reported that the
famous director had come at the instance of his "brother" Robert Fielding,
a Chino Copper Company engineer: "Manager Fielding has been attracted
to this country by the descriptions of it given by his brother" (St. George
Cooke 1970, 3). Both Silver City newspapers, *The Enterprise* and *The Independent*, reported that the Lubin Company would be making an industrial
picture "of the copper mining operations being carried on at Santa Rita
and Hurley" (St. George Cooke 1970, 3).

Fielding's troupe stirred commotion in and around Silver City as it set
about to create action scenes that required sending a local house up in
flames, blowing up a narrow-gauge railroad bridge, and dispatching two
water tanks "fully 200 feet in the air" (St. George Cooke 1970, 12). Building
his plots around staged and raw footage such as large blasts that were produced at the Chino Copper Company mines, Fielding created high drama
that in turn fueled intense performances. Two of his Silver City flickers
are *Riot at the Smelter* (1913) and *The Clod* (1913). *Riot at the Smelter* and the
companion film *The Golden God* represent the start of an abiding interest
by filmmakers in labor and mining in Grant County that would culminate
in the classic labor film *Salt of the Earth* (1954). *The Silver City Enterprise* for
June 16, 1913, provides a full description of the film's action:

Sunday was a thrilling day for Silver City people. The Lubin Stock
Co. enacted a drama at the smelter below town, blew up the narrow
gauge railroad bridge and two large water tanks and incidentally

furnished amusement for 2,000 people scattered over the surrounding hills watching the interesting events. A riot scene, in which
200 men dressed in old clothes took part, preceded the explosion.
Mason Kelly and E. A. Blevins were pressed into service as labor agitators, after which the entire crew rushed up to the water tanks, set
fire to them and then, as they rushed down the hill, the tanks blew
up. (St. George Cooke 1970, 11)

Fielding's *The Clod* drew its subject matter from the Mexican Revolution. The picture contained elaborate reenactments of battles that suggest
that disorder and chaos are symptomatic of Mexican border struggles and
antagonistic to the order imposed by Americanism. A Silver City reporter
observing the staging of the movie concluded:

Romaine Fielding and his Lubin Motion Picture players put in another
strenuous time last week. For a spectator to follow the thread of a
motion picture special such as Mr. Fielding has just completed, the
hunting for the proverbial needle in the haystack is beat a thousand
and one ways. One thing is certain, judging from the bunch of murderous looking insurrectos which he has rounded up, the scene of
action was somewhere in Mexico during the recent, or more strictly
speaking, ever present, revolution. (St. George Cooke 1970, 20)

If Fielding did produce film dramas that meant to challenge racial
assumptions about Mexicans, *The Clod* does not illustrate this side of his
film work. To the contrary, and judging from the plot synopsis included
with a theatrical poster made for the release of the movie, *The Clod* is as
base a representation of Mexicans as could be had in 1913. The protagonist of the film, Pedro Mendez, is presented as a dupe, an utterly passive
and fatalistic person who lacks any form of assertiveness. The billboard
informs filmgoers that Pedro is "a simple-minded Mexican farmer, strong,
but so dull mentally as to be a mere clod," and plots out his story in detail:

He goes to town to get supplies and learns of the intended revolution and is asked to join the recruits. He can't understand what it
is all about, he has all he wants and why should he fight. He goes
back home and says nothing to his wife and crippled mother. Later
a troop of revolutionists passing by confiscate his horses. He would

protest but the gold lace and commanding tone of the commanding officer cow him. Next day a band of guerillas raid his house and
make off with his chickens and cattle. A battle takes place near
the farm and a band of rebels takes possession of the house and
make a barricade of it. The house is shot to pieces and takes fire
and Mendez's wife is killed by one of the bullets. He picks up his
crippled mother and carries her out, then returns for his dead wife.
Again reaching his mother he finds her also dead. His dormant passion and strength is aroused, his wife and mother dead, his farm in
ashes, he wrenches a gun from a dead soldier and plunges into the
fight, clubbing the gun he attacks anybody not knowing which side
he is fighting. At last he is shot and staggering to the place where his
mother lies rolls over on his face dead. (*The Clod*, release bulletin)

The message to film audiences is unambiguous: Pedro represents the
masses of Mexicans and his actions show that he is incapable of standing
up for himself in the face of those who despoil his home and kill his loved
ones. As Carlos Cortes would remind us, the movie curriculum at work
here suggests that Pedro Mendez's passivity is an inborn characteristic of
his race and culture. Pedro's failure to act even in the face of the most egregious insults and attacks on his person and family would not have been
lost on audiences of the day. Pedro Mendez's final response only confirms
his endemic passivity, for in the end he "attacks anybody, not knowing
which side he is fighting." The message to film audiences of 1913 comes as
an object lesson on what ought and what ought not to be the appropriate
behavior of the individual in civil society. Pedro's failure to act on his own
behalf is condemned as repulsive and anathema to the way in which Anglo
Americans view themselves. For uninitiated audiences on the eastern sea-
board without any real notion of the social and economic conditions in
Mexico or on the U.S.-Mexico border, such films constituted the whole of
their knowledge about this part of the world and its inhabitants. *The Clod*,
like most films of this time, provides a depiction that coincides with popular racist views of Mexicans.

In the summer of 1913, Fielding moved the Lubin Company to Las
Vegas, then a booming town located in northeastern New Mexico. Fielding
installed his production company in the Plaza Hotel, audaciously renaming

it "Hotel Romaine" ("100 Years," 14). With Fielding and the Selig Polyscope Company—led by actor and director Tom Mix—in residence in Las Vegas in 1914, New Mexico came as close as it ever would to becoming a permanent home for the production of motion pictures in the West ("100 Years," 14). Before leaving Silver City, Fielding had told a reporter that he had every desire to continue making movies in the region: "I know and like the people of the southwest. . . . They are of my kind. I understand them; they understand me. We work together beautifully, and I get better results here than any other place in the country" (St. George Cooke 1970, 24).

The Golden God, a film done in Las Vegas, may be a better example of what Linda and Michael Woal call Fielding's "allegorical realism" and his "working class narratives," a progressive strand in Fielding's work that his defenders argue typifies his work. As with other lost Fielding films, what can be surmised about the theme of The Golden God comes from accounts in the local press and a few still photographs, the only items to have survived an explosion in the film vaults of the Lubin headquarters in Philadelphia, where most of Fielding's films were lost (Woal and Woal 1995, 32).

The Golden God was to be a landmark social epic that reviewers anticipated would rival D. W. Griffith's plans for Intolerance (1916). The Lubin Company billed it as its first feature-length domestic production. Accounts from area papers indicate that the film was a high-budget, large-scale production that employed some ten thousand extras drawn from the ranks of the residents of Las Vegas, the state militia, "trainloads of people," and the National Guard, all of whom were to be paid two dollars a day (Woal 1995, 32).

The film, a story of labor uprising, called for a large number of extras to capture the sense of a mass movement of workers pitted against the interests of a few magnates who control the world's industrial base. The Woals contend that The Golden God is one of a handful of social melodramas from the period that they deem pro-labor films. Indeed, the film's synopsis suggests that Fielding had a prophetic sense of class struggle when conceiving the story of Myton Powers (the Golden God) and his dominion over the laboring class. Set in 1950, the film forecasts the "climax of the world-old struggle between capital and labor reach[ing] its culmination in the awaking of the sleeping giant, the people, and a titanic world-wide struggle between them and the armies controlled by 'Consolidated Industries,' headed by the Golden God" (Las Vegas Optic, qtd. in Woal 1995, 30).

As the film progresses, Powers's daughter, Eleanor, who "sorrows for the masses," takes up the cause of the workers along with her lover, Richin Manlove, a journalist and the Golden God's severest critic and adversary. The climax of the film comes as the Golden God's armies clash with the striking workers. Myton Powers "enters the firing line with a cannon-mounted automobile," only to find his own daughter leading the people against him. The encounter proves to be the deciding moment that affects a change of heart in Powers, who determines to turn "his forces from the field and give that which is rightfully its own—Freedom" (*Optic*, qtd. in Woal 1995, 30).

From the descriptions we have of the film it is difficult to determine to what extent race and ethnicity enter into this story of workers and their struggle for just treatment. While *The Golden God* purports to contend for the rights of the working class, members of that class are not the protagonists of the story. When the film does show us the workers, they appear as the unruly mobs that rise up against their bosses. The masses remain undifferentiated and unidentified. If class is decentered, we would not expect race or ethnicity to be represented in the storyline either, since the film is about showing the humanity of Myton Powers, his daughter, Eleanor, and her suitor, Manlove, and of their redemption and transformation of spirit in the manner of Charles Dickens's classic tale *A Christmas Carol*.

Despite the fact that *The Golden God*'s intended release came just before one of the bloodiest incidents in U.S. labor history, the Ludlow Massacre in the coal fields of southern Colorado, there simply is no sure evidence to suggest that Fielding makes any specific reference to the people who struggled and died at Ludlow some three hours by rail from where *The Golden God* was filmed. In the case of Ludlow we know that on April 20, 1914, the Colorado National Guard was mobilized by the governor of Colorado at the behest of John D. Rockefeller, the owner of Colorado Fuel and Iron Coal Works, and ordered to attack a tent colony of some twelve hundred striking miners. The skirmish lasted fourteen hours and ended in the death of more than twenty-five people. The dead included three militiamen, but even more tragic were the deaths of twelve children and the wives of miners in a fire that erupted in their tents. The strikers were mainly ethnic workers: Greeks, Italians, Slavs, and a high percentage of Mexicans who had emigrated from both Mexico and New Mexico.

The strike that prompted the Ludlow resistance was one of many that typified the struggle for workers' rights against corporate interests. A general outline of the Colorado strike against the plutocrat Rockefeller does suggest itself in the outward contours of the plot of *The Golden God.* Is it possible that Rockefeller provided the model for Myton Powers? Perhaps, and yet as we have seen the protagonists still remain the members of the privileged classes. It would be nice to assume that *The Golden God* operates in solidarity with the struggle of the miners who were on strike during the very months that the film was shot, just three hours from Ludlow down the Santa Fe line in Las Vegas, New Mexico, but there is little to support this contention. It would be another fifty years until a film shot in New Mexico, *Salt of the Earth*, could claim not only that it was pro-labor but that it was made in solidarity and with respect for the struggle of the laboring classes.

The Rattlesnake, Species Exotica

Film historian Joseph Eckhardt credits Fielding with moving beyond expected portrayals in Mexican-themed films, a move that turns Fielding's films away from the greaser fare that was a standard of other American film directors. According to Eckhardt, the films Fielding shot in New Mexico "dealt with superstition, drug-induced madness, fatal attractions, triumphs of the spirit, interracial romances that end in disaster, and other human tragedies of the sort not previously seen in movies" (150). *The Rattlesnake, A Psychical Species* (1913) is one of the eight surviving Fielding films shot in the Southwest, and in it Fielding intentionally deals with some aspect of all these themes.

Fielding is an interesting case among those filmmakers of his generation who used the landscape and human-scape of the Southwest in their films. Based on the few Fielding films that survive, one can deduce that he was not primarily concerned with creating canned stereotypes of mexicanos and nuevomexicanos, as Enrique Lamadrid argues at one point;[6] rather, Fielding's portrayals in *The Rattlesnake* reflect the kind of filmic disposition noted by Carlos Cortes, in which filmmakers "have simply taken advantage of existing audience predispositions in order to provoke conditioned emotional responses" (1992, 87).

The plot of *The Rattlesnake* is rather convoluted. Part I opens with a shot of a diamondback rattler slithering over some rocky ground. Viewers

FIG. 2. Lobby Card for Romaine Fielding's *The Rattlesnake* (1913). Used with the permission of the Free Library of Philadelphia.

are next introduced to the quartet who will form the Mexican entourage of characters (José, Happy Tony, the Mexican maiden, and her father, the Mexican patriarch). José and Happy Tony are rival suitors who fawn over the daughter of a hacienda grandee. A few frames later a smitten José attacks Happy Tony at a stream where he has stooped over to take a drink of water. As José prepares to finish Happy Tony off, a rattlesnake quite unexpectedly bites him. Stumbling to his feet, Happy Tony picks up the snake, which coils about him with some mysterious air of loyalty. For most of what remains of the film, Happy Tony and the rattler will be attached to one another by some weird symbiotic thread. The film cuts back to the arrival of the *americano* surveyor, John Gordon, at the hacienda. After Gordon talks to the don, he is set upon by the flirtatious señorita, who is more than happy to show Gordon the way to a mine he has come to inspect. Halfway up the road the pair encounters Happy Tony at the place of José's death. Tony explains the scene by saying in broken English, "He tried to kill me and snake killed him." Like the snake of the story, the plot twists itself around the inciting incident sparked by the rivalry between John Gordon and Happy Tony. The americano and the señorita are both taken aback by the sight of Tony and the snake. The señorita rebuffs Tony and vows never to see him again unless he gets rid of the snake, while Gordon, upstanding and honorable, wins the opportunity to court her.

Part 2 picks up the story seven years later. Gordon and the señorita, now married, have a daughter and live in the hacienda. A demented and debauched Tony lives in a cave-like stone house, having become a totally despicable and repulsive figure who spies menacingly on the home of his former love interest. The climax of the film comes on the night Tony attempts to kill Gordon by putting the rattlesnake in his bed. Tony's plan goes awry when the little girl rather than her father jumps in bed with the snake. In a fit of remorse, Tony, who cannot accept the thought of killing the little girl, reverses course and rescues her before the snake is able to bite her. After he is found out, and before being led away by a policeman, Tony is able to confess to the girl's mother, "My love for the child is greater than my hate was for you."

The film's epilogue is set six months later. Tony has lost an arm (how this happens is not clear) and he is rid of the rattlesnake. All is happiness and light at a garden party where all the players are brought together.

Here the adults mingle and talk and Tony and the child embrace. With the trusting child in hand, Tony suddenly and furtively walks off with her into some bushes. Their absence is noticed by the mother, who finds them coming back out of the shrubbery. The film closes with an iris shot that fades around Tony and the girl. No further explanation is given and the viewers are left with questions about Tony's intentions and motives.

Presumably several greaser movies were shot in New Mexico and in neighboring Arizona at the time of this early infatuation of filmmakers with western themes. While *The Rattlesnake* does not repeat the standard greaser plot, it does rely, as I have noted, on audience predispositions triggered by the greaser tag that is put on the Mexican male in film. At the outset of the film José and Tony are festooned in caballero attire: vaquero boots, embroidered vests, and sombreros. The Mexican maiden's dress and attire more closely resembles that of a gypsy woman. The loose connection links village woman to exotic dancer as ordinary peasant dress is transformed into the festive and bedecked version associated with the gypsy female. This common way of representing the Latin woman in early film is not surprising, but it seems such tinkering with the image still has a contemporary ring. The same imagery was recycled in a 2002 Jennifer Lopez music video, where "J-Lo," all rings and bangles, enters an eroticized dance with a handsome caballero.

Fielding's renderings of New Mexico reach far beyond the use of ethnic traits to create "pseudo-environment."[7] Enrique Lamadrid goes on to say that the depiction of the mexicano is articulated in deliberately "profound psychological and symbolic terms" (1992, 13). It is a case where "Fielding anticipates Ingmar Bergman in his overt use of symbols, creating a kind of psycho-greaser-western" (13). Fielding's challenge in *The Rattlesnake* is to produce psychological or pseudo-psychological drama that communicates the message that there is an "imponderable" nature to the mexicano.

Fortunately, not all is neatly squared in such experimentation, something that makes the film much more interesting than later Hollywood representations that send forth pat, essentialist, and dangerous messages about the character and disposition of Latinos. The trigger for drama in *The Rattlesnake* is sexual conquest, an unresolved consequence of the American takeover of the Southwest. Lamadrid notes that this is "a major preoccupation, both overt and subliminal, of the 19th century popular culture and political discourse that underlies these films" (1992, 15). In other words, the story of Anglo suitor, Mexican maiden, and Mexican lover had already been told countless times in dime novels and Mexican War pulp fiction.[8] In nearly every one of these fictions, ethnic identity is impaled upon the spike of racism and whiteness. The Mexican woman, nearly always represented as "half-Castilian," is whitened to make her an eligible mate for the Anglo suitor who must save her from the raw vengeance of a spurned Mexican male. Fielding's "dark lady" is no different and, indeed, it's transparent that actions of the maiden in *The Rattlesnake* are scripted from Anglo conquest novels set in the Borderlands both before and after the U.S. war with Mexico. Arthur Pettit has written that "the function of many New Mexican dark ladies is to hand over the title deeds of the family haciendas to their Yankee suitors. To qualify as loyal aides in the foreign conquest of their county these beauties must be rich" (1980, 69). If there is a variation in *The Rattlesnake*, it comes from the preexisting requirement that Mexican women recognize the superior qualities of Anglo Saxon thinking and society; thus, in Fielding's film, the audience is made to understand that the dark lady is seduced not just by the Anglo male's virility but by the prosperity of his world and of the social order he represents. But as Pettit reminds us, "Whatever the variations on the theme, the outcome is the same. The dark lady gains the hero only by renouncing her past" (142). Social mobility as a function of sexual exchange is put before the audience allegorically in the contrasting views of Happy Tony living in his cave-house and the parallel scene of the Mexican woman in a prosperous and clean home shared with her American husband. If Romaine Fielding pushed against this racist logic at all, it is by providing the possibility of redemption for Happy Tony. When Tony reverses his plan to kill John Gordon (1913 audiences must have gasped), we are happy to know that some humanity still beats in his dastardly heart. Audiences may have momentarily concluded that his debasement stems from the blow to his head that leads to an "unnatural" alliance with evil transfigured as the rattlesnake. Tony may gain redemption, but it comes with a price. How and when Tony loses his arm is not nearly as important as the fact that the price has been paid. Had Fielding really been about overturning the Social Darwinism that infected his age, *The Rattlesnake* would end here. It does not. Rather, a kind of deterministic recidivism is suggested by Tony's predatory interest in the girl at the garden party. Read as a sign of backsliding, the film's conclusion suggests the ever-constant fear that the Mexican male will return to vile ways via the abnormal stirrings of the unconscious (the emblematic rattlesnake) that still resides inside Tony. The final scene of *The Rattlesnake* is so filled with uncertainty that even into the present it suggests that Tony—that is, the Mexican male—is incorrigible, unredeemable, and unworthy of public trust.

For all its avoidance of trite stereotype, Fielding's film nonetheless compounds the suspicion of the Mexican male in American popular culture. These early films shot and cast in New Mexico were likely to have gone unnoticed by nuevomexicanos who during this period participated only nominally in American life and culture. Fear, suspicion, trepidation, and loathing of things Mexican in the Southwest would amplify in the next decades. It is somewhat ironic, then, as I show in my next chapter, that xenophobia would be most steeply pitched in matters related to the business of mexicanos in their private search for salvation and redemption.

2

Ill Will Hunting (Penitentes)

It is just past three in the afternoon, the hour the gospels record as the moment Christ was nailed and left to die on the cross. The year is 1888, nearly two millennia after that crucifixion. Charles F. Lummis is the man with his head draped by the black cloth of a Prosch camera obscura. He has just completed a successful New Mexican safari hunt in search of elusive evidence of penitents having bagged the "first ever" photographs of a crucifixion as purportedly carried out by New Mexicans in their Holy Week observances. Lummis himself describes the scene: "And there we stood facing each other, the crucified and I—the one playing with the most wonderful toy of modern progress, the other racked by the barbarous device of twenty centuries ago" ([1893] 1952, 75).

This intrusion by an outsider at the village of San Mateo is one of the most aggravated instances of Penitente hunting in New Mexico history. It is an instance marked by the taking of photographs at gunpoint with the assistance of local residents Ireneo and Amado Chaves. The act also marks the beginning of a sustained period of lurid interest in New Mexico's religious brotherhood of penitents. For the next three decades, "Penitente hunting" would be a yearly pastime for travelers and anthropologists who racked up a number of egregious intrusions and violations of the Lenten observances of what was and is a private religious and mutual aid association of long standing in New Mexico.

Marta Weigle notes, "By the end of World War I, the Penitentes had become a regular stop on tourist itineraries and an inevitable highlight in

regional travelogues" (1976, 114). To illustrate how the annual ritual of Penitente sightings evidences the disregard of curiosity mongers, Weigle cites
the example in the *Santa Fe New Mexican* of a district judge responding to
a complaint filed by the Hermanos against some Penitente hunters. Judge
Miguel Otero explained, "The Penitentes complained to me that they did
not object to having people come around to watch them if they did so in a
respectful way, but what they did object to was having people come around
their morada [chapel] and flashing automobile search lights on them and
laughing at them and in other ways making themselves obnoxious" (qtd.
in Weigle 1976, 116).

The Brotherhood of Penitentes, officially known as La Cofradía Piad-
osa de Nuestro Padre Jesús Nazareno (The Pious Confraternity of Our
Father Jesus of Nazareth), has a history of policing its religious activities
from unwanted intrusion and unwarranted speculation. Surprisingly, the
greater part of that history includes operating through ordinary legal and
political channels. Still, it is plausible to think (though we have no knowledge of this) that the wardens (celadores) present at San Mateo on Good
Friday 1888 would have acted to stop Charles Lummis from taking his photos had they been asked to do so or had they not been staring down a pistol
barrel and had Ireneo Chaves not menaced them, in Clint Eastwood fashion, saying that "if any one attempts to hurt him [Lummis] or his instruments, I will blow his head off." Any resulting action would have been, in
good conscience, an act of self-defense. At San Mateo things could have
gotten physical, but save for incidents of being accosted or held up as in
the Lummis case, members of the Brotherhood were most likely to defend
their religious integrity by seeking legal redress from local courts or officers of the law on the basis of religious freedom or anti-defamation claims.

The authenticity of Lummis's San Mateo photos, as I demonstrate,
must now be understood in the context of how they came to be made.
Nonetheless, they remain a potent example of the power of image making
and of technology's ability to outstrip the safeguards of the native subject
to protect his or her privacy and image. Southwest scholars have generally
accepted the Lummis photographs as prima facie evidence of a crucifixion
of a penitent by his own brethren, but a close examination of the photos
does not square with the tale Lummis told of them in his famous travelogue, *The Land of Poco Tiempo*, published in 1893.

To begin with, Lummis did not appear at the photo-shoot cold. He had in fact spent the previous several weeks residing just a mile outside of San Mateo at the home of his friend, Amado Chaves. Lummis was there convalescing from a mysterious attack of muscular paralysis in his left side and arm. His malady had manifested itself in Los Angeles in December of 1887 while he was working as a reporter for the *Los Angeles Times*.

This was Lummis's second visit to New Mexico, the first having occurred when he was on his famous tramp across the continent in 1884, when he walked the 1,500 miles from Chillicothe, Ohio, to Los Angeles to take a job as a reporter at the *Times*. On the tramp, Lummis sent dispatches of his adventures along the way to his former newspaper in Ohio. His second stay in New Mexico would last a full four years. During this time he redirected his life, restored his health, embarked on a successful career as a freelance journalist/photographer, saw his work legitimized, and found himself catapulted to the stature of a leading authority on the cultures of the Southwest. The greatest part of his notoriety would come from his photos and exposé of the Penitentes that he first published under the title "The Penitent Brothers," in *Cosmopolitan* in May 1889.

In a recent biography, Mark Thompson explains how it was generally believed that Lummis's relentless work pace at the *Times* had caused his physical collapse and brought on the onset of his paralysis. At the urging of his wife, Dorothea (Dolly), and other close friends Lummis decided to leave the *Times* and recuperate in New Mexico. Despite his attempts to deny his affliction and continue to work, Lummis eventually succumbed to the reality that he was very sick.

On his first go-round through the Southwest, Lummis had made a quick but deep friendship with the patriarch of the Chaves ranch, Manuel "El Leoncito" Chaves, and with his sons, Amado and Ireneo. When the Chaveses heard of their friend's plight they welcomed him back with open arms, inviting him to stay in San Mateo as long as he needed. Mark Thompson describes the convivial life Lummis experienced back in New Mexico:

> In early afternoon, they reached the Chaves hacienda. Lummis felt like he had come home. The sprawling adobe with its twelve-foot wide central hallway, floors carpeted with Navajo blankets, windows covered with lace, roaring fireplaces, and fun-loving members

of the extended Chaves clan, two dozen in all including several
seductive señoritas—this was where, during his brief stopover as a
tramp, Lummis's lifelong affair with Spanish American culture had
begun. (2001, 95)

Soon after his arrival in New Mexico, Lummis's health improved to the
point that he was able to roam about the mesas and hills near San Mateo,
hunting rabbits and coyotes and building enough stamina to rifle through
nearby Indian ruins digging up rare pots and other artifacts. Throughout,
Lummis remained the ever-mindful reporter attuned to learning whatever
he could about the lore of the region as he went about his daily encounters with both Indians and nuevomexicanos. In all this he counted on the
patronage and influence of his hosts. The advice and counsel he received
from Amado Chaves was especially useful to him. Years later, when writing to his son Win, Amado described the entrée Lummis had to the residents of San Mateo. It is through Amado that one learns that the villagers
remembered Lummis from his first trek, and that, upon his return, they
expressed concern for him and inquired after his health and well-being:

> The people of San Mateo were delighted to know that he was allright
> [sic]. They all loved him and thought there was no cure for him. The
> young people started to take him to the village where they would play
> games and sing. All went well. He was getting well fast. He learned
> to make cigarettes with one hand. He carried a guapre (a small bag
> made of hide) full of tobacco and a piece of steel and a flint to strike
> fire to light his cigarettes. (Amado Chaves, October 28, 1929)

Lummis was beside himself over his good fortune at finding himself
back in the company of his New Mexican friends and let it be known that
life in San Mateo was a delight:

> If a contented animal could keep a diary it would be a good deal like
> mine. Hunting, riding, digging in prehistoric ruins, photographing
> beautiful landscapes, quaint habitations and quainter inhabitants,
> rounding up cattle, eating chile, frijoles and carne machado, talking
> rheumatic Spanish, learning queer folksongs of the shepherds, and
> paralyzing them with Irish imitations, sleeping like a log and eating
> like a coyote—that's about the bill. (qtd. in Thompson 2001, 101)

Presumably, Lummis had already met a good number of Penitentes on his return to New Mexico. He would have encountered them among the men and women servants and the ranch hands at the Chaves hacienda or among the "quainter inhabitants" of the village itself. Nonetheless, Lummis notes in his diary that he first learned of the Penitentes and their Lenten observances on March 7, 1888, three weeks ahead of *Semana Santa* in San Mateo. Holy Week, the culmination of Lent, promised to be the most active time for his neighbors to engage in penitential rites at the morada in San Mateo canyon. Anticipating the penitential activities at San Mateo during Holy Week, Lummis resolved: "Then I will photograph them! *Por dios amigo*, but they will kill you if you think of such a foolhardy thing! But who ever knew an enthusiast to be a coward in the line of his hobby? If I had been certain of being killed the next moment, it is not sure I should not have tried to take the photographs first, so wrought up was I" ([1893] 1952, 92–93).

Not only did Lummis get the photos he wanted, but in the process he spun a powerful liminal tale of vengeance and malevolence that he placed on the residents of San Mateo, the same people with whom he had just spent weeks in convivial splendor. In "Penitent Brothers" he disparaged all of San Mateo by calling it "the most unreclaimed Mexican village in New Mexico." Lummis's story would bring forth subsequent dramas and violence whose effects endure to this day.

Lummis's Fiction of a Crucifixion

The hunt for Penitente ceremonies took up a good part of the month of March. In his diary Lummis records that Amado and Ireneo Chaves first mentioned the Penitentes to him on March 7, 1888. Four days later, with Dolly visiting from Los Angeles, Lummis wrote in his diary: "Dolly y yo andamos á pie á San Mateo (la plaza) y visitamos el Molino y la morada de los penitentes. También la casa de Lorenzo Sánchez. [Dolly and I walk over to the plaza at San Mateo and we visit the old mill and the morada of the Penitentes. We also stop at Lorenzo Sánchez's house]" (Lummis Diary, March 11, 1888).[1] Lummis later turned these prosaic visits to San Mateo into more dramatic renderings that tantalized his magazine readers:

I had been watching feverishly for Holy Week to come. No photographer had ever caught the Penitentes with his sun-lasso, and
I was assured of death in various unattractive forms at the first hint
of an attempt. But when the ululation of the *pito* filled the ear at
night, enthusiasm crowded prudence to the wall. The village air
grew heavy with mysterious whisperings and solemn expectancy.
Whatever they talked about, the people were evidently thinking of
nothing else. I wandered through the fields and arroyos at all hours
of the night, trying to trail the mysterious whistle whose echoes
seemed to come from all points of the compass; but in vain. My
utmost reward was a glimpse of three ghostly figures just disappearing into Juanito's house on the hill. (1889, 44)

On Holy Thursday movement and activity at the morada at San Mateo
intensified, and the day provided Lummis with the opportunity he sought
to catch the "Penitentes with his sun-lasso." However, Lummis's diary entry
for Thursday the twenty-ninth is sparse and underwhelming. He wrote:

De mañanita Amado y yo vamos a pie a la plaza y Ireneo trae mi
máquina de retratos en el bogh. Vemos a los penitentes con azotes,
maderos y lid [sic]. Tomo 14 retratos y arruino 2 vidrios también.
Vuelvo a casa Chaves para hacer listos otros vidros. Los penitentes van a la capilla y no vuelo a la plaza. Acabo cinco retratos de
penitentes.

[Early in the morning, Amado and I walk to the plaza and Ireneo
brings my photo camera in the buggy. We see the Penitentes with
lashes, crosses, and commotion (?). I take fourteen pictures and
ruin two glass plates as well. I go back to the Chaves house to make
ready some other plates. The Penitentes go to the chapel and I do
not return to the plaza. I finish five photographs of Penitentes.
("Diaries," March 29, 1888)]

While managing to take his photographs at a guarded distance from a
hilltop overlooking the *camposanto* to which groups of villagers and penitents had been making sacred pilgrimages all that day, Lummis resolved
to get closer to the action. In stark contrast to Lummis's descriptions of
elusive and clannish Penitentes hiding away from view and moving as

"strange specters flit[ting] through the loneliest mountain gorges," that afternoon the Hermanos quite literally paid Lummis a visit. It was late in the afternoon of Holy Thursday as Lummis prepared his glass plates for the next day's shoot that a procession of penitents led by the *Hermano Mayor* (chief brother), José Salazar, made its annual pilgrimage to the chapel at the Chaves home. Lummis's biographer tells how Lummis seized the opportunity to set the stage for his scoop the next day:

> At the end of the day, the Penitente procession made its way to the Chaves family compound, a customary stop. The flagellants waddled on their knees into the small family chapel in the shade of two old oak trees a hundred yards from the house and lay prone on the floor for an hour while the rest of the people in the procession sang hymns. Then the flagellants entered a room in the Chaves home, plugged the keyhole to prevent anyone from looking in and discovering their identity, removed their hoods and ate a meal. The rest of those in the procession milled around outside for a couple of hours with nothing to do, which gave Lummis a "golden opportunity" to win over the leaders of the cult. (Thompson 2001, 104–105)

Years later Lummis gave his version of the meeting: "But that night [Holy Thursday] thanks to Don Amado and his brother, I got the Hermano Mayor (chief brother) and some of the Brothers of Light over to the Chaves home. There I plied them with cigarettes and good words, photos of other strange things I had taken and a good deal of 'soft Sawder and Human Natur' and they were mine" (qtd. in *Centennial Exhibition*, 29). In *Cosmopolitan*, Lummis continues his story, "On the morning of Good Friday, March 30, I was in the village bright and early; and so was every one else for twenty miles around" (1889, 46). Apparently the negotiations of the evening before were working in his favor. At around ten o'clock, Lummis set up his camera some two hundred feet southeast of the morada on a nearby rise and shot photos of the morning processions going in and out of the morada. Around two o'clock, José Salazar came out of the morada and, approaching Lummis, "marked a spot about one hundred feet from the door where I might stand." The two men had a curt exchange: "'Sta bueno?' he asked through Juan and when I replied that it was, he gave orders that no man should stir a finger until the pictures were taken" (1889, 48).

At three in the afternoon, the holy hour set to reenact the crucifixion, Lummis found himself standing in front of the morada when, he later wrote, "in gracious response to my request, the Hermano Mayor had paced off thirty feet from the foot of the cross and marked a spot to which I might advance in order to get a larger picture" (50). From there Lummis snapped his photographs of the mock crucifixion that would make him famous in his own lifetime.

Ireneo's menacing warning and at least three pistols would underwrite Lummis's "soft Sawder and Human Natur." Lummis later confessed, "Don Ireneo and a peon stood near me, each with a six-shooter cocked in his hand. As I needed my only hand for the camera, my gun lay cocked on top of the camera box" ([1893] 1952, 29).

If one "reads" the photos without referring to the Lummis narrative, the images are of an undefined hulk bound to a cross. The figure is wrapped like a burrito in what at first glance seems to be a sheet or shroud. The figure's head, wrapped in a black veil, pops out of the burrito like a black olive. Another black blob rests at the foot of the cross. Two brothers hold the cross up by guy ropes and six others are nearby. In addition to the fact that the white sheets obscure the figure beneath, it seems that Lummis or someone else doctored these images. When they are digitized and augmented it is possible to see that the white and black cloth Lummis reported to be sheets and hoods were manually touched up in the photos. At close range, the cloth forms are blockish and angular and have no folds of the kind that would drape naturally around a human body. And the black olive at the base of the cross? Lummis tells us that it is a penitent, who "lay down with his feet against the cross and his head pillowed upon the stone, where a mass of *entraña* [cactus] kept his back sixteen or eighteen inches above the ground" ([1893] 1952, 74). The angle at which the photo was shot keeps us from really knowing what the shape is.

Since the Lummis photos do not represent what they purport to represent, "a crucified [Penitente Cristo]," one must ask: What do they represent? Clearly, they represent Lummis's maniacal obsession with bagging a trophy-photograph of a live crucifixion as supposedly practiced by the Penitent Brothers of New Mexico, but the scene captured in the photo is, by one measure or another, a staged representation. Two explanations seem plausible. The event could in actuality be a simulated crucifixion as practiced by the Hermanos, wherein representations of the Passion of Christ often involved the raising of a life-size *bulto* of Christ in the Sepulcher known as "El Santo Entierro" at the fourteenth or last installment of the Stations of the Cross. In common practice, at this point in the ceremony, a reclining figure of Christ, with moveable arms and legs, would often be laid out and bound to a cross to represent the crucified Cristo. This is a spiritual exercise the Hermanos would have commonly enacted at three o'clock on Good Friday. If the figure beneath the sheet were really that of a wooden statue, it would explain why Lummis felt a need to mask the image. The alternative explanation is that the photo is of a completely hostage event, one performed for Lummis by the Hermanos by force, intimidation, coercion, or acquiescence. This, as I will show, is the more probable of my two suppositions.

When one gives full attention to Lummis's accompanying narrative script, as a means to equilibrate the image and the text, more questions arise regarding what actually transpired at San Mateo. Quite remarkably, in "The Penitent Brothers" and in other published accounts of the San Mateo incident, Lummis is careful to provide detail—however pressed through his highly impressionistic imagination—regarding the manner in which the rituals he saw played themselves out in real time. His Holy Thursday observations, for example, are closely drawn descriptions of his surveillance of Penitente ceremonies from beginning to end. Lummis notes,

> It was two P.M. when a stir in the crowd on the hill-top told us that it was coming at last; and the camera was straightaway planted behind the adobe ramparts of the door-yard. In five minutes more a fifer came over the ridge, followed by five women singing hymns; and behind them a half-naked figure with a bagged head, swinging his deliberate whip, *swish, thud, swish, thud!* we could hear plainly two hundred yards away, punctuating the weird music. In measured step the pilgrims paced along the reeling footpath, and disappeared around a spur toward the *morada*. (1889, 45)

Likewise, the glass plates he produced that day attest to the fact that before him had passed a highly structured and formally arranged religious entourage, one formed by members of the brotherhood, members of the women's sodalities, and members of the community-at-large. Lummis was observing a "procesión," one of "the four named rituals" that Penitente communities staged each year during Holy Week. The act of moving in procession from one sacred shrine to another was and continues to be the most common of all Penitente rituals. At San Mateo, the object of this particular devotion was to visit the graves of the dead at the community camposanto, and, once there, to offer prayer and sacrifice for the repose of the souls of departed loved ones. Lummis could see, if not completely understand, that the camposanto held great significance in the activities on this day. He goes on to note: "Slowly and solemnly they strode down the slope to the stone-walled graveyard, filed through the roofed entrance, whipped themselves throughout all the paths, knelt in prayer at each grave and filed out again. These services lasted twenty minutes" (46).

Lummis's photos of the procession bear out his observations. In them one sees the penitents, the *pitero* (fifer), the *rezador* (prayer leader), the female members of the Carmelitas (the women's sodality), the *verónicas* (young girls representing Veronica), and members of the community bringing up the end of the procession. These photos not only represent the penitents; they also bring into view the range and placement of the various participants who form the ritual context that Lummis observed, but the same cannot be said of his Good Friday plates of the "self-crucifixion."

Lummis's dearth of narrative explaining how things on Good Friday unfolded in real time is more than just an oversight. Students and scholars of Lummis uniformly point out that he was compulsive about logging his observations in his diaries, yet he consigns not a word about the rite or ritual leading to his most important "discovery" in any of his published or unpublished writings. Odd too, but not surprising, he consigns nothing to his diary that would give us an indication of just what arrangement he and the Hermano Mayor came to at their Holy Thursday meeting. In his published accounts, Lummis led his readers to conclude that what he got from José Salazar was permission to photograph on Good Friday and to set up his camera out in the open and at comfortable distance from the action.

The omission of the ritual context to the San Mateo crucifixion is, however, not a small lapse of memory. Indeed, it suggests that the climactic moment of a mock crucifixion did not follow the ritual cadence of a reenactment that would have required time and space to complete. This brings further importance to the question of what exactly Lummis asked

José Salazar to do on Good Friday, making it entirely plausible to believe that he asked him to perform a rite that the Hermanos themselves had not contemplated doing at all. Lummis could have done this with a mere suggestion that he was interested in understanding how the Cristo was put on the cross in the past.

The plates themselves are quite telling, precisely for what they omit over what they include. By Lummis's count there are eight individuals in the frame, all of whom he identifies by name. They are, from left to right, Juan Baca, José Salazar, Jesús Mirabal, Filomeno, Cisto, Santiago Jaramillo, "Cuate," and "Melito." Juan Baca and José Salazar pose for the camera, clearly aware that they are in the loop of the "sun-lasso," and they return an inquiring look at the photographer's gaze. Filomeno averts his gaze and casts his sight downward as though he is an unenthusiastic participant. Cisto, Cuate, and Melito have their backs to Lummis. Jesús Mirabal is at the far distant end of the circle of men surrounding the cross and only a sliver of his right side is visible; the rest of his body is blocked by the men with their backs to the camera. All the men are dressed in ordinary street attire. Lummis reported that he later discovered that Santiago Jaramillo, the cook at the home of Ramón A. Baca, played the Christo at the center of the photo. Lummis does not name the black blimp at the foot of the cross and, as already mentioned, it is not clear what the form is. Other individuals may be just outside the frame, unless they were specifically asked to distance themselves from the scene in such a way that no one of the fifty-one women and children from the morning processions, the numerous other villagers bearing the chromos of saints, the hundreds of spectators Lummis reported to have been there, or the dozen or so *ayundantes* cast even a shadow into the field of the camera's gaze. Mind you, it is not that I think that they are not there; surely some of them would have ambled about in clumps and groups around the scene. I just don't think they are there as participants in a ritualized observance of Christ's Passion and, particularly, one sanctioned as Lummis reported by the Cofradía itself. A rite such as this, with deep religious and cultural significance, would have quite naturally brought them into the scene of the action and into the frame of the photo.

Thus, Lummis's famous photograph that he captioned "The only authentic photograph of a Penitente crucifixion ever taken" is for many

FIG. 3. Charles Lummis's photo of a mock crucifixion at San Mateo, New Mexico, Good Friday, March 30, 1888. Courtesy of the Braun Research Library, Autry National Center of the American West, Los Angeles; N30747.

reasons not what it purports to be. Devoid and detached from the village ceremony at San Mateo, it is akin to a single frame of film pulled from celluloid footage to produce a useful publicity still. In this case, there is only the still, severed and detached from the sequential motion of the ritual itself. Despite Lummis's assurances to the contrary, he gives us a publicity still without a movie.

This, too, is the moment of fabrication of Lummis's dramatic tale of Penitentes taking out vengeance on prying journalists. In Lummis's recollections, the tale of retribution grew out of his resolve to uncover the Penitentes and expose their rites to the world. But if the means that Lummis employed to take his San Mateo photos is convoluted and confused by the various accounts he gives of the disposition of the residents of San Mateo toward him, so too is the whole matter of the grudge Lummis told his readers the Penitentes had for him. The Penitentes, he maintained, had resolved to do him great harm, perhaps even kill him. Given Lummis's betrayal of the trust of the residents of San Mateo, they no doubt had good reason to change their initial opinion of him.

In September 1888, while Lummis was still staying at the Chaves compound, he determined that he simply had to have an example of the *disciplina*, the scourge made of soft-plaited yucca that the Penitentes used in their exercises. Apparently, he was interested in a capturing an adventure trophy to accompany his photographs, and so one evening in September, after having spent the afternoon photographing the morada and taking portraits of "some of the Penitentes themselves," Lummis stole away and, under cover of darkness, broke into the morada and took two of the yucca whips. Lummis made a feat of daring out of this act of common larceny, a tale he obviously relished telling over and over again. He consigned the event to his journals on at least two occasions. His journal entry describes the incident: "That night with a brave boy, burgle the Moradas and steal 2 only Penitente scourges ever acquired by museum or collector. We are detected and fired on 6 times as we bound over the rocky ridge behind the Morada" ("Journals" 1888, 1). Thirty years later in Los Angeles, when asked by Garnet Holmes to speak to a group of students, Lummis noted in his journal: "He asked me to speak to one of his classes about the Penitentes and their strange ceremonials; so I took one of the Penitente whips—of which I have the only 2 in the world outside the Brotherhood, and which I had to burgle the Morada to secure" ("Journals" 1921, 2).

Lummis summed up his Holy Week adventure at San Mateo in *The Land of Poco Tiempo*. In it he made a point to impress upon his readers how he had risked life and limb to get his story and photos. He did this while continuing to live at the Chaves home. For six months, from March to September 1888, he resided there without fear of reprisal from his immediate neighbors, the Penitentes of San Mateo, and still enjoyed good relations with them, even though Lummis had already planted the seed of his narrative of hostile Mexican commoners and Penitente revenge in his *Cosmopolitan* article. He was also aware that the book would have far greater impact on the American reading public and, in *The Land of Poco Tiempo*, did not lose the opportunity to hype up his encounter with the Penitentes:

> And make the photographs I did, twenty-five of them, with my own useful hand quaking on the bulb of the Prosch shutter and now and then snapping an instantaneous picture of the marvelous sight, with a cocked six-shooter on the top of the camera box, and lion-like Don Ireneo and a stalwart peon with revolvers in hand facing back the murderous mob. Perhaps the pictures were not worth the risk of that day and the many subsequent months when repeated

attempts were made to assassinate me; but they are the only photographs that were ever made of the strangest of the strange corners of our country and I grudged the price. I afterward got photographs of several of the chief Penitentes. ([1893] 1952, 92–93)

Nearly a full year later while Lummis was residing at Isleta Pueblo, ten miles south of Albuquerque, the whole cycle of his story seemingly played itself out just as he scripted it. Culling the details from the Lummis diaries, biographer Mark Thompson relates how Lummis's new life at Isleta almost came to an end in a most unexpected and dramatic way. It was early in February when, as was his habit, Lummis got up just after midnight from where he had been writing next to a wood-burning stove to take a break, stretch, and admire the night sky. With his right arm raised above his head and his mouth in a wide-open yawn, he was suddenly hit with a spray of pellets from a shotgun blast. Though dazed and bleeding, Lummis was able to spot the silhouette of his assailant as he fled the scene (Thompson 2001, 126). The attack was enough to leave Lummis bed-ridden for several days, mending from the most serious of his wounds, a pellet shot that pierced his open mouth and lodged itself at the base of his neck, where it would remain for the rest of his life.

To many it appeared that the Penitentes had exacted their revenge on the nosy *americano.* Lummis did little to remove this idea from public view, even while he consigned the real motive for the attack to several enigmatic entries in his journal. The idea that the Penitentes were involved in the assault on Lummis was so persistent that years later several interested parties pressed Amado Chaves for information on what he knew about the matter. When Albuquerque resident Laurence Lee asked Amado to clear up the matter for him, Chaves wrote back: "Lummis always believed that the San Mateo Penitentes had sent someone to shoot him. I never could find out whether that was true or not. They were very angry and may have done that. I do not know" ("Amado Chaves"). It is of course not unimportant that Chaves, who lived a mile away from San Mateo and knew most of the Penitentes personally, could not say if Lummis was telling the truth or not.

If not the Penitentes, who else in New Mexico held a grudge against Charles Lummis in 1889? Lummis consigns the core of that matter to his journal, in which he relived the night of his attack in detail, transmitting the entire entry in an intimate letter to his wife, Dolly. He names his attacker:

> Liberato's peons [are] superstitious about me, and believe I lead a charmed life, escape their bullets so many times—and especially because in dead of winter at lambing camp, I chop holes through foot of ice to take my morning bath at 10 below zero. So Liberato imports a pelon [*sic*] from old Mexico who lies around the pueblo some days to get a line on me; learns about midnight, I always step outside my 'dobe room to take fresh air a few minutes and swing my one arm to open my lung. ("Journals" 1889, 2)

Throughout his time in New Mexico, Lummis supported himself by continuing to work as an investigative reporter and his copy articles covered a gamut of newsworthy scandals in territorial politics, education, and race relations. His no-holds-barred exposés of life in the territory resulted in far more bitter entanglements than those involving the penitents at San Mateo. Mark Thompson gives a full account of the circumstances that led to his being shot at Isleta:

> By the end of the summer of 1888, Lummis was on the trail of a story that was far more dangerous than his exposé of the Penitente ritual. It was a story about five unresolved murders committed over the previous couple of years in Valencia County, which in those days covered a vast expanse from the Rio Grande valley south of Albuquerque to the rangelands around San Mateo. Plenty of people knew who was behind the killings but no one dared name the culprits. The opportunity to blow the story open was one Lummis simply couldn't resist. It didn't seem to faze him that the prime suspects were the Chaveses' neighbors, the heads of the family that had been intertwined with that of his hosts for generations, Roman and Liberato Baca. (2001, 109)

Lummis's New Mexico sojourn involved a web of personal and public associations that converge in complex and intricate ways in his relationships. That he managed to get his hand in so many things is a remarkable testimony to his ability to play the end against the center in any number of situations. Clearly, Lummis was living in a social and cultural context thick with complex social relationships involving issues of race, class, social power, and white privilege. Throughout, Lummis took risks and was able to survive and promote his career. He did this largely by evolving contingent strategies for dealing with the different kinds of people he met while in New Mexico. He took advantage of class and racial divides, for example, whenever these suited his ends and thus was able to play one group of folks off another, just as he did at San Mateo in his engagement with the elite families (the Chaveses and Bacas) and the New Mexico commoners in the villages. To explain the hostility he experienced from the townspeople on the day he went about photographing the Penitentes, it became imperative for Lummis to mark and divide nuevomexicano society into two mutually exclusive social strata by which he could make his essentialized notions of each group fit his narrative. His hosts, the Chaveses, are represented in his writings as the upright example of "Spanish gentility and hospitality," while folks living adjacent to them are depicted as despotic tyrants (the Bacas) or wretched peasants (the villagers). In contrast to the permanent residents of New Mexico who, owing to their class and racial identities, lived in fixed relationship to one another, Lummis enjoyed the advantage of the social mobility that came to him as the outsider. Thus, he was able to move in and out of circumstances where others were not. His residence at the Chaves hacienda and open entrée to the village folk is one example; the other is his residence at Isleta Pueblo, which becomes even more astounding given that the Pueblos were then extremely wary of outsiders.

Lummis fancied himself an ethnologist, a student of living cultures, and to the extent that he recorded elements of Hispanic and Native American culture that were unknown to white Americans, he qualifies as a privileged chronicler of Borderlands culture. The exigency placed on him by virtue of his profession as a journalist, however, made it impossible for him to acquire, let alone study, the full dimension of life pathways that, at times, he was the first among his people to see. In the end, it was his fables that took root, his narratives of adventure and retribution, and not his overall appreciation for the peoples of the Southwest that he so strongly espoused in later years.

I am, of course, most interested here in the story of Penitente vengeance, not merely because it made Lummis's freelance career, but because of how it was created and how it came to endure over time. Clearly, as I have shown, Lummis's liminal narrative functions as drama, the fuel of commercial film, precisely because it leaves the complicated interface between Lummis and the Penitentes out of the telling. In much the same way any good scriptwriter would have done, Lummis boiled the story down to antagonisms between barbarism and modernity, between the familiar and the strange. Neatly, surgically, Lummis edits away mention of the friendships he made with the common folk at San Mateo, avoids any mention of his betrayal of their kindness or of his theft of ritual objects from their holy places. Nor does he mention his run-in with the Bacas, their close familial ties to the Chaveses, and many more elements that make the offscreen elements of his time at San Mateo a far more compelling narrative than anything that would end up in films made of the Penitentes in later decades, films that to one degree or another owe their existence to Lummis's originating encounter narrative.

D. W. Griffith in the Borderlands

Director D. W. Griffith supervised the filming of the first commercial motion picture to feature the Penitentes. His film *The Penitentes* was completed in 1915 and released by Triangle Pictures in the same year. No copies of the film are known to have survived and what is known of the production comes from several film reviews published in November and December of 1915. Interestingly, the film did not depend exclusively on Lummis's San Mateo chronicles; rather, Griffith used the Penitentes as the backdrop to stage a convoluted action-packed plot taken from a novel by Ellis Wales. The film fictionalizes and embellishes on sensational accounts of New Mexico Penitentes while setting the action of the film in the distant past.

The film opens with an Indian attack on a Mexican village. The inhabitants of the village, except for two monks and a child named Manuel, all die in the attack. Soon after, Penitentes living nearby claim the property belonging to Manuel's family and take the boy away. Years later, at a regional fiesta, a priest notices Manuel, now grown, and questions the Penitente leader about his background. Fearing that the truth of the kidnapping will be revealed, the leader induces his followers to choose Manuel to be the sacrificial Christo on Good Friday. Manuel's girlfriend, Dolores, tries to dissuade him from participating but he insists that it is something he must do. The priest pleads with a Colonel Baca to save Manuel, which leads to the colonel's troops descending on the village and stopping the ceremony. The film ends with one of the old monks revealing Manuel's true identity and heritage, thus allowing him to return to his accorded place in society.

Film scholars have pointed to the disturbing representations of ethnic groups that repeatedly show up in Griffith's films. Known almost entirely for his negative depictions of African Americans during Reconstruction in his tour-de-force *The Birth of a Nation*, Griffith has received less scholarly attention for his representations of other ethnic populations in the United States. The director's Mexican-themed productions, *The Penitentes* and *Martyrs of the Alamo*, illustrate his penchant for racializing history and culture. An early film critic, writing in *Variety* about *The Penitentes*, was obviously aware of such linkages: "The filmization was directed by Jack Conway under the supervision of D. W. Griffith and in a great many ways reminds one of the note which the master director struck when he worked out the screen version of the Ku-Klux Clan in 'The Birth of a Nation'" ("Penitentes" 1915, 1). Be that as it may, the reviewer in *Variety* also put readers on notice that Lummis had a hand in the making of the film: "On the leader to the film version of Mr. Wales's story there is a brief recital of the beliefs of the faith which the Penitentes follow and someone is accorded acknowledgement for aid in furnishing historical data for the feature. Mr. Wales's tale, while a work of fiction, has a certain convincing basis of historic fact and on the strength of this alone the picture will undoubtedly attack" (1).

Although the reviewer does not name the film consultant, it was none other than Charles Lummis who lent the film its "convincing basis of historical fact." Lummis was hired to assist with the details of staging this film, a matter that called for the creation of a Mexican village. The reviewer of the film notes the village was built in Chatsworth Park north of downtown Los Angeles. The Lummis photo collection at the Southwest Museum in Los Angeles contains the unusual photo of what appears to be a young boy, hooded and wearing thin, white cotton pants, carrying a cross penitent-style. It is the only photo of its kind among the historical material Lummis shot in-situ in New Mexico or elsewhere in the Southwest. The "penitent boy" photo is a staged shot taken inside a house, perhaps at Lummis's El Alisal home. In the photo the boy stands before a white drop cloth draped above a sheepskin rug. To the left are a bookcase and desk. Flanking the cross bearer are the barely visible figures of two men standing on chairs and holding up the white sheet. There is nothing to indicate when or where the photo was taken, but a plausible explanation is that the staging of this penitent act was done in connection with Lummis's consultation with the Griffith film people.

This was not the first time that Lummis had been asked to consult on films. As one of only a handful of experts on the Southwest at that time, he was often called upon to add authenticity to feature films dealing with Native American and Hispanic subjects. Before *The Penitentes*, he worked on the film adaptation of *Ramona*, Helen Hunt Jackson's famous novel of early California. He no doubt had several reasons to engage in this kind of work, one being that he could earn extra income by contracting with film companies to shoot on location at his Los Angeles home. Lummis never got used to working with film people. According to his biographer, much of his discomfort stemmed from the fact that he was "a man accustomed to having full control over his creative output [and] wasn't cut out for the collaborative

FIG. 4. Staged photo of boy penitent carrying cross inside a dwelling. Courtesy of the Braun Research Library, Autry National Center of the American West, Los Angeles; N20142.

nature of that sort of work" (Thompson 2001, 293). He revealed his total antipathy for film people in a letter to Amado Chaves in May 1917. Lummis writes: "I have had experience with them in quite a number of cases—including 'Ramona,' and 'The Penitentes' and various other things—some of which they summoned me to advise them about at their studios, and some of which they staged here at my home. And of all the pirates I ever encountered they take the loot" (Lummis Letter, May 6, 1917).

Given Lummis's grandiose self-image, perhaps he was miffed that the plot of *The Penitentes* completely left out the story of his own exploits among the group. In a most ironic twist of fate it turns out that Lummis's narrative of Penitente vengeance and retribution would eventually turn up in a film that a group of Hollywood filmmakers released in 1936. Shameless and sensationalistic, *The Lash of the Penitentes*, produced nearly a decade after Lummis's death, proposed to "once again expose the secret cult of the Penitentes" to the American public. This film and the offscreen tragedies it produced is the subject of my next chapter. But, before turning to a discussion of *Lash*, I would be remiss if I did not mention the fact that back in New Mexico the Brotherhood of Penitentes had taken notice of Lummis's publications and photos and resolved to do something about them. Their response, however, had nothing to do with exacting vengeance and everything to do with defending and protecting themselves under the guarantees of the U.S. Constitution.

Just two years after the San Mateo incident, Brotherhood constitutions would begin to resound with the first signs of defense and protest. At a general meeting on June 7, 1890, the membership of the Concilio de Santa Gertrudis in Mora, New Mexico, added three articles to its governing constitution. The language of their resolutions appears as a direct response to Lummis's foray into New Mexico, calling upon members of the Brotherhood as follows:

Rule 2: To vigorously and carefully enforce each and every right granted by the Constitution and laws of the United States which favor every member of this Fraternity as each is a citizen.

Rule 3: To energetically prosecute by all legal and just means any individual or group of men who commit any violence, assault or disregard against the virtue, honor or sensibilities that is to be accorded to a member of this Fraternity.

Rule 4: To respond or cause a response to be issued to any article or publication that contains any remark against the honor, reputation, or
character of the members of this Fraternity, or their families, or
of this Fraternity in general as may appear in any publication, be
it inside or out of this territory and to demand and require of the
editor or manager of such a publication to explain and name the
author of such defamation. (Meléndez, Personal papers)

Following New Mexico's admission into statehood, its newly organized
legislature adopted an act in 1915 to protect religious organizations from
the kind of libel described above. While not making reference to any religious association in particular, the language of this first-of-its-kind hate
crime bill in the area of religious protection appears most directly aimed
at curbing the troubles the Penitente brotherhoods were experiencing, or
so Section 1 of the act suggests:

Section 1. Any person who, with intent to injure, publishes or circulates any malicious statement in writing with reference to or concerning any fraternal or religious order or society shall be guilty of
criminal libel. (Weigle 1971, 508)

It seems, too, that Hermanos were not merely given to rhetoric, as later
they defended themselves publicly and as the following example clearly
illustrates. On April 1, 1939, *The Horse Fly*, a small English-language newspaper published in Taos, New Mexico, published a woodblock print by Man-
ville Chapman of a black-hooded man writhing and bound to a cross. The
woodblock, entitled "Penitente Crucifixion," ran with this caption: "Once
Upon a Time, Good Friday was celebrated like this in good old Taos." In the
following week's issue there appeared a vehement protest from Taos-area
Hermanos, in which they challenged the editor, Walter "Spud" Johnson, to
"get down to brass tacks":

Mr. Johnson, we know that there are a few unknown writers in Taos
& would-be friends of the native people or the penitentes that have
made great efforts to enrich their bins with gold, writing great falsi-
fications and exaggerations about the penitentes.

  We believe that our doings are in accord with the Christian religion of which we are members and we resent criticism on the part

of would-be friends like you, Chapman and others now living in Taos. We could cite many religions and their practices, but feel it uncalled for. Let us keep in mind the greatest charter ever written by civilized man in this continent, the Constitution of America. Do also unto others, as you would have them do unto you. Let us work together in the right way, which is the only way.

Spud Johnson offered a weak apology in response to the letter: "It was no more than an historical note and we are sorry if we offended" (Weigle 1982, 168–169). Protest and challenges to defamatory and miscon-strued images would follow the distribution of *The Lash of the Penitentes* and later films that proposed to use knowledge of sacred ritual against the Brotherhood.

3

A Lie Halfway around the World

The successor in film to Charles Lummis's vengeance narrative is the 1936 road show exploitation film *The Lash of the Penitentes*, produced by Mike J. Levinson and shot by Roland C. Price. Also released as *The Penitente Murder Case*, the film opens with journalist George Mack beseeching his editor at the Metropolitan Syndicate to let him go to New Mexico and uncover the secrets of the Penitentes. Unmoved, Mack's boss is skeptical that the United States could harbor the kind of "wild, primitive men" the Penitentes are said to be. Mack's insistence grows as he declares that the government is about to do an investigation that will "root them out" and that he knows of a vagabond cameraman who shot footage of the Penitentes two years earlier. The editor relents and Mack is on his way.

An ominous narrator assumes control of the storyline as the film crosscuts between stock footage of travel by train and car taken from other films set in the West. As Mack's sedan snakes its way across the mountains and valleys of New Mexico, the narrator amplifies his descriptions, coding the landscape with enough mystery, suspense, and eeriness to weaken the resolve of the most valiant viewer. The narration echoes with the recognizable speech taken from Lummis's *Land of Poco Tiempo*. Lummis's famous encapsulation, "Sun, silence, and adobe is New Mexico in three words," is delivered here as "New Mexico is a land of sunshine, solitude, and silence." In *Lash*, New Mexico is shown to be lonely and primitive, with the villages of the north being the mountain fastness of the Penitentes. The often-photographed *calvario* at Truchas, New Mexico (which later inspired a

Georgia O'Keeffe canvas), makes its debut appearance in *Lash*. The narrator notes, "This is our first sign of the penitentes."

In the scenes that follow, *Lash* works to establish authenticity through a series of filmic forays into the customs and traditions in these villages. The population, we are told, "follows the customs handed down to them through centuries of the past." Lent is a season of high activity when, as the narrator reminds us, "signals flash between the Penitente brothers and they keep a sharp eye out for strangers." Oddly, considering the lack of dramatic potency of the built environment, the film pans the structures of a village and entertains a brief discussion of adobe as an ideal building material, "cool in the summer, warm in the winter." Shots inside village homes of native women grinding corn on a *metate* occasion the remark that "women's work is dull routine." Other aspects of village social life are fleetingly touched upon. That "Latin blood flows freely in these lowly peons" is cause for the festive (romance and singing) and solemn (penance and fatalism) aspects of the villager's existence.

The village scenes in *Lash* combine actual footage juxtaposed against purely staged elements. Some unintended invention also stems from the indiscriminate use of footage of Hispanic villages and of Native Americans at Taos Pueblo. Group and individual portraits of nuevomexicano villagers are used here, but also shots of the natives of Taos Pueblo draped in traditional native blankets. Particularly jarring is the superimposition of a belfry-like tower with radiating animal horns above a low adobe façade. The composite shot is meant to represent a morada. A re-creation of the interior of the morada employs New Mexican santos and other religious items shot against bare, exterior adobe walls.

At last George Mack arrives at his destination. At a plaza (Taos, New Mexico) the journalist approaches a young nuevomexicano named Chico. Mack quickly enlists him to secure a cabin and to work for him during his stay. Mack bolts off to find the morada (which he pronounces "Miradha"). Here the plot cuts away from Mack to supply other "authenticating gems" on tradition and custom. The altars of the morada are shown and described as the repository of "gruesome idols" where "the whip is enshrined as a symbol of salvation." Similar nonsense is invoked when suggesting "the Penitentes canonize their own saints" and the "Christos with skirts are for both men and women." Moving outside the Lenten motif, the film proceeds to show a "corrida de gallos" (a rooster pull), an event described as "a sport close to every peon's heart and for which they cannot restrain their enthusiasm." Here is further evidence of the villagers' strange ways. George Mack appears on the scene asking Chico to explain the corrida but also to ask, "Can you help me get inside the Miradha [morada]?" "No, señor, they will keel [kill] you," answers his informant. In an inter-scene, the film cuts to a procession of hooded druid-like men (no New Mexican equivalent exists). The druids pull a "carreta del muerto" (actually *carreta de la muerte*) that they will leave at the door of a reluctant Penitente novice. Their motive, the narrator says, is to intimidate the young men of the village to join the Penitentes. A second scene outside the Lenten drama places George Mack at the performance of the Matachines dance. The scene employs actual footage of matachines to which the filmmakers add some inventive staging at the point where a set of masked dancers wind around a totem-like idol and peer ghoulishly at the camera, first over one and then the other shoulder of the statue before them. Mack cynically scrutinizes Chico, who is also in attendance. When asked, Chico tells his boss that the dancers will make their way to the morada to do penance. "Can you fix it for me to see it?" Mack asks. "Oh no, no, no, señor," responds his helpmate, "it is very dangerous."

The last third of the film focuses on "the day of orgy," presumably Good Friday, when the Penitentes elect a "white-robed Penitente" to be the "chosen one" whom they "worship as divine on the procession to the *calvario*" (needless to say, no New Mexican equivalents are known to have existed). With his knowledge as a native informant, Chico places Mack at strategic viewing points along the march to Calvary. Here Mack is witness to all forms of violence preceding the simulated crucifixion of the Christo. Mack now has his story, but the film's narrator alerts the audience that he has been spied on all along. Several minutes of the original film are missing from available copies; fortunately, this loss does not diminish the full sense of the plot. The last third of the film is hybrid footage built from staged reenactments of a procession and a mock crucifixion set on coastal California landscapes. A detail compromises the filmmakers' claim that "actual footage of a Penitente scourging and crucifixion shot at great risk by Roland C. Price was dusted off" and sutured into a film to tell the story of the murder of writer and journalist Carl N. Taylor.

Once found out, Chico is surrounded by Penitentes who accuse him of betraying their secrets. "You know what you must do," they warn as the film cuts ahead to Chico sneaking up to Mack's cabin as the journalist types out the final page of his story "The Bloody Trail." Chico treacherously shoots the journalist from the window. Following Mack's death the local sheriff tracks down Chico and forces a confession from the boy, who screams, "I had to do it."

Lash's epilogue begins with a newsroom scene, which shows the presses of a large newspaper running at full tilt. An intertitle informs the viewers: "The giant Press grinds on and thrives upon the adventure that lives in the hearts of men." Cutting away we are taken to a large city in the United States where paperboys bark out the sensational headline "Penitente Writer Murdered." Disbelieving newspaper readers at street corners ask themselves: Who are the Penitentes? The film makes a point of illustrating that this news is reaching a wholly uninformed and unsuspecting American public. The film takes a last, perplexing twist with its parting message directed at the viewing audience. As Alberto López-Pulido has observed, *Lash* "ends with a disturbing racist scene. A large cross is burning in the dark of night and the film's narrator states authoritatively: 'Wake up, America. Here in our own country we can see the heart of Africa pounding against the ribs of the Rockies.'"

Despite widespread misunderstandings of the Penitente brothers, no New Mexican equivalent of a large burning cross is ever mentioned even in the most virulent anti-Penitente literature. The burning cross, uniformly associated with Ku Klux Klan intimidation and retribution, is difficult to explain in relation to the kind of specialized sensationalism *Lash* aims to provoke. The "heart of Africa" tag is, however, easier to explain. It is a quote lifted verbatim from *The Land of Poco Tiempo.* Lummis himself had embedded the remark in an extended description of the Southwest, which he tinged with exotic orientalism: "It is a land of quaint swart faces, of Oriental dress and unspelled speech; a land where distance is lost, and the eye is a liar, a land of ineffable lights and sudden shadows of polytheism and superstition, where the rattlesnake is a demigod, and the cigarette a means of grace, and where Christians mangle and crucify themselves—the heart of Africa beating against the ribs of the Rockies" (3).

Word of the self-proclaimed exposé on the Penitentes reached the governor of New Mexico, Clyde Tingley, who vehemently protested the film in a letter to the chairman of the National Board of Censorship (López-Pulido 2000; Weigle 1976). In his letter, Tingley exculpates the Penitentes, pointing out that the motive in the Taylor murder "was robbery, not religion." Tingley's objections include the use of nudity in the advertisement for the film. Calling the work "cheap sensationalism," he vows to use his police power to ban it from being shown in New Mexico. It is not clear if the Penitentes themselves weighed in on Governor Tingley's protest. It is possible to think that they exerted some influence in the matter, since at the time of the filming a young, charismatic, and gentle figure, Miguel Archibeque, was at work organizing the Hermanos in regional networks and brotherhood councils. Archibeque was himself a state employee in Santa Fe and was widely known and respected by Santa Fe locals and Santa Fe socialites. It is not unconceivable to think that this real Hermano—with a hard-working and Gandhi-like presence—could have culled sympathy for the Hermanos from even high-ranking state officials.[1]

Carl Taylor, Adventurer-Hunter-Martyr

For the better part of three years, Carl Taylor had been living a less than harrowing life among nuevomexicano neighbors in the Sandia mountain community of Cedar Crest, some thirty minutes away from Albuquerque. Taylor came to New Mexico from Milltown, Indiana, in 1926 to pursue a master's degree in English at the University of New Mexico. He completed his studies in 1928 and took a position as an assistant professor at the University of the Philippines in Manila, where he taught for about a year before turning his attention full-time to his writings about out-of-the-way places. He returned to the United States in 1930 and spent two unprofitable years writing before returning to the Philippines to gather additional materials for his book *Odyssey of the Islands.* Taylor took up permanent residence in New Mexico in 1933, electing to live in Cedar Crest, an early Hispanic settlement that until recent times bore the traditional name San Antonito.[2]

Come the Carl Taylor case or not, it is likely that the dramatic plot of *Lash,* or one rather like it (*Indiana Jones Meets the Penitentes* comes to mind), would have made it to Hollywood and celluloid. In the classic way of "a lie going halfway around the world before the truth can get its boots on," the story of Penitente retribution in the Carl Taylor case sizzled in the press in the days after the murder and then was turned into a movie with dazzling speed, hitting theaters before the year was out. But in a real sense, and as we have seen, it was a story scripted decades before Modesto Trujillo and Carl Taylor ever met. While we may never know the exact nature of their relationship, it can be said that the conditions of their encounter were ruled by rigid sociocultural norms, by what Curtis Marez has identified as a complicated set of "neocolonial service relationships" that helped to make New Mexico an attractive destination for artists and tourists in the 1920s and 1930s (Marez 2004, 117). Seemingly nonsequential linkages between New Mexico's mestizo culture, its poverty, and its status as a cultural arts mecca would lead to a series of unexpected outcomes in the story of Modesto Trujillo and his writer-employer, Carl Taylor, a real-world drama that far outstrips anything Hollywood could conjure up.

Carl Taylor was murdered at his mountain cabin in Cedar Crest, New Mexico, on Wednesday, February 5, 1936, as he readied himself that evening to attend the Satiric Ball at the University of New Mexico. The following morning the *Albuquerque Journal* reported the story under the banner headline: "Carl Taylor Is Mysteriously Slain; Writer Found Shot in Mountain Cabin; Suspect Penitentes." The local paper cast about for suspects and, finding that Taylor was preparing an article on the Hermanos Penitentes for *Today Magazine* and that he had just taken some photos of the interior of a morada, immediately sought to blame the Penitentes in the area for his murder. Modesto Trujillo, Taylor's Mexican houseboy, told officials that two masked men had broken into the cabin and that he had heard shots as he ran away from the scene. Two days after the murder, both the *Albuquerque Journal* and the *Santa Fe New Mexican* reported that Modesto Trujillo had recanted his earlier tale of the masked assailants attacking the writer and confessed to having killed him. Modesto, who was tagged "the mountain boy" in the newspapers, lived with his mother and had been employed by Taylor to chop wood and do other menial chores around the cabin for several months.

Local papers reported that Modesto "broke down after long hours of questioning when officers confronted him with a small pistol found in a trash heap near the cabin. Trujillo first admitted ownership of the gun and then made a full confession to the sheriff" (*Santa Fe New Mexican*, February 6, 1936). The papers filled in the details of how Taylor was set to leave Albuquerque to do a story in Big Bend, Texas. Modesto Trujillo, they reported, had accompanied Taylor to town earlier in the day and had seen him draw out a large amount of money when cashing some traveler's checks at the bank. By this time, the police had questioned a second boy, Cresencio Gutiérrez, who admitted having sold the gun used to kill Taylor to Modesto Trujillo just weeks earlier. On February 17, Modesto Trujillo appeared in District Court before Judge Fred E. Wilson. Trujillo's lawyers, Owen B. Maron and Waldo Rogers, entered a guilty plea on behalf of their client, and Judge Wilson sentenced "the mountain boy" to ninety-nine years in prison on a second-degree murder charge. District Attorney Thomas J. Mabry told reporters he had accepted the second-degree plea because of the boy's "youth and his stupid, though rational mentality."

At the same time Mabry made a special effort to put the facts of the case before the public: "Mabry said the boy's confession and an investigation by himself and his assistants had proved to him without a doubt that Trujillo alone was responsible and that members of the Penitentes who had been suspected by some of Taylor's friends because Taylor had been writing an article about their brotherhood for an eastern press, had nothing to do with the murder" (*Albuquerque Journal*, February 18, 1936). Still, Taylor's university friends and, in particular, his editor and literary agent clung to the belief that Taylor had met a violent death at the hands of the "Penitente cult." That they arrived at this outcome was the result of the vagabond-explorer stories that Carl Taylor had often used to impress friends and readers, in which he added to his reputation by recounting the perils of living with and writing about exotic peoples. Taylor, who had last visited the Philippines in 1932, liked to regale his friends with stories of the dangers he had encountered as a travel writer.

Taylor's friends and acquaintances stirred further speculation in the press. Immediately following the murder, the *New Haven Evening Register* connected the dots: "Taylor's friends say he had a penchant for penetrating primitive places for the subject of his writings. Dr. George St. Clair, head of the University of New Mexico English Department, told reporters that Taylor had discussed an article on the tribes of the interior of the Philippine Islands. 'After that is published I can never go back to the Philippines,' he said Taylor told him" (*New Haven Evening Register*, February 6, 1936). With regard to this theory, the *Albuquerque Journal* noted, "The manuscript has

FIG. 5. Carl Taylor (kneeling) on javelin hunt with pygmy guide; (facing page), Taylor "the hunter" emerging from the bush. From Taylor, *Odyssey of the Islands.*

been sent to the publishers and the idea that some person whose feet had been stepped-on in the Philippines article, had seen it and determined to kill the author was regarded as fantastic" (February 7, 1936). While retribution from the distant Orient was considered implausible, the same skepticism did not hold for the Penitentes.

The image of a traveler-explorer risking life and limb among the barbarians completely shrouded Taylor; it was, after all, an image located at the center of the master narrative of the traveling anthropologist as cultural authority, and in 1936 it still had the power to sway public opinion. It was especially potent when buoyed, as it often was, by intensifying the elements of mystery, death, and drugs. This, then, was the story the print media chose to present to the national reading public. The example it held out of lurid spectacle and horror was heightened by the fact that this story was happening in a "free America."

Throughout the early months of 1936, the national press churned out story after story about Carl Taylor's fateful death while disregarding the actual motive for the murder. The *Los Angeles Examiner* began the onslaught with "'Penitentes' Vengeance for Exposé Blamed in Taylor's Death," a story it published three days after Taylor's death. That same day, the *Cleveland News* sensationalized earlier new reports by interjecting distorted views of

the New Mexico penitents, painting them as both fanatics and dope fiends: "In the strange, marijuana-maddened minds of the Mexican Indians who call themselves the Penitentes, they are Brothers of the Blood of Christ" (February 8, 1934). The print media was led headlong into the story by Taylor's literary agent, Roy De S. Horn, and by his editor at *Today Magazine*, Raymond Moley. Refusing to admit that robbery was the sole motive in Taylor's death, Horn told the press he had received letters in New York sent by Taylor the day before he was killed that contained three "never before shot" photos of the interior of a Penitente chapter house. Moley culled bits of text from "Agony in New Mexico," the manuscript found at Taylor's cabin, in an attempt to connect Modesto Trujillo to the brotherhood. "The boy who chops wood for me," Taylor had matter-of-factly written, "I think, secretly cherishes an ambition someday to be elected the village Christo and hang upon a cross" (Taylor 1936b, 3).

The most colorful of the items in the national press was a piece in *Famous Detective Cases* called "The Strange Murder in the Penitente Hills." The crime installment, authored by Robert Sothern, ran in July 1936. The crime magazine dramatized the events leading up to Taylor's death by employing an eyewitness point-of-view that placed the reader at Taylor's side at his mountain cabin on the night of his murder. Readers were treated to blood-curdling sounds and strange movements in the dark of night, said to be the work of the Penitentes. Written as if he were standing next to Taylor, Sothern's prose booms with gravitas:

> Voices rose over the bleak New Mexico hills. Deep violet crags caught and hurled them back, a cabalistic rhapsody that swelled and awed in the abyss of a desert night. Far distant they were, these voices that wailed in hellish, screaming cadence, as though some fiend danced on the piping notes of a monster organ.
>
> But Carl Taylor knew them. . . .
>
> He knew, too, that the singers were mad men by night, that they belonged to *Los Hermanos Penitentes*, and that blood soaked the ground on which they danced and shouted unholy hymns. And tonight as they twisted and shrieked in the red rites of their sect, he recalled legends of men lashed for daring to look at forbidden things, of others who died horribly because they crept into the foul, dark temples where bits of human flesh and blood rotted on stone floors. . . .
>
> Carl Taylor turned away from the window laughing at his own doubts. He had written of strange things before, had taken greater risks in other lands to learn the secrets of men and women who lived in barbaric traditions of centuries long dead. But this was his own land, and the Penitentes, although cloistered in their own weird world, lived and worked as their neighbors in Albuquerque, a scant twenty miles away. (34)

To advance the theory of Penitente involvement, the *Famous Detective* story (as did the others) conveniently ignored the fact that the start of Lent was a full month away from Taylor's death and that penitential activities of any kind among his Catholic neighbors would not have been occurring at this time of the year. The most sensationalistic stories were accompanied by a set of photographs reported to be authentic representations of Penitente rites. Sothern's story made use of two historical photographs, a nineteenth-century photo of a Penitente ceremony and an aerial shot of a morada in northern New Mexico, but it also included a set of staged photographs taken by Roland C. Price made for the film *The Lash of the Penitentes*. Price, the "vagabond cameraman," reported that he spent the two years prior to Taylor's death pulling footage together for the film. It is now clear that Price was working the story from a number of angles. In a piece for the *Los Angeles Examiner*, Price presented himself as an eyewitness to penitential rites in New Mexico. The newspaper reported: "Price spent two months amid the bloody brotherhood in 1934, obtaining some of the most remarkable and terrifying pictures ever to be captured by a camera, some of which are being published by the *Examiner*" (February 8, 1936). Price spiced up the drama by suggesting that the Penitentes "exercised grim control" over politics in New Mexico.

More recently, cultural critic Curtis Marez has lucidly shown how New Mexico in the 1930s faced a crosscurrent of social conundrums, each having the potential to drastically determine the future of the region. Largely a consequence of the work of the artist colonies in Santa Fe and Taos, tourism had come to be seen as the foundation of the state's future economic well-being. Away from the tourist centers of Taos and Santa Fe, the state was experiencing economic distress and chronic poverty sharpened by the labor strife that was in turn exacerbated by the Depression. The picture

FIG. 6. Roland C. Price's staged movie scene, "Penitente Altar." Marie de Forest (kneeling) plays *Lash*'s Raquel. Blackington Southwest Photograph Collection, Fort Lewis College, Center of Southwest Studies; P0492074.

in rural New Mexico and other parts of the Borderlands was one of labor strikes, red-baiting, state repression of labor activity, and aggressive drug enforcement. Hispanic and Indian New Mexico was poverty-riddled, hungry, and destitute, and, in an effort to keep the state safe for tourism, government and cultural leaders lumped their fears together and called for an all-out war on dope fiends, Bolsheviks, labor agitators, and immigrants. In this climate, all foreign others—and in the Southwest this could as easily mean Mexican or New Mexican–born brown people—could be turned into the criminal other.

If national news outlets were averse to serving up fear and sensationalism to their readers, Hollywood stood ready to exploit those conditions. It is telling that Roland C. Price's other film achievement in 1936, the year *Lash* was released, was a B-movie called *Marijuana*, for which Price did the camerawork. Price's *Marijuana* does not have a New Mexico connection, but like *Lash* it draws heavily on tropes of depravity and moral license. A standard disclaimer was required in all exploitation films from the period and was to be found in what industry insiders referred to as the "square-up" script, where filmmakers disavowed any aim to exploit the subject, declaring that, to the contrary, their sole mission was to educate by exposing a threatening menace in the hopes that the public would stamp it out. The "square up" was a kind of boilerplate statement into which the particular cause for public outcry could be tailored to whatever social menace the exploitation film proposed to examine, be it a sex exposé, a narcotic exposé, or any number of threats to society.

Among the coterie of exploitation actors and crews, Price's stock-in-trade camerawork was the nude scene, and both *Lash* and *Marijuana* titillated filmgoers with suggestive and lewd material. In this vein, *Marijuana* is still considered an over-the-top film for the period in terms of the number and frequency of racy and sexualized scenes involving marijuana users. Ironically, this same film was unscathed by the Hays Office and was allowed to be distributed uncensored when, according to one reviewer, it was the nude scenes of Marie de Forest, who plays Raquel in *Lash*—scenes missing from the abridged versions—that also influenced Governor Tingley's call to have the film banned in New Mexico. In the end, the Hays Office of the National Board of Censorship ordered that scenes be cut but "refused to give the film its seal of purity."

The charge of marijuana-induced depravity was clearly at play in the Taylor case, and came as an overlay of the intense condemnation of marijuana being fostered during the period by social, clinical, religious, and educational authorities nationwide. Federal and state governmental agencies promoted the notion that smoking dope led to a mind-altered state, a mental derangement that opened the user to moral abandonment and physical violence. Price's *Marijuana* film scrolls forth an intertitle warning: "Did you know that the youthful criminal element is our greatest problem today? And that—*marijuana* gives the user false courage and destroys the conscience, thereby making crime alluring, smart? Marijuana: hashish of the orient, is commonly distributed as a doped cigarette. Its most terrifying effect is that it fires the user to extreme cruelty and license."

The charge that New Mexico's penitents were "strange, marijuana-maddened Mexican Indians" was an easy one to frontload into public thinking given that New Mexico and other border states had so thoroughly criminalized the use of marijuana, deeming it a menace to civil society. As Curtis Marez notes, the public's war on hemp rested on a number of suppositions that tied marijuana use to Mexicans and Mexican Americans:

> The drug was a Mexican import now well established in the U.S. Southwest; marijuana use was especially common among male laborers, who became murderers and rapists after smoking it; Mexican marijuana dealers sold the drug to white schoolchildren; and finally marijuana was spreading from the Southwest to the rest of the nation. Marijuana supposedly removed inhibitions and unleashed the most primitive physical impulses. Or as the FBI warned, the marijuana user "becomes a fiend with savage or 'cave man tendencies.'" (131)

Carl Taylor, Freelance Writer

After his permanent relocation to New Mexico in 1933, Taylor supplemented his career as a freelance journalist by teaching an occasional English class at the university. During his time in Albuquerque he made the acquaintance of George St. Clair, Thomas M. Pearce, Conrad Richter, Arthur L. Campa, and the painter Carl Redin. Each of these men was ensconced in

New Mexico literary and arts circles and they helped Taylor sustain his career as a writer and teacher.

In preparing the *Today Magazine* article, Taylor entertained conversations with the well-known Hispanist, Arthur L. Campa, then a faculty member at the University of New Mexico. The talks with Campa on the subject of the Penitentes would prove to be decisive. After Taylor's death, Carl Redin told the *Albuquerque Journal* that "Taylor had recently finished a story on the Penitentes, a religious sect that still prevails in secluded districts of New Mexico," but, Redin added, "Taylor had not made his investigation personally, getting his information through Dr. A. L. Campa of Modern Languages at the University" (*Albuquerque Journal*, February 6, 1936). The comment is telling since, despite the newspaper reports that conclude Taylor was somehow surrounded by a "Penitente colony," Taylor's cabin was located some six miles away from the nearest morada, and the only indication we have that Taylor had any face-to-face encounters with Hermanos Penitentes is the fact that he had taken some photos of the interior of the morada in Tijeras, New Mexico, with the permission of the Hermano Mayor there. More telling is the fact that Campa had been the more active of the pair in having himself engaged in what had become the rage in 1930s New Mexico: Penitente hunting. Here, then, was a connection that interested Taylor and later gave him cause to write, "Strange adventures have befallen people of my acquaintance who have ventured forth on 'Penitente hunts' and allowed curiosity to overcome their discretion" (Taylor 1936b, 3).

In an unpublished manuscript titled "Back to Barbarism," Campa tells of succumbing to the excitement of "the chase." Campa's verve in his telling is pronounced: "Hunting Penitentes is a well-known sport around Albuquerque, and it carries with it the thrills of a real hunt." Despite his training as a philologist and folklorist specializing in New Mexico Hispanic culture, Campa penned his exploits in the sensationalistic style typical of the yellow journalists of his day. Campa begins his account by saying, "We had organized a party of six to 'hunt' Penitentes but had also arranged beforehand with the 'Hermano Mayor' (Elder Brother) to see the services held in the 'Morada'" (Campa n.d.). Campa's account, like most others of the time, tells of being welcomed into the morada to attend religious services inside the chapel. Typically, such services included devotions such as a recitation of the Rosary, the singing of sacred alabados, the Tinieblas ritual (Darkness

Symbolizing the Death of Christ), the recitation of the Stations of the Cross, and other spiritual exercises, none of which was the stuff of "bits of human flesh and blood" that so excited Penitente hunters. It was just too ordinary to walk away from such prosaic encounters without seeing blood. Invariably, accounts of Penitente hunting repudiate the courtesy extended to visitors to the morada and script out voyeuristic scenes of spying on the more private rituals of the group. Campa's account is no different in this regard; for example, on the night he visited the morada he writes:

> We thanked the Hermano Mayor for the courtesy extended to us and went home only to return by a different road, being careful not to turn on the lights of the car. About a hundred yards from the Morada we concealed ourselves against a ruined "adobe" wall and waited for hours. At about one in the morning the moon came up and made matters worse, for by the light of the moon we could be easily detected. The doleful note of the Pitero once more was heard, and one by one the Penitentes came out of the Morada administering strokes as they walked. One of the members of the party suggested that we move closer to try a picture by moonlight, but no sooner did we come out of our hiding place than a shower of rocks came whizzing by. The cars had been left on the highway and our exit was blocked by rocks that continued to rain on us. One of the members of the party opened fire with his automatic followed by the rest, and we made a rapid retreat. After a good sprint we were out of the village and on the road. From there we reached the cars and sped home to the hotel some fifteen miles away. There were enough of us to stand a good number of assailants, but if we were detected our chances for the following night would be spoiled. (Campa n.d.)

Campa ends his tale by saying, "It had been a successful hunt and no one had been hurt." This was a fortunate outcome, indeed, considering that it was a member of the party of hunters that "opened fire" on the East Mountain villagers that night, blindly shooting into the dark. It was fortunate that in the ensuing chaos a member of Campa's hunting party was not hit.

Campa's account, like many others from the period, exhibits a schizoid view of the Penitentes that, on the one hand, alternates between the "hunters" concealing themselves out of a blind fear of being detected by the "fanatics," and, on the other, has them showing up at the door of the village morada and being received as religious pilgrims. Mabel DelaMater Scacheri published the most telling example of the split narrative account in *Family Circle* in March 1936. Scacheri's account of "Penitente hunting" builds to a climax as she and her husband tool along the mountain byways of northern New Mexico, happening upon one and then another strange indication of penitential activity in several of the mountain villages. But the account unmasks its own artifice as an exposé of the lurid, hidden, and occult by including the author's testimonial of the gentle nature of the villagers and their deep religious orientation. While snapping away pictures from concealed locations with her husband, who has brought along a camera for "taking a motion picture of their processions," Scacheri undoes her own mystification of the villages when, in sober realization, she must report in all honesty:

> But in Cordoba [*sic*], where we snapped the sacred morada or chapel from the highway and then concealed our cameras, they invited us into their houses for dinner. Later they invited us into the morada itself, the holy of holies, where we sat with them through a long eerie service of the tenebrae (symbolic of the Darkness during the suffering and death of Christ). They offered us free lodging for the night, patched our flat tire, showed us their beautiful wood-carving, blessed us and prayed for our dead, and sent us on our way with a courteous "You will always be welcome in this house."
>
> When I think about the gentle little Mexican woman who slipped my hand in hers as the church went dark during the tenebrae, so that I would not be frightened, I can hardly look upon these people as dangerous wild beasts whose vicious practices should be made the occasion of a police investigation. Rather, they are something rare in this age of hokum—perfectly sincere, simple people, who really act according to their deep belief. (14)

Carl Taylor had recently completed the monograph "Agony in New Mexico." A copy was found neatly stacked and undisturbed on the table of his mountain cabin the night he was murdered. "Agony" would eventually be published in the July 1936 issue of *Today Magazine*, a move that allowed the publisher to cash in on the publicity surrounding the writer's murder.

Like other tracts of popular journalism dealing with the Penitentes, Taylor indulges in some degree of sensationalism about the Brotherhood, but the *Today Magazine* article is not filled with the scandal-bent prose of the self-proclaimed exposés from this same period. Taylor had in fact opted to bring forth a deeper understanding of the religious faith that he witnessed in his "Penitente neighbors." He had specifically turned his sights toward trying to get to "the question of what their religion really is" (Taylor 1936, 3).

In the course of the article Taylor moves from trepidation to greater appreciation and empathy for the Brotherhood. Taylor opens the article by telling of his recent experiences in the Philippines. He begins, "On Easter Sunday three years ago I stood beside a dusty lane in the Philippine Islands busily photographing a strange procession. Along a bull-cart trail a hundred members of the Brotherhood of Flagellants were scourging themselves with barbarous cat-o-nine-tail whips in imitation of Christ's agony" (3). Taylor thinks to himself, "I'm glad to be going back to the United States where such things can't happen," only to find himself writing about a similar tradition just a few miles outside of Albuquerque, New Mexico, one maintained, to his surprise, by "the voting citizens of the republic" who "upon recovering from their self-torture would return to work upon the nearby projects of the New Deal" (3). For Taylor, New Mexico was cause for him to rethink the whole matter of his formal education and to consider what had been left out of his school textbooks as he went about discovering how so much of the United States could remain unknown to him. His interrogations at one point become self-reflexive in a way that is quite unusual in Penitente writings from this period. Taylor reflects, "A subject of this nature is difficult to write about fairly and intelligently. If you see it, as I have had the opportunity of doing, you may turn away sick and disgusted. But you can hardly fail to admire the abounding faith at the bottom of it. Reading about it is something else again" (3).

Taylor's account is uncharacteristic in yet another way, since unlike other reporters he has a number of good things to say about his experience living close to the Penitentes:

> If you are surrounded by Penitente neighbors, as I am, and if those
> neighbors come and nurse you when you are sick—as mine have

done—you perceive that they are quite human. And that is exactly what I want to convey.

My Penitente neighbors are honest, simple and cheerful people. Among them you will rarely see a dour face. Most of them possess a highly-developed sense of community obligation; when someone is ill, a baby is being born, or a corpse is to be laid away, there is no lack of neighborly assistance; when hunger stalks through their barren hills, everyone tightens his belt that all may have a little to eat.

The boy who chops wood for me, and who, I think secretly cherishes an ambition some day to be elected the village *Christo* and hang on a cross is immensely proud of his shiny new bicycle.

Some (though by no means all) of these people amuse themselves with radios, drive automobiles, get up by alarm clock, use lipstick and hair tonic, and take considerable pride in their mastery of current slang. (3)

Taylor, it appears, was attempting to convey the sense of an ordinary and commonplace humanity that he encountered on a day-to-day basis in the Hispano residents of the Sandias, something that makes his article one of the first attempts to draw out some minimal sociocultural understanding of the Brotherhood and to describe its mutual aid functions in Hispano communities. Taylor moves away from the tendency of most other writers of his day to denigrate the Hermanos Penitentes. He even chastises the voyeuristic indulgences of the Penitente hunters: "To judge from the antics of some persons who go out each year drunk, disorderly and insolent—bent upon making a Roman holiday out of what is tremendously sacred to these people—the wonder is that killings are not regular Lenten occurrences. That they are not is due in the main, I think to the fact that Penitente faith is exceeded only by Penitente forbearance" (3).

"Agony in New Mexico" does go on to describe penitential practices, but it is hardly the exposé that it was made out to be in the press and it was certainly tamer than the film the Taylor story spawned. It is important to recall that the manuscript for the article, the supposed object of Penitente retribution, was found neatly stacked, untouched and undamaged, at Taylor's cabin, and not even the three "never before seen" photos of the interior of Penitente morada, which Raymond Moley claimed led to Taylor's death, were published with the piece. In the end there was no exposé, no pictures, and there was no vengeance that could be exacted from the horrific death of Carl N. Taylor at the hands of the "mountain boy." It remains tragic that a series of unforeseen events ended Taylor's life and left Modesto Trujillo without a future, and in this sense each is equally a victim of circumstances.

Modesto, Modestito?—"If You Want to Know Who I Am, Just Ask the Jailer"

News reports provide this picture of Modesto awaiting arraignment after being detained.

> Meanwhile, young Trujillo sits unconcerned, composing verses of a song in his jail cell. The verses are being written to a folk tune he picked up from a friend before the murder. He is writing in Spanish, as he does not speak or write fluently in English. The one verse he showed officers, when translated into English without the rhyme, says, "If you want to know who I am, just ask the jailer: I am Modesto Trujillo, who has just come from San Antonio." (*Albuquerque Journal*, February 1936)

One would expect to find a photograph of Carl Taylor, the eyewitness-informant and intrepid adventurer, or at a minimum the photo of some "bloodied Penitentes" on the cover of "Agony in New Mexico"; however, no such images appear. Instead, the article is bedecked with a photo of Taylor's slayer, young Modesto Trujillo. The photo is remarkable in many ways, for it presents Modesto as a dapper, stylishly dressed young man. He sports a golf cap, a safari shirt, a silver-studded belt, a sleek pair of well-pressed slacks, and, most curious of all, a smoking pipe that dangles from his mouth as from the lips of a young preppy college student. Though unintentionally, the photo momentarily causes the viewer to confuse Modesto with his writer-patron, so patent are the accouterments of the writer upon the body of the boy. The photo is so atypical that it raises the question whether this could really be the "mountain boy" described in earlier news reports: "The boy wore a battered sombrero, an old brown suit-coat, denim trousers with frayed edges and muddy shoes" (*Albuquerque Journal*, February 6, 1936). The disparity between photo and news descriptions is so marked as to make the content of the corrido that Modesto was composing all the more intriguing, for it may have contained some disclosure that would allow us to know something about who Modesto really was and how it was he came to find himself in this jam. Imagine the experience of the third eye that Modesto Trujillo would have experienced if he had had occasion to see the article at some point in his life.

Like his counterparts in the artist-writer communities of Santa Fe and Taos, Taylor found it beneficial to hire a neighbor boy, Maria Trujillo's son Modesto, to do chores for him around the mountain cabin. Modesto spent most of his time chopping wood to heat the cabin and to warm water for Taylor's weekly baths. Modesto was likely not a menace to his neighbors, but he did have a penchant for taking things that did not belong to him. Mrs. Ruth Finley, a schoolteacher at Gallup, New Mexico, and one of the few females who kept company with Taylor, had misgivings about the boy. When reporters asked, she remembered sharing her apprehensions with Taylor on a visit to Albuquerque to take in the movie *Tobacco Road*: "Isn't it strange," she said. "I warned Carl about that boy long ago. I said I didn't trust Trujillo and said I hoped he would let him go. But Carl only laughed and said: 'Oh, he's stolen things from me once in a while, but I think I have him in hand now. I'm not afraid of him'" (Sothern 1936, 66).

Modesto Trujillo was a good-looking young man who lived with his mother and two younger siblings at Cedar Crest. His father, José León

FIG. 7. "Dapper Modesto," Carl Taylor's photo of Modesto Trujillo, published in "Agony in New Mexico," *Today Magazine*, February 15, 1936.

Trujillo, lived away from the family for extended periods of time due to his work as a sheepherder for the Fernández Company Ranch at San Mateo, New Mexico. The papers in New Mexico took to describing Modesto as "child-like" and "the sheepherder's son who quit school in the fourth grade." On the day of his son's arrest, José León could not even manage to be at his side since he could not leave his post until a replacement was able to come to tend to the flocks of sheep under his care. Thomas M. Pearce, who collected New Mexico anecdotes, had heard a rumor about Modesto's father. It was a story Pearce felt said something about José León's character.

> I heard this story of Trujillo's father, at present a sheepherder near San Mateo, sixty miles west of Albuquerque. At the death of Trujillo's mother, the man claimed she had left his house and some other possessions to him alone, without any mention of his brothers or sisters. These brought suit and came to court to testify against their oldest brother. The latter entered the courtroom with a gunnysack filled with something. When his turn came to produce witnesses of his mother's bequest, he opened the gunnysack. In it were a dozen or more santos, wooden saints collected from his house and the church. "These are my witnesses," he said. (Pearce 1936)

Pearce ends his story of José León with a wry note on the disposition of nuevomexicanos and tersely suggests that it should not surprise anyone if a few more santos (New Mexican religious carvings) might not be enlisted in some courtroom antic to aid Modesto's defense.

No doubt that Modesto was proving to be a tough child for a mother with two younger children to raise on her own. Modesto was acquiring a reputation in the East Mountains for getting into trouble, and under questioning he admitted breaking into the home of Carl Webb at Casa Loma, saying he had taken fifty cents on one occasion and a pack of playing cards on another.

Like their neighbors, the Trujillos were socially and economically distressed. The land company that employed him as a sheepherder bound the head of the household, José Trujillo, in poverty and peonage. His wife, María, was left to raise the children and supplement her family's income by working as Taylor's washerwoman. The portrait is of a family caught in a Depression-strapped service economy supporting the twin pillars of New

Mexico's economy in the 1930s: stock raising and art tourism. Modesto's family could well be the poster image of the way of life Curtis Marez tells us typified New Mexico in this era:

> The real counterparts of the shepherds featured in literature and paintings owned neither land nor herds, but instead leased both from large livestock concerns. The resulting form of livestock "sharecropping" effectively bound shepherds in debt to leasing companies. In 1935, for example, after thirty-five years under a sharecropping contract with the appropriately named "Bond Company," sheepherder Amarante Serna remained in debt and therefore tied to the company. Even closer to artists' homes and studios, Mexicans served as day laborers, servants, cooks, and maids within a dual-wage service economy. In 1931 Mexican labor cost $2.50 to $3.00 a day, and skilled labor was valued at $6.00 to $9.00 a day— roughly two dollars less than the respective rates for white labor. Art colonists often hired labor at these racialized rates to work in their homes as gardeners, handymen, cooks, maids, and washerwomen. And in many cases these same workers sat for painters and served as sources of folktales and songs for writers. (2004, 118)

The enigma of Carl Taylor and the "mountain boy" was a topic of conversation in Albuquerque, especially among Taylor's university friends, for a good time after the murder. Pearce, an English professor at the university, knew something of Taylor's habits and sat down after the writer's death to pen some of his observations into his journal. He begins by describing how the news of Taylor's death reached friends gathered at Carlisle Gym on the University of New Mexico campus as the Art League's Satiric Ball was in full swing. Pearce's description of the Satiric Ball has a film noir quality and could well be the opening scene of a murder mystery movie. Like the climatic carnival scene in the Brazilian classic *Ofeu Negro* (Black Orpheus), the revelry is suddenly hushed as the news of Taylor's death filters among the partygoers. As Pearce has it, George St. Clair's party is gathered in a box on the balcony of Carlisle Gym watching the spectacle below. The gymnasium is filled with milling crowds donning paper hats and blowing whistles and horns. One of the evening's pageants, a satire on Russia for which local poet Witter Bynner has just recited his clever poem "Stalin, Stalin All the

While," is coming to a close. A group of men and women in tunics and caps stage a dance and are joined by a "machine-like figure" that pirouettes and parades around an allegorical mock-up of "the five year plan" before a masked dancer portraying Stalin. And then, suddenly, a visibly agitated Carl Redin runs through the gym and rushes up to the box to speak to St. Clair, but the noise of the revelers makes it impossible to hear what he is saying. Seconds later, St. Clair turns to Pearce: "'Carl Taylor has been murdered at his cabin in the mountains. The sheriff has just confirmed the report. Redin came to tell me.' Unbelieving I could only repeat, astounded, 'Murdered!' and Saint again said 'Murdered. He's been murdered'" (Pearce 1936). Pearce continues, "Now, seven days later, the facts are known. After speculation has run the gamut from motives of revenge by Penitentes to more personal complications, the truth is stranger than all else." But perhaps because Pearce could not possibly know the most intricate details of the truth, he reflects on the tremendous irony in the fact that Taylor, the globe-trotting travel writer who has faced headhunters, wild tribesmen, hoboes in slums, and gangs of thugs on waterfronts, should be killed while sitting and reading a newspaper in front of his fireplace by a Mexican houseboy whom he trusted to prepare his bath and warm his cabin.

There was a ritual in preparing the bath, one born of the sparse living conditions of Taylor's neighbors, but one, as Pearce describes it, that borders on a homoerotic encounter. The bathing ritual between Carl Taylor and the strapping "mountain boy" had been reenacted on a weekly basis for some time:

Bathing in the mountain cabin at Cedar Crest was a matter of borrowing a washtub and filling it with water heated at the woodstove. The houseboy carried the tub from his mother's, the tub in which she had done Taylor's washing for four years. About eight o'clock, Carl told the boy to bring the tub; an hour was adequate time for a bath and dressing when between nine and ten Carl would join Redin and his party, and the rest of us. It was while bringing the tub into the main room of the cabin that the boy paused, not two feet from Taylor, and there discharged his revolver in the man's head. The shot did not kill Carl. He fell and still conscious lifted his arm to ward off a second shot, but he was so dazed and stunned

that he was helpless to do more than lift his arm. The boy placed
the pistol to Taylor's temple and pulled the trigger a second time.
(Pearce 1936)

Pearce, like so many others who knew Taylor, was perplexed by the
enormity of Modesto Trujillo's unthinkable act. Pearce was all the more
vexed by the anecdotes he heard about the boy, which did not square with
the image of the callous and unfeeling murderer that the papers had made
Modesto out to be. Pearce had his own view of the boy: "Modesto Trujillo,
fifteen years of age, houseboy of Carl Taylor, internationally known corre-
spondent and writer, says, 'You're welcome' and 'Thank you' to examiners
who visit him in the County Jail. He has begun to compose *décimas* about
himself as a local hero from San Antonio" (Pearce 1936).

Pearce noted that seven days after the murder, Modesto had not
remarked about his deed nor expressed concern about himself or his dead
employer. The judicial system was equally mystified by the case. The newspaper stories carry the idea of how utterly ill equipped the justice system
was to handle young offenders like Modesto. Perhaps Modesto was beginning to understand that his life belonged to the state and seemed to be
saying as much in his *corrido*: "If you want to know who I am just ask the
jailer." In sentencing Modesto, Judge Wilson told reporters, "I doubt very
much, from what I have been able to find out about the boy's history and
the crime he has committed, if it is possible to rehabilitate him or make
him a useful member of society. We must think about other juveniles who
might be influenced by what he has done and who should be made to realize that if they commit a real crime they must suffer punishment" (*Albuquerque Journal*, February 18, 1936). District Attorney Thomas J. Mabry could
only remand Modesto to the crude machinations of the state penitentiary:
"It may be in years to come, some system may be developed whereby boys
even of this type may be rehabilitated. I doubt that somewhat. . . . Anyway,
it is for the future. I think that for the benefit of society that this boy will
be isolated for the rest of his life" (*Albuquerque Journal*, February 18, 1936).

As he waited in jail Modesto had let himself be photographed by news
agencies, and photos of him circulated in the local and national press,
each shot presenting him in a different guise. A Paramount News cameraman was sent from Los Angeles to take "talking pictures of the boy" and

of his jailer, Sheriff Ross Salazar. D.A. Marby ordered that the footage be destroyed when, according to a news report, "Sheriff Salazar balked at some questions he [the cameraman] was to ask." The papers reported that the Paramount cameraman would still be permitted to film the crime scene and the boy, with the proviso that the filming would not compromise the investigation by discussing the details of the case. Had the movie film not been exposed, we might have even heard Modesto singing his *corrido*. Fortunately, several of the still photos taken of Modesto were published and survive. In one, Modesto is standing with Sheriff Ross Salazar before a jail cell, looking every bit the part of the outlaw Billy the Kid. In another photo, Modesto is holding a cigarette to his mouth pachuco-style, looking the part of the incorrigible Chicano "dope fiend"; in a couple more, Modesto is seated across from his interrogators, visibly frightened and appearing as though he has just come to understand the enormity of what he has done.

In the days before his sentencing, the papers reported that Modesto appeared unmoved and unrepentant as he worked on a beaded belt and "ate and slept well and was apparently unworried" (*Albuquerque Journal*, January 18, 1936). But after being sentenced he broke down and "cried in his cell." In public Modesto kept a stoic front, and so too, it seems, did his parents. On February 18, the *Albuquerque Journal* noted: "The boy who will reach his sixteenth birthday next Saturday did not seem affected while in the court chambers. His parents, Mr. and Mrs. José León Trujillo, who were among the spectators seemed rather stunned and bewildered, but gave no outward signs of deep emotion."

What more could be expected of a boy in his predicament? As it was, Modesto displayed an amazing range of emotions and thoughts. As photos of him reveal, he could be alternately polite, stoic, resigned, filled with bravado or filled with anguish. In all likelihood he had felt each of these different emotions well up in him as he faced his accusers and an uncertain future. Nowhere is that range of sentiments better represented than on the day Modestito (surely his mother called out to him this way) was being transferred to the New Mexico state prison in Santa Fe. Modesto put on a good face for the media, but also let the public in on experiences that were already pointing him toward the life that someone of his ethnicity, class, and religion all too frequently met up with. It is surprising to learn that by the time he was fifteen Modesto had already tasted the hard life of being a migrant worker, something that he found matched his current circumstances as a convict of the state of New Mexico:

> "This reminds me of the time I hitch-hiked and bummed train rides to California," Modesto Trujillo, 15-year old slayer of Carl Taylor, writer, said Tuesday as Sheriff Ross Salazar and two deputies were taking him to state prison in Santa Fe to begin a 99 year sentence.
>
> "I worked in the tomato fields out there," the boy continued, "and it was hard work and the sun was hot."
>
> The boy had a box of candy, given him by a friend and offered the officers some, but they declined, thinking it might be a long time before he has any luxuries.
>
> The boy's eyes grew misty at times as he apparently realized he was taking his last automobile ride and enjoying the last look at the Sandias which were his home since birth, for perhaps the remainder of his life. But he didn't shed tears, as he had when he bade his mother good bye.
>
> The sheriff said the boy was brave about the ordeal of entering the prison, where he will spend his sixteenth birthday next Saturday. (*Albuquerque Journal*, February 19, 1936)

Finally, when Modesto was asked if he harbored any hatred for his boss, he replied directly in his coarse and broken English: "No sir. I didn't. He was alright. He treated me pretty good, but once in a while spoke harshly to me. I just wanted his money" (Sothern 1936, 66). If there were other motives, other secrets in the relationship between the writer and the mountain boy, they remained unvoiced and they most certainly remained too taboo a subject even for the exploitation B-movies Hollywood could churn out.

Modesto's family did not abandon him after he was sent to the state penitentiary in Santa Fe. The visitor's register for the New Mexico Penitentiary logs the visits of large parties of family members visiting Modesto in July and October of 1936.[3] Three years into his sentence, residents of Cedar Crest and other east mountain villages drafted and circulated a petition asking that Modesto be paroled and allowed to return to his home. The petition, dated August 14, 1939, includes the signatures of 138 individuals. That the list should include both Anglo and Spanish surnames suggests that local sympathies outweighed the image of Modesto in news reports as a fiend and Anglo-hating monster. The petitioners asked Governor John E. Miles to use his office to intervene in the matter, believing that Modesto had been "punished enough." They pleaded,

> On account of his age we figure that the boy should be given a chance and be parole [*sic*] to his parents here in Albuq, NM. His parents are getting old and they need their son to help them with their work. This boy [*sic*] parents are people that have always lived in the Mountains east of Albuq and they are poor and humble people. Nobody felt worse than them at the time that this crime was committed if there had been any way to remedy it they would have gone far and near to see it remedied [*sic*]. (Citizens' Petition)

Despite the fact that a month later the New Mexico Board of Parole denied a request for parole, family members continued to write Governor Miles and subsequent New Mexico governors asking for clemency in the case. Modesto would serve nine years of his original sentence of ninety-nine to one hundred years before it was first commuted in February 1944 to twenty-five to ninety-nine years. Modesto received a conditional release from prison in October 1946 and his sentence was commuted twice more, once in July 1948 and again in August 1949. After serving sixteen years, he was finally discharged from the prison system in January 1951.[4]

The shallow mysteries, such as the ones District Attorney Mabry alluded to in the *Santa Fe New Mexican*, linger: "The boy had in his possession a new bicycle and a camera and other articles believed to have been stolen for the reason that the boy had no money with which to purchase these things" (February 6, 1936). If the items mentioned here were indeed stolen and if some of the goods belonged to Carl Taylor, then quite naturally this would have damaged the master–chore boy relationship and turned it toward its tragic ending. But it is likely that the bike was not stolen since Modesto had no qualms in riding it through the village, giving the impression that he was "immensely proud of his shiny new bicycle." Perhaps Carl Taylor bought him things or lent him things, just as he had let him dress up preppy-style and pose for the photo for the article he was writing. Perhaps Modesto felt that the items he got from Taylor were his to keep. Perhaps Carl Taylor could not bring himself to ask his impoverished neighbors to return the lent items. We do know that Taylor had no qualms about issuing an occasional reprimand to Modesto by speaking harshly to him. The intricate and complex master–chore boy relationship the case denotes is material of deep and complicated sociohistorical significance. Too profound, unfortunately, for the makers of the exploitation films like *Lash*, who in their haste to turn a buck forever barred the human dimensions of this tragedy from their film, driven as they were by their zeal to exploit the Penitentes and the "marijuana-minded Mexicans."

4

Lives and Faces
Plying through Exotica

Then I knew we had won something they could never take away—
something I could leave to our children—and they, the salt of the earth,
would inherit it.
> – Esperanza Quintero, *Salt of the Earth*, 1954

You are the salt of the earth.
> –Matthew 5:13

In contrast to Native Americans, who have been the subject of a great many ethnographic films and photographic surveys, there is a comparatively small amount of ethnographic materials related to the Mexican Americans of the Southwest before the 1960s.[1] As a rule, the visual ethnographies that do exist, at best, are ad hoc assessments of Chicano material culture (i.e., photo surveys of religious iconography, shrines, courtyards, home altars, roadside memorials, and so on). The documentation of these places and artifacts is almost always severed from the people and their cultural ways. As such, exceptions to this pattern are fundamentally important in augmenting the visual representations that are available of Mexican-origin peoples in the United States. Despite its shortcomings, visual documentation still affords the possibility to see how members of subaltern communities lived out their lives in subtle tension with greater American society. The collection of Farm Security Administration (FSA) photographs of towns and villages in the Southwest stand out as the exception to omission of Mexican Americans in the Depression-era ethnographic record of the nation. For this reason the work of FSA photographers Russell Lee and John Collier Jr. merit consideration here.

Russell Lee came to New Mexico in 1939 and returned in 1940 as a photographer employed by the Farm Security Administration, a New Deal project devoted to documenting the devastation the Depression visited upon the nation's rural populations (Wroth 1985, 1). Other FSA notables include Dorothea Lange, Walker Evans, Maynard Dixon, and Gordon Parks. Lee's images of the nuevomexicanos and of *tejanos* are imbued with qualities that set them apart from the aesthetically conscious photos by other Southwestern devotees such as Ansel Adams, Eliot Porter, and Edward Weston.

In considering the New Mexico portion of Lee's work, William Wroth observes that the photographs "constitute an important visual document of a way of life that was and is still little known and appreciated by the larger society" (1985, 2). Lee's work, to a photo, privileges depictions of people over those of the landscape and the built environment. In Lee's photographs men, women, and children can be found completely absorbed in work, play, and ritual. Put another way, the people of the communities he photographed can be seen, asserting agency in any number of culture-making endeavors. Lee records human activity in the pursuit of self-sufficiency and independence, an approach that ties his work to a school of socially relevant documentary photography that had begun with the documentation of immigrant tenements in New York at the turn of the twentieth century.

Photographing America's Forgotten People

My specific aim in discussing Lee here is to show that his work allows the image of the Spanish-speaking Borderlands communities to ply through the layers of postcolonial exotic imagery that had been brokered and fashioned into the adventure and vengeance narratives of earlier eras. I do this even as on the face of things this view contradicts Rosa Linda Fregoso's estimation of Lee's presence in the Borderlands. Fregoso asserts that Lee was a border crosser (more a transgressor), "an image maker crossed the border into Mexican Texas, inserting tejano bodies into representational space" (Fregoso 1999, 186). Given the nature of Lee's New Mexico and Texas photographic commissions, I would argue that Lee's presence, equally in the villages of Taos and Rio Arriba counties in 1940 or a few year later in Corpus Christi, was meant to sensitize the public at large and to change public policy and spur government interventions on behalf of the populations he photographed. I also contend that by inserting tejano and nuevomexicano bodies "into representational space," as Fregoso offers, Lee sought to provide America at large its first glimpse into mexicano lives in the Borderlands by publishing these same photographs in national publications such as *Survey Graphic, U.S. Camera,* and *Look.* Lee did not sensationalize his subjects, and in both Texas and New Mexico he knew better than to intrude on Indo-Hispano religion and cultural practices as the vagabond photographers of the Penitentes had done in years past. As Wroth notes, Lee's photos are about "ordered life in the villages" as expressed in "everyday tasks" (1985, 3).

Despite the benign, even salubrious effect of Lee's Mexican American portfolio, something all three of us (Wroth, Fregoso, and I) agree upon is evident. Fregoso charges Lee with "recycl[ing] an available colonist fantasy on the Borderlands" and in so doing transfigures him from "border crosser" into a colonizer or perhaps re-colonizer, making the charge stand only long enough to immediately resuscitate a kinder assessment of him: "Lee was a border-crosser who inhabited the world of the Spanish-speaking people for a brief moment, injecting memories with his presence and sharing as well in the generalized visibility of a Tejana/o public culture" (1999, 188). Lee's photographic interventions in Tejas trouble Fregoso on two counts. First, Fregoso believes Lee did not go as far as required to unmask racism and segregation as the root cause of tejano second-class citizenship. While noting that some of his photographs make visible the poverty tejanos are subjected to, most, she adds, do not; thus, "The reader/viewer has to surmise that poverty is an effect of racism and segregation, since this interpretation is not conveyed directly by the content of the photos" (199, 188).

A second deficit Fregoso sees in Lee is his failure to identify his subjects by name. Fregoso is doubly right to point out this lacuna, for in truth members of the México-tejano community are never named, and in most instances the same is true in the nuevomexicano case, an act that erases a major aspect of their activity and personhood. Fregoso, it should be noted, is personally concerned with how this omission came to be. She relates how on a hot, humid day in 1949 an Anglo man carrying a camera approached and asked her mother, Lucía Orea, if he could take her photograph. That man, Fregoso later came to know, was Russell Lee. Fregoso's mother recalls that the man left without giving his name and took her image with him. Lee was following the conventions of documentary photography or, as I term this work, ethnographic photography in this period. It is a convention that results in the kind of distancing that erects and maintains a formidable divide between the documentary photographer and his or her subjects, and it is an act that ensures that the representational (documentary) proxemics of these encounters can only be partial, giving sight only to the outsider's gaze as witness to the workings of these communities. The same convention is at work in Lee's photographs of nuevomexicano villages, where most of the villagers remain anonymous. There, members of the community are identified through group membership: "Chamisal. Home of Spanish-American Farmers," "Young Spanish-American cow herder," "Spanish-American women waiting to see the doctor."

Champions of Lee's work are apt to declare that these are "color-blind images," which result from the photographer's internal fortitude and his personal antipathy for racial inequality. Ironically, Fregoso reaches the opposite conclusion, insisting, "Texas as Whiteness fills the entire frame of reference" (1999, 187). Fregoso's characterization of Lee's Texas portfolio as photographic naturalism is akin to declarations by Lee's defenders, in that she too wishes to see observational truth driving Lee's photography. Even while the eyes of Russell Lee are upon Texas mexicanos, Fregoso maintains that the proxemics Lee employed merely recycled another convention in documentary photography, the one meant to heighten the exteriority of the subject. It is a matter that causes Fregoso to opine, "Lee's photographic naturalism inscribes Tejanos/as in otherness and alterity" (1999, 188).

In his evocative treatise on photography, *Camera Lucida* (1980), Roland Barthes offers the spectator of photography a way to monitor his or her relationship to the object by considering what Barthes calls the "studium" and "punctum" of any given photograph. In Barthes's estimation, a photograph's "studium is that very wide field of unconcerned desire, of various interest, of inconsequential taste" (1980, 27). Elsewhere Barthes remarks, "It is by *studium* that I am interested in so many photographs, whether I received them as political testimony or enjoy them as good historical scenes" (1980, 26). Barthes employs the idea of "punctum" to communicate the ability of any given photograph to tap the spectator's sensibilities when, with lightning-like speed, some sensitive detail of the photograph punctures the viewer's more general interest. For Barthes it is the "punctum" moment that provides for a more expansive contextualization of the photograph.

By this schema, both Lee's defenders and detractors are piqued by the "punctum" of Lee's nuevomexicano and tejanos photos. The "punctum," too, will also allow for the possibility of a more expansive "third eye" encounter, when at some future moment the subjects finally gaze upon themselves in the image. Lee's professional and public charge—to record the effects of poverty and economic stagnation of the nation's rural poor—controlled the major aesthetic and documentary decisions that shape his work. The "punctum" found in the details of the photographs is, by means of Barthes's logic, a way for the Chicano spectator to find him- or herself in these photographs. In this way Lee's photodocumentation becomes an important source of self-knowledge for Chicanos and Chicanas.

Less manifest in his work, but very significant, is the influence of native scholars who carry Lee across the threshold of the cultural divide and onto the plain of a fuller epistemology of Indo-Hispano life in the Southwest. In early 1940, native-born educator George I. Sánchez briefed Lee on how to bring about a successful photographic assessment of rural New Mexico. According to Wroth, Lee got "a real understanding of the rural Hispanic culture of northern New Mexico" from Sánchez (1985, 134).[2] In effect, the photographs that Lee would go on to make could easily be paired with the social history Sánchez laid out in *Forgotten People*, a classic study of New Mexicans also published in 1940, or with the many reports issued by Sánchez's *Study of the Spanish Speaking People of Texas* a few years later.

In *Forgotten People*, Sánchez described in incisive detail the legacy of conquest, social inequity, and educational neglect that was the common experience of nuevomexicanos in their homeland. For several years prior, Sánchez had been studying the situation in Taos County and came to the conclusion that socioeconomic factors there mirrored those that New Mexico's Spanish-speaking population faced across the state. In a chapter entitled "The Taoseños," Sánchez writes:

> The Spanish-speaking population there is typical of that found in other counties. The social and economic level of that population is much like that attained by other New Mexican communities.

It is the sense of this report that a portrayal of the *taoseños* is, in effect, a portrayal of New Mexicans generally. The differences that may be observed when the *taoseños* is compared with New Mexicans elsewhere—in the poorer sections of Albuquerque, in Rio Arriba County, in Valencia County, in Santa Fe—are differences of degree rather than of kind. Furthermore, it is to be observed that, in general, differences in the degree of underprivilege that exist among the New Mexicans in these and similar sections are small differences. Taken by and large, they are all about equally poor in health, in wealth, and in education, from much the same causes and due to highly similar circumstances. ([1940] 1996, 43)

William Wroth contends that Russell Lee's photographs of New Mexicans should be recognized for the way they "transcend the documentary purpose for which they were made" (Wroth 1985, 2). To underscore this point, Wroth calls attention to the fact that the photographs are quite beautiful and aesthetically engaging. As important as their technical quality—which Wroth describes as resulting in "seemingly effortless photographs"—is their remarkable unbiased spirit, one that runs decidedly against the abhorred tainting of "otherness" so often at play in the rendering of ethnic minorities in commercial projects during this period. It is to Lee's credit that he allowed for the expression of the "quality of life" that he found remarkably preserved in "the spirit of strong independence" that characterized the village life he observed in 1940.

Of course, Lee inflected subjectivity into these images; after all, it was his professional charge to register the "plight of rural Americans," but there is a refreshing absence of xenophobia and race bias in his work. I rest this assertion on the fact that it is difficult to find any appreciable difference in his treatment of the distinct people he photographed. One need only compare Lee's photographs of rural New Mexicans to his photographs of rural Anglos in his Pie Town, New Mexico, series produced in the summer of 1940. The people in both series are busy and engaged in a variety of activities. The nuevomexicanos tend to their fields, fish, unload farm equipment, construct adobe homes, can fruit, herd their livestock, deliver mail, get examined at the local health clinic, converse with the county agricultural agent, make their own music, attend traveling *carpa* performances, take meals as families, lead processions, and bury their dead. The rural Anglos can fruit, converse after evening meals, attend Farm Bureau meetings, engage in community sings, square dance at home, make their own music, pick up their mail from rural mail boxes, and herd their livestock. In economic terms the Pie Town Anglos that Lee described as "migrants from Texas and Oklahoma—dry land farmers raising Pinto Beans and corn" (qtd. in Colson 1993, 4) —could not have been much better off economically than the New Mexican farmers. Interestingly, as Lee's photographs show, the Anglos do not have a corner on nobility of character, industriousness, respect, or generosity. For William Wroth it is important that Lee depicted the nuevomexicanos "not as statistics for relief roles or as stereotypic poverty cases but as strong, often joyful human beings carrying out their daily tasks" (1985, 3). Similarly, Rosa Linda Fregoso finds honesty in Lee's photos of tejanos and tejanas. Upon viewing Lee's photos of Texas Mexicans, she remarks,

> [They] capture the very centrality of Tejanos/as to Texas history and culture: Tejanos engaged in all facets of public life, as active citizens and productive members of Texas society, selling their wares, participating in Church bingos and parades, reading newspapers and books, shining shoes, selling fruit and vegetables, mourning their dead in public. These photographic images conjure up a refusal of their invisibility, a rejection on the part of Tejanas and Tejanos of their erasure. (1999, 188)

Clearly, Lee affords his viewers a way of understanding the daily life of minority populations that were, in his day, considered marginal and living outside of the great middle of American life. Wroth, Lee's curator, is convinced that these images hold no stake in racial misrepresentation. While this may be true, it is my view that Lee's professional and public charge—to record the effects of poverty and economic stagnation of the nation's rural poor—controlled the major aesthetic and documentary decisions that shape his work. These things above all else create the imperative to center the eye of his camera on the workaday lives of ethnic and minority subjects.

In this we see the very decisive role that Roy Stryker, head of the historical unit of FSA, played with Lee and with each of the photographers the

FSA employed. In his correspondence, Lee mentions the detailed instructions Stryker sent him. Stryker was effusive, sometimes composing ten to twelve handwritten pages of suggestions. And as Wroth notes: "Stryker also emphasized the need for the photographer to understand the broader significance of what he was seeing and not simply photograph whatever came before the camera in the hope of presenting a coherent and meaningful picture of a culture" (1985, 126). Whether one is inclined to give greater credence to one cause or the other, Lee's resulting view of poor and marginal people is amazingly uplifting: "The strength of his personality has prevented Lee from falling victim to stereotypes. Even in his work in the most depressed areas of the country (or the world) his photographs do not overstress the hopelessness of his subjects. Indeed, he often depicts them leading comparatively serene and dignified lives, although the evidence shows that they should be reduced to abject misery" (Wroth 1985, 136).

The Taos County FSA photographs stand equidistant from two subsequent visual representations that become interpolated into the dialectic of Indo-Hispano representation in the Borderlands in the Cold War period. Occupying competing social realist camps, nurtured and fostered in the Cold War years, *Salt of the Earth* (1954) and *And Now, Miguel* (1953) tug at Lee's photo-documentary work from opposing vectors of belief and ideology. Still, I assert that all three representations provide for an increasing discernment of the actual condition of Mexican Americans in New Mexico and in adjacent Borderlands states during this period of time.

Zinc Town, USA

Salt of the Earth, the better known of the films, has become *de rigueur* in the canon of films shown in ethnic studies, women's studies, Chicano studies, sociology, and other academic disciplines. *Salt of the Earth* tells the story of the 1950 mining strike by the members of the New Mexico Local 890 of the International Union of Mine, Mill, and Smelter Workers in Hanover, New Mexico. The strike was but one in a series of labor struggles in the mining districts of southern New Mexico and Arizona that go back well over a century. In her landmark study of the making of *Salt*, Deborah Rosenfelt notes the major reasons for the fifteen-month strike:

The specific issues were the workers' demands for portal-to-portal pay and parity in the number of paid holidays with other mines in the district. The company insisted that it would never pay for time not worked—including lunch periods and travel to and from the surface of the mine. This issue is less dramatic than the issue of safety emphasized in *Salt of the Earth*; however, safety had been paramount in the other union struggles in the district. The film does accurately accentuate the underlying issues of the Empire Zinc strike; the company's arrogance toward the workers; its resistance to their efforts to negotiate their own demands; the history in the area as a whole of discrimination against Mexican-American workers; the larger struggle for power between labor and management. (Rosenfelt and Wilson 1972, 117)

That a film should take as its focus a labor struggle in New Mexico's mining districts where some 60 percent of the common labor came from Mexican American workers is indeed a major rotation in the choice of the subjects that prior generations of filmmakers and photographers had found alluring in the "exotic" Southwest. Students of *Salt of the Earth* know that the film's radical readjustments to formulaic commercial film portrayals do not end here. James J. Lorence calls the film "an enduring document of Cold War America and an emblem of determined independence." Lorence straightaway points out the vanguard characteristics that make the work an extraordinary film achievement: "The remarkably contemporary film based on the Empire Zinc strike, *Salt of the Earth* (1954), stands as a revealing celluloid document, a record that chronicles a determined effort by socially committed men and women to question the accepted gender and racial relations of their time and to build better lives for themselves and their families through the medium of socially conscious unionism" (Lorence 1999, 2). The red-baited and blacklisted Hollywood filmmakers who came to Silver City to film *Salt*—Paul Jarrico, Sylvia Jarrico, Herbert Biberman, Sonya Dahl Biberman, Michael and Zulema Wilson—were not, of course, concerned with exotica, nostalgia, or romance, the standard elements that had been applied successively in films about New Mexico and nuevomexicanos. In every way imaginable their work condemns the trite clichés that preceded them.

An informal meeting at the Craig Vincent ranch in San Cristobal, New Mexico, in the summer of 1951 brought screenwriters Paul and Sylvia Jarrico together with Grant County union organizers Clint and Virginia Jencks (Baker 2007; Lorence 1999; Rosenfelt and Wilson 1972). The Jarricos were so taken with the story of the Empire Zinc strike that had just been called 300 miles to the south in Silver City that they decided to visit the area on the return trip to California. Once in Hanover, the Jarricos came to know first-hand the elements of the strike, and they left convinced that they had hit upon exactly the kind of story their colleagues in the Independent Production Company (IPC) would like to make into a film. When Paul Jarrico met with Henry Biberman back in Los Angeles, his enthusiasm for the project could not be contained: "This is a story that's got everything. It's labor's rights, women's rights, minority rights, all in a dynamic package" (qtd. in Lorence 1999, 58).

The fifteen-month strike at Empire Zinc brought up a host of issues that affected the Mexican American communities in the copper mining regions of Arizona and New Mexico. Residents of copper towns, writes James Lorence, "lived out social and economic relationships that were the product of centuries of exploitation and inequality" (1999, 13). In 1950, the copper industry was the largest employer in Grant County and its presence had converted ancestral communities into company towns. Thus, the scene was set in historical terms for a David and Goliath story, one IPC believed would move the conscience of American filmgoers. But what would make *Salt* a truly remarkable undertaking was the way it brought the participation of women in the strike to the forefront. Ellen Baker suggests that this is the film's defining theme: "Women's rebellion against male domination lies at the heart of both the Empire Zinc strike and *Salt of the Earth*. It deserves exploration coming as it did from Mexican Americans (whose culture had a powerful, if complicated patriarchal authority) and during a period when the 'feminine mystique' permeated Anglo-American culture" (2007, 10). The Jarricos, with Sylvia joining the women's picket line on their initial visit to Hanover at the height of the Empire Zinc strike, felt strongly that the film should also be an account of women's emergence (2007, 57).

Here was a project that deliberately sought to get things right in historical, economic, and cultural terms. The filmmakers were able to achieve this through sustained and close working collaborations with the people whose story they wished to bring to film. The willingness of the filmmakers to give up authorial control in favor of "getting the story right" is rare in the history of U.S. film.

Even before the residents of the mining communities became aware that some of them would actually appear on screen, they began to express concern about the outcome of the film. Virginia Chacón cautioned, "If a movie was to be made, they did not want 'Hollywood shenanigans'" (Lorence 1999; Rosenfelt and Wilson 1972). Screenwriter Michael Wilson went to great lengths to put the collaboration between members of Local 890 and the professional crew of *Salt* into practice. Wilson held opening meetings where union members could critique his treatment of the screenplay. According to Baker a strong collaborative spirit infused the project:

> Michael Wilson understood his task to be honoring the people of Grant County, and he believed that to do them justice meant to defer to them—albeit after rigorous discussion—on critical matters. Whatever beliefs about the workers or ethnic minorities he brought with him, he did not apply them indiscriminately to a passive and inarticulate people. He listened carefully to the historical actors and tried to recast his own thinking to match their situation. (2007, 194)

In New Mexico, a production committee made up of union members and members of the IPC was organized to vent both large and small matters concerning the filming of *Salt*. The committee had "policy-making" duties and was responsible for "seeing that [the] picture ran true to life from start to finish" (Lorence 1999, 73). Community approval was especially important since many mine families were operating from a deep conviction that the film project was a testament to their "burning desire for an end to racial discrimination" in southern New Mexico. They also saw their identity as mine families and workers in the labor struggle as "an extension of Mexican American culture and community solidarity" (Lorence 1999, 44).

Salt opens with a shot of the film's protagonist, Esperanza Quintero (Rosaura Revueltas), chopping wood in the backyard of her company house. Esperanza's voiceover narration, close shots of the Quintero home, and vista shots of "Zinc Town" lay bare the film's key assignments of struggle and dignity:

ESPERANZA'S VOICE: My name is Esperanza Quintero. I am a miner's wife.

This is our home. This is not our house. But the flowers . . . the flowers are ours.

This is my village. When I was a child, it was called San Marcos.

The Anglos changed the name to Zinc Town. Zinc Town, New Mexico, U.S.A.

Our roots go deep in this place, deeper than the pines, deeper than the mine shaft.

In these arroyos my great-grandfather raised cattle before the Anglos ever came.

The land where the mine stands—that was owned by my husband's grandfather.

NOW it belongs to the company. Eighteen years my husband has given to that mine.

The action of the film bolts back to a day Esperanza recalls as the beginning of her story:

ESPERANZA'S VOICE: It was my Saint's Day. I was thirty-five years old. A day of celebration. And I was seven months gone with my third child.

It is a fateful day, one on which Esperanza will entertain the frightful thought that it would be better if her child would not be born, not into the misery that surrounds her in Zinc Town. The day following her birthday, the stillness of Zinc Town is interrupted by the wailing of sirens from the mine, a signal that another in a string of mining accidents has injured, perhaps killed, another mine worker. In an exchange between the company foreman and angry mine workers, Ramón Quintero (Juan Chacón), Esperanza's husband, articulates the workers' grievance with the company's cost-saving policy that requires miners to work alone even when doing the hazardous work of detonating explosives. This day's accident could have been avoided, Quintero insists. This most recent injury of a brother miner initiates Salt's dramatic conflict when on Ramón's signal his co-workers shut down operations and walk out on strike.

The remainder of the film presents the tedious progress of the strike and the work of union organizers to gain support from labor unions and political organizations nationwide. Several months into the strike, the company wins a court injunction under the Taft-Hartley Act that prevents members of the union from crossing state lines to picket at Hanover. A crucial and bitterly contested vote is then taken by the union local to allow the women, members of the 890's Ladies Auxiliary, to replace the miners on the picket line, an act meant to keep the strike alive. Lorence sees this action as having "transformed the strike and determined the outcome" (1999, 29). From this point to the final resolution, *Salt* illuminates the questions of gender equality and personal growth, matters that are seen as equal to the union's workplace demands. Esperanza's growth results from her involvement in union activities and suggests that a higher level of equality is to be achieved. *Salt's* boldest treatment of gender inequality is at the point where the work roles of the men and women of the mining community are reversed. After a few days of caring for the children and doing the household chores, Ramón comes to see how the women's grievances about sanitation, lack of child care, and lack of running water are equal to the safety and pay issues in the mine. But Ramón is chagrined by Esperanza's newfound assertiveness and, at one point after a night of drinking, he rebukes Esperanza for neglecting the family and threatens to hit her. This critical scene illuminates the intertwined themes of labor and gender inequity:

FIG. 8. "Ramón Quintero and Neighbor Hanging Clothes," still from 16mm film print of *Salt of the Earth*. New Mexico Historical Film Collection, image number 11949. Courtesy of the New Mexico State Records Center and Archives.

ESPERANZA: No you don't. Have you not learned anything from this strike? Why are you afraid to have me at your side? Do you still think you can have dignity only if I have none?

RAMÓN: You talk of dignity? After what you've been doing?

ESPERANZA: Yes, I talk of dignity. The Anglo bosses look down on you, and you hate them for it. "Stay in your place, you dirty Mexican"—that's what they tell you. But why must you say to me, "Stay in your place"? Do you feel better having someone lower than you?

RAMÓN: Shut up, you're talking crazy.

ESPERANZA: Whose neck shall I stand on, to make me feel superior? And what will I get out of it? I don't want anything lower than I am. I'm low enough already. I want to rise. And push everything up with me as I go . . .

RAMÓN: Will you be still?

ESPERANZA: And if you can't understand this you're a fool—because you can't win this strike without me. You can't win anything without me!

(He seizes her shoulder with one hand and raises the other to slap her. Esperanza's body goes rigid. She stares straight at him, defiant and unflinching. Ramón drops his hand.)

ESPERANZA: That would have been the old way. Never try it on me again— never. (Rosenfelt and Wilson 1972, 81–82)

A deflated Ramón goes off on a hunting trip with his union brothers the next morning just as he had threatened to do the night before. But while walking down a forest path, he has his own revelation as he hears the voice, but more important, comes to understand the logic of Esperanza's remonstrance of the night before: "I want to rise. And push everything up with me as I go." A shot is heard ringing through the arroyo and Ramón calls out, "We've got to go back, brothers." Ramón and the others arrive back at his home just as the local sheriff (Will Geer) is in the process of evicting a mining family. Hearing of the eviction, a stream of other miners and their families arrive on the scene. The group eventually swells to a hundred or more women, children, and miners who block the sheriff and his men. In the face of the crowd amassed against him, the sheriff backs down and the residents burst into celebration. The final exchange between Esperanza and Ramón brings closure to the parallel effects of the strike in the lives of the residents of Zinc Town:

RAMÓN: Esperanza . . . thank you . . . thank you for your dignity. You were right. Together we can push everything up as we go.

ESPERANZA: Then I knew we had won something they could never take away—something I could leave to my children—and they, the salt of the earth, would inherit it. (Rosenfelt and Wilson 1972, 90)

Whenever I teach *Salt of the Earth* in my film classes, I insist upon calling the work a Chicano/a film, despite the admonition from Chicana film critic Rosa Linda Fregoso that Chicano/a films can only be those "by, for, and about Chicanos." I argue for including *Salt* as a Chicano film on the basis of its significance to Chicano communities and its collaboration with Chicano communities. In terms of the film's significance to Chicanos, it is obvious that its very creation was meant to ameliorate the conditions faced by Chicano workers and their families in particular. As "a record of people (Chicanos) striving to make their own history" (Lorence 1999, 61), *Salt* is exemplary. Clearly, it was a film known and of great use to legendary labor leaders like Bert Corona, who made use of the film in his own organizing in the 1950s. Lorence argues, "The Chicano/a community of the Southwest embraced *Salt of the Earth* as an expression of Mexican American cultural resilience and strength. Their supportive response to the film paralleled Mexican American loyalty to Mill-Mine in the troubled union's years of greatest peril" (1999, 202).

By the mid-1960s *Salt* became an important cultural and educational document that would serve to educate and raise the consciousness of a generation of university students. In New Mexico, *Salt*, for example, was screened at one of the early organizational meetings of the United Mexican American Student Association (UMAS) in 1968.

The extensive participation of Mexican Americans on- and offscreen qualifies *Salt* as a bi-cultural text in the sense that Arnold Krupat has applied the term: native raconteurs collaborating with white chroniclers to produce Native American autobiographical writings.[3] The influence of the mining families in Grant County is decisive especially when one considers that their approbation accounts for equal parts of what appears and what does not appear in the film. Deborah Rosenfelt lists the impact of community decision making on the film's final form:

Scenes that did not ring true to them were excised or re-written: "No Hollywood Shenanigans," they said. Some incidents they feared would perpetuate negative stereotypes of the passionate and drunken Mexican. They objected, for example, to a sub-plot involving Ramón's infidelity with a woman whose husband had gone to Korea; it was eliminated. They objected to the characterization of Ramón as a heavy drinker, buying a bottle of whiskey with his last paycheck; Ramón as a *borracho* (drunkard) came out; but the scenes in the bar, crucial in suggesting the male refuge from both work and home, remained. (Rosenfelt and Wilson 1972, 127)

But the most enduring shaping of *Salt* by the residents of southern New Mexico comes from their onscreen participation as principal and secondary protagonists. The selection of Local 890 president Juan Chacón to play the male lead certainly broke with film conventions of the day. It was director Herbert Biberman who argued loudly for the use of amateurs drawn from the community; as Lorence notes, "Biberman balked at the idea of Anglos in the lead roles" (1999, 69). Chacón's energy and enthusiasm won over Biberman and the professional crew. Lorence writes,

The greatest shock came when Juan Chacón proved to be "just incredible," as "sensitive a human being as can be." Perhaps exaggerating, Biberman told his family that he had "never, never, seen such a miracle." When the nonprofessionals were complimented on their work some asserted that as minority workers who had often experienced punishment for open expression of their true thoughts, they learned to act before Herbert Biberman ever entered their lives. (1999, 75)

Thirteen of the nineteen members of the nonprofessional cast were local Mexican American residents and union members. An unknown number of members of Local 890 appeared in the film as unnamed extras. The dignity of their participation on film suggests that finally the image of Chicanos, in this case of nuevomexicanos, had plied its way through the layers of distortion to form a more fully rounded view of men and women creating their own history and acting on their own agency and determination.

Brown Men/Cold War: USIA's Upstanding Upland Villagers

The 1953 film *And Now, Miguel* is as much a preemption of *Salt of the Earth* as it is a continuation of a persistent image of nuevomexicanos as noble and idealized mountain villagers living in a timeless, ahistorical setting. Shot in the northern village of Los Córdovas, a community located some seven miles south of Taos, New Mexico, *And Now, Miguel* became the basis of a novel for young adults that Joseph Krumgold published 1953 and for which he received a Newbery Medal. The film version by Krumgold and his associates tells the story of Miguel Chávez, a young boy who grows up in the shepherding tradition of his New Mexican ancestors. It is Miguel's dream to join his father, uncles, and older brothers in the annual practice of taking the family herds of sheep from winter pastures in the valley to the alpine meadows of the Sangre de Cristo Mountains. As Miguel nears puberty he becomes aware that completing the summer trek will confirm his ascendancy to manhood and responsibility in the tradition of his fore-bears. To be able to make the pilgrimage into the mountains, as in all coming-of-age stories, Miguel must prove his worth before he can take his place in the tradition that precedes him.[4]

And Now, Miguel's ethnographic touches and depiction of villagers engaged in the age-old practice of transhumance provides the film its social realist bent and links the work to the photos of Taos County by Russell Lee and John Collier Jr. The distribution and sponsorship of the earlier version of *Miguel* by the United States Information Service (USIS) of the United States Information Agency (USIA) also brings forth important considerations about its intended use at home and abroad. *And Now, Miguel* is at a distant and opposite end from *Salt* within the triad of representations that includes the FSA photographs. *Miguel* is, in fact, a kind of counter to *Salt of the Earth*. *Miguel*'s gentle theme and idyllic portrayal of nuevomexi-canos dismantles the more radical and activist politics underpinning *Salt*.

And Now, Miguel is prefaced by a shot of a mountain trail winding through an aspen grove in the Sangre de Cristo Mountains. The Arcadian scene is accompanied by the following intertitle:

> This is a path in New Mexico in the Southwest part of the United States. It leads up into the high mountains where the sheep go to summer pasture. The sheep are driven by men of the Valley who

have grown up as shepherds, among them the men of the Chavez family.

A shot of individual aspens carved with names and dates follows:

G. Chavez 1901/ Blas Chavez June 25, 1919/ Gabriel Chavez 7/21/1948/ Blank tree.

And a second short intertitle lists the film credits.[5]

Miguel opens with a shot of a ewe and her newly born lamb standing in the wind and cold next to a borreguero's (nuevomexicano sheepherder's) camp wagon. The scene carries no narration and lingers on the face of a borreguero who, hearing the bleating of ewe and lamb, rises from his bed-roll. The voiceover narration begins with Miguel jumping up from bed at the same moment in the nearby farmhouse. Miguel tells of the importance of the first birth of the lambing season. His mother and sisters leave to go see the first birth, but Miguel must stay at home to watch his younger siblings, a determination that causes Miguel to lament his position in the family as a middle child, too young to attend to the sheep, too old to remain in bed. The film scans headshots of Miguel's father, Blas, his Uncle Bonefacio, and his older and younger siblings. The portraits of his family and a vista shot of the Sangre de Cristo Mountains, shot at a low camera angle, add stature to the images and are more than mere reminders of the Lee and Collier photos of Taos County residents.

John Collier Jr., son of the renowned commissioner of Indian Affairs John Collier Sr., an untiring advocate of Native American cultural sover-eignty and education, was not a newcomer to New Mexico. His father's resi-dency in New Mexico provided John Jr. with a great deal of early experience among the Pueblo and Spanish-speaking peoples of the state, a strength Roy Stryker saw when he hired Collier to work as a FSA photographer in 1941. Indeed, his assignment to New Mexico, in the words of Malcolm Col-lier, placed John "in the unusual position of working in his home terri-tory" (1993, 15). Malcolm Collier recalls that John Jr. had made his home in a rural New Mexican community since 1936. His status as a resident of northern New Mexico provided him "close relationships with a number of families" (15). Malcolm Collier suggests his "connections crossed cultural and social boundaries in what was, and still is, a culturally and socially

compartmentalized region. It's difficult to assess the impact of this position on his photography, but it must have facilitated his work, and certainly provided insight into local circumstances" (15). In point of fact, and
presumably because of his connections to local communities, John Collier
Jr. arrived and photographed the Chávez sheep operation at Los Córdovas
a full ten years ahead of the making of *And Now, Miguel*. Whether through
planning or chance, the convergence of Collier, Russell Lee, and Joseph
Krumgold at the Chávez home remains a fascinating coincidence.

Indeed, these random encounters, along with a monumental number
of uncatalogued FSA photographs, prompted the photo historian Cavalliere Ketchum at the University of Wisconsin to retrace the movements of
Collier and his fellow FSA photographers in New Mexico. Ketchum's specific aim continues to be to name the hundreds of nuevomexicanos listed
only as Spanish Americans in the FSA collections. In a piece in *On Wisconsin*, Ketchum tells how, after having spent several summers combing
the mountain villages of northern New Mexico trying to identify a Collier
photo of two smiling nuevomexicano farm boys, he unraveled the mystery
without having to leave his own campus. Some time in the late 1990s, Ketchum took a chance and strolled over to the office of a new colleague to
talk about his research and show her some of the Collier photos of Taos
residents and their homes. Ketchum's new colleague, Alicia Chávez, was a
professor of educational administration and a New Mexico native. Chávez,
it turned out, was immediately able to identify the location and subjects in
Collier's photos; as chance would have it, the photos were of her father and
uncle. The *On Wisconsin* article notes: "Although Ketchum did not know it,
it was the house in which Alicia Chávez's father grew up. The young boy
with the devilish smile was Gabriel, standing next to his big brother Blas,
Jr." (Penn 2002, 54). Like Lee's photos of nuevomexicanos, Collier's photos are dignified and uplifting portraits that run against the grain of most
views of ethnic minorities at the time. Malcolm Collier maintains that
some of John's sensitivity toward excluded populations accrued to him
from his father's work as a champion of Native American rights: "Though
most people would have seen these groups as curiosities, John was predis-
posed to see them as significant, vibrant peoples with a future" (1993, 14).

Cavalliere Ketchum believes that Blas Chávez Sr., the patriarch of the
Chávez home, was a favorite subject for Collier, and at least three of his

Taos photographs show this to be the case. One photo is of Blas Chávez and his daughter, Faustina, standing in front of the family home surrounded by a herd of sheep. Its vantage point is surprisingly similar to shots Krumgold used in *And Now, Miguel.* Another is the photo of Gabriel and Blas Chávez Jr. standing against the mud-plastered wall of the Los Córdovas house. The boys are so close in appearance as to be twins. They are scrubbed and neatly groomed, dressed in matching wool sweaters and posed with all the formality that would be required for a First Holy Communion photo. Among the most evocative images in the series is a family portrait taken

FIG. 9. John Collier Jr., "Chavez family portrait." Library of Congress, Prints and Photographs Division, #LC USW3–19219-C.

by Collier inside the Chávez home. In this photo, Blas Sr. is flanked by his wife, Fedelina, and daughter, Faustina, the trio sitting on the living room sofa. Fedelina sits on the armrest and Faustina nuzzles in as Blas reads a letter with news that the family has won an animal husbandry competition for raising a prize ram. The photo is an especially clear example of the kind of scene Roy Stryker advised his photographers to record. The photo is, indeed, a kind of cultural chronotype, filled as it is with the social and cultural signposts that mark rural Hispanic life. The photos are so close in spirit to the scenes depicted in *And Now, Miguel* that one is inclined to think that Krumgold took suggestions from Roy Stryker prior to shooting the film. Krumgold's mise-en-scène shots at Los Córdovas are equally evocative of the social and cultural values that underpin the Chávez household, linked to ethnographic moments in the film that are established through Miguel's narration of the "patterns of life" that dictate the norms of the Chávez and other families in Los Córdovas.

As Miguel recounts family stories, he accounts for the origin of the patterns of family, work, and environment. The affinity of the family to their natural environment is brought forth in Miguel's own view of the Sangre de Cristos. "I think of them as my mountains," he says with pride. Later he will relate how his grandfather, who worked for a *patrón*, started the flock long ago and "now has too many sheep to count." It is through Miguel that the audience learns the details of the yearly cycle of caring for the flocks of sheep. During the lambing, ewes and lambs are branded with painted numbers to identify each pair. Miguel's sisters take in some of the orphan lambs (the *pencos*) when possible. Other strays are matched to ewes by fitting the orphan with the fleece of a dead lamb so as to fool the mother into believing her lost offspring has returned. On May 15 the village of Los Córdovas celebrates the feast day of San Isidro, the patron saint of farmers and agriculturalists. The film follows the villagers as they honor their patron saint with an evening procession. After Mass, the next morning, San Isidro is taken out to bless the fields. Scenes of the village fiesta replete with beer, music, and the staging of native dances like *la varsoviana* and *las chapanecas* follow the religious observances. The scene provides one of the few places in the film where local musical forms are employed.

The next major event in the Chávez home comes with the arrival of the Márquez brothers who have come down from Colorado to shear the sheep. As the music of *corridos* plays in the background, Miguel tells how these particular workers shear with electric shears and mechanical methods. The time of shearing is also an opportunity for Miguel to prove his worth as a *pastor*. He sweeps the stalls and gathers bundles of wool into huge canvas sacks that hang from timbers above the corrals. Just as the workers are taking notice of his hard work, however, Miguel decides to pack down the wool by jumping down into the sack, only to find that he is not able to get out of it again. The predicament is evidence of his youth and inexperience. Later, however, it is the shearers that recognize Miguel's hard work by inviting him to eat with them at the dinner his mother has prepared for the workers. Miguel is overjoyed as he hears them "tell stories of shepherding up and down the Rio Grande Valley."

Each installment of the film reiterates Miguel's yearning to join the *pastores* in their trek to the Sangre de Cristos. Miguel has a chance to prove himself in the wake of a spring snowstorm. The storm forces the sheepmen to build fire at night to warm the sheep. The next day news comes that the storm has scattered the flocks and many sheep are missing. Later, while on the playground at school, a friend named Cubi informs Miguel that he has seen the sheep and knows where they are. Miguel bolts out of the schoolyard, books in hand, while his teacher tries to call him back. When Miguel does find the strays, we are offered a generous shot of Miguel (as the Good Shepherd) carrying a young lamb in his arms back to the Chávez home. Mrs. Mertian, the schoolteacher, has already been to visit Miguel's parents. Miguel's father thanks him for attending to the lost sheep but reprimands him for cutting school. "What about summer?" Miguel asks, only to have his father answer, "No," and he will have to wait.

Miguel is set back to praying to San Isidro to grant him his wish to go to the mountains. Miguel's prayer is answered when a letter from the U.S. Selective Services arrives for his older brother Gabriel. As Gabriel's situation becomes clear, Miguel blames himself for his brother's imminent departure and prays to San Isidro to make the letter disappear. When the letter doesn't go away, Miguel hides it, but this will not undo its effect. In a long heart-to-heart talk, Gabriel explains that his leaving for the army is prompted by the current danger that looms in the world. Gabriel's speech evokes the spirit of service to the country that is transmitted to the viewing audience as the natural inclination of the *taoseños*. He tells Miguel that

the Chávezes' way of life, which includes their use of Forest Service per-
mits to graze sheep in the mountains, is at risk and must be defended.
Miguel repeats Gabriel's explanation of service to country. Miguel tells us
that Gabriel's journey in the "big world" parallels Miguel's steps on the
path into the mountains. The day of Gabriel's departure is also the day the
pastores start their journey to the mountains. *And Now, Miguel* ends with
scenes of mountain meadows, grazing sheep, and the men of the Chávez
family, among them Miguel.

There is much to appreciate about the accuracy of the ethnographic
detail encased in this small film. Like the photos by Lee and Collier Jr., it
remains a window onto a history of livelihoods that today are the stuff
of memory for all but a few northern New Mexicans. It should be kept
in mind that recalling this past need not fall into the realm of nostalgia.
After all, the film evokes the lives of working families in the 1950s and is
not a distant recall of things that transpired in the past. *And Now, Miguel*'s
veracity in this way could only have come from the field investigation that
Krumgold undertook before making the film. Though not the subject of
the film itself, it is the history of sheep agriculture by Hispanos in the Taos
Valley, as Krumgold came to learn about it, that gives the film its corner-
stone realism.

In an interview, older brother Gabriel Chávez, a key participant in the
film, shared his recollections of the making of *And Now, Miguel*. Gabriel's
account is especially rich in detail concerning the months that led up to
the making of the film. His memories of how his father, mother, and siblings all took time to share the Chávez story with Krumgold explains a great
deal about how the film came to find its cultural and historical anchor.
Gabriel Chávez spoke of the generations of family members engaged in the
sheep industry:

GABRIEL CHÁVEZ: We were pretty much wrapped around our raising sheep
    and making a living that way with my dad, you know. That's what we
    did. We raised hay and the garden and things like that . . . but most
    of our concentration was on the sheep. That's what gave us our liveli-
    hood. And so we, ourselves, spent a lot of time out on the range all
    around here and then in the summers as the movie shows we went
    up into what is now the Pecos Wilderness and we spent the summers
    up there. That is where you see all those carvings on the aspen trees

with our names on them. Our life was not, for the rest of the people in the community . . . was not totally, was pretty much, whereas there are very few sheep in this valley now, I think there used to be around 20,000 head of sheep in this valley in those days. So, very many of the people were involved in that activity. (Chávez interview)

In an interview at Temple University in 1971, Krumgold recounted how his first contact with the Chávez family came by way of the efforts of the county agricultural extension agent (Krumgold 1971, 2), whom he does not name. Years later, Gabriel Chávez would confirm the specifics of that meeting:[6]

GC: It would have happened in Fifty. Or maybe late Forty-nine. Because the movie was made starting in Fifty-one, finished in Fifty-two. And then he ended up here in Taos and from here he was directed by the county agent at the time, a fellow by the name of Ernesto Gutiérrez. As a matter of fact, he shows up in the movie also, to come and talk to my dad I guess. Apparently he found what he was looking for. He came back and spent some six months with us. Not living with us, but daily, on a daily basis talking with us and to people in the community. (Chávez interview)

Krumgold's version of setting up in the Taos Valley also makes note of an extended period of research and time spent at the Chávez ranch getting to know his subject:

JACQUELYN SCHACHTER: You spent a long time with them, didn't you?

KRUMGOLD: From the inception, from the writing of the script through the shooting of the picture, some six or seven months. Got to know how to raise sheep very, very well. I thought we would finish up raising sheep more than making a movie half the time, but it was a lengthy process and thank the Lord for that because I enjoyed every minute of it. (Krumgold 1971, 2)

It is reasonable to assume that during the time Krumgold spent preparing for the filming of *And Now, Miguel* he would have had occasion to view Lee and Collier's FSA photos of Taos and surrounding areas. FSA photos continued to be widely disseminated in newspapers, magazines, USDA county extension newsletters, and other publications. Indeed, it would have been hard for anyone interested in the area not to come upon them in one fashion or another. FSA photos were also prominently and routinely featured in national publications such as *Look, Life,* and *Fortune,* and in exhibits at the Museum of Modern Art (Penn 2002, 23).

Krumgold's screenplay includes a significant culminating speech on the importance of patriotic duty to nation voiced by the Chávez sons, but it is one that Krumgold did not include in the novel. Where the film clearly amplifies Gabriel Chávez's resolve to fulfill his duty to home and country, the novel is mute on the threat that a distant war could have on the Chávezes' way of life. The omission is best explained by Krumgold's admission that he conceived of the film and novel as separate projects with distinct purposes, but it may also have something to do with the fact that as he went along Krumgold learned about the especially high regard nuevomexicanos had for military service. Gabriel Chávez recalls that patriotism was a vital part of his upbringing:

GC: Very, very special. Very great. And, of course, now we talk about the military, we talk about the Hispanics, now you really open it up. Now we're not only talking about Northern New Mexico or New Mexico, because it's very different as you well know even from Puerto Rico. It's totally different, but it's a big connection there. All of it I felt was very loyal, even more so than a lot of the other ethnic cultures, you might say, or people. (Chávez interview)

Krumgold was aware that the film was intended for the use of its chief sponsor, the U.S. Information Service, but when asked in 1971 about why he turned to writing children's books, he responded in a surprisingly frank and honest manner:

To make money . . . I have produced very few. When I said to make money . . . it was a shrewd act of business. I had just finished the picture, a publisher saw the shooting script and said wouldn't I write this as a children's book and it seemed an utterly simple possibility of picking up some extra revenue out of work that I'd already done . . . that this could be done very quickly, so that was my original intention. I had no notion of saying anything, but I soon discovered that one undertakes the writing of a children's book in any serious fashion at his peril. (Krumgold 1971, 2)

Casting the story as a piece of children's literature called for the omission of heavy ideological and political messages that would take away from the book as a good read for young adults. In addition to the business of monetary gain, redirecting the project away from government sponsorship also required Krumgold to confer a literary pedigree on his new children's book. This was a matter Krumgold felt compelled to address in the Temple interview, where he speaks about Miguel's story using the language of 1950's New Criticism:

> And the story that the family was living was then so meaningful that it fitted the program that I was doing, but much more important than that, as I discovered later when I put it into a book, was that it had a universality that went far beyond any government program and started to take on real meaning and dimension of itself. (Krumgold 1971, 2)

In the film, Gabriel's explanation to his younger brother of communism as an external world threat is larded with a fair amount of Cold War rhetoric. Keeping with the focus on life as apprenticeship, it is Miguel who voices Gabriel's explanation of the global threat as an allegory of the Good Shepherd protecting his flock. Miguel's voiceover is at once poignant and pithy:

> Down there, by the river Gabriel talked to me for the first time as though I was full grown. The letter, he explained, made no difference. It told him where to report, that is all. He was going because sometimes when there is danger far off, your flocks may be lost. A shepherd must leave his flock to stop the killer before any sheep are lost. Just so, beyond the oceans into which this river flowed, there is now a danger not only to the flock but to our whole family and other families like us who lived with the freedom to make the wish that was in their hearts, like my wish to go to the mountains, come true. There were those who would put an end to such a freedom and destroy everyone's wish but their own. Gabriel was going as a Shepherd must to face them, so that one day, he and I, we could be pastores together.

The political message here is the clearest nod to the support of the film by USIS and raises the question as to why USIS, a network of field posts

FIG. 10. "Miguel and Gabriel Chavez, Heart-to-Heart," still from 16mm film print of *And Now, Miguel*. New Mexico Historical Film Collection, image numbers 11157, 11158. Courtesy of the New Mexico State Records Center and Archives.

headquartered at U.S. embassies around the world, would turn *And Now, Miguel* into one of its informational films. We know that copies of the film were deposited at USIS libraries across the globe and were kept on hand to assist USIS country affairs officers in their foreign information campaigns. The inclusion of *And Now, Miguel* among USIS titles, at first glance, appears rather incongruous, and yet a look at USIA's criteria for selecting film subjects suggests that it fit neatly into the agency's mission.

Writing in 1976 Leo Bogart affirmed, "Projecting America is the USIA's biggest job," insisting that "USIA dedicates a substantial part of its activity to cultivating familiarity (and by implication friendship) with the United States and its institutions" (1976, 88–89). Bogart notes that while USIA operators often disagreed on whether both the attractive and unattractive aspects of American life should be projected to the world, they did come to find that Americana of various types could help them in creating familiarity and friendliness with the United States. The motives of USIA during the Cold War were straightforward, as can be seen in the ideas that the agency wished to convey to the world about the United States:

1. Americans are nice people.
2. America is generous and altruistic.
3. America is democratic.
    a. In America all races and creeds live happily together.
    b. Americans don't consider it beneath a man to work with his hands.
4. Americans believe in equality for other people.
5. American life has a spiritual quality.
6. Americans are a cultured people.
7. The U.S. economy is successful.
8. America is a peaceable country. (Bogart 1976, 89–90)

A chief USIA concern was to avoid projections that showed too high a standard of living. The agency feared that an emphasis on the material progress of the United States could incite hostile reactions in foreign peoples who would take these depictions as a sign of boasting. Bogart provides the cautionary note: "The 'green-tiled bathroom' image should be counteracted, wherever possible, by showing that some Americans live under simple conditions, or by stressing the survival of handicrafts in the Appalachian highlands" (1976, 94). Other USIA procedures stipulated that "anything put out under U.S. government imprint should be calm, factual, and non-combative," thus opening the door for the use of Americana: "Anything that's a history of the United States, Americans at work or play, any and all of these subjects should be USIA" (Bogart 1976, 123).

Joseph Krumgold confirms that he and the others responsible for making *And Now, Miguel* were totally cognizant of how the film's content and message served the goals of USIA. When host Jacquelyn Schachter inquired as to how he came to meet the Chávez family, Krumgold notes the details of the movie's genesis:

> Well, it had to do with the purpose for which the film was being made. This was done for the U.S. Information Service who was making a program of films under the direction of Margaret Mead the anthropologist. One of the purposes of the program was to show that the family in American life still constituted to a considerable extent, if not a majority extent, that the family unit still continued as an economic and a social unit that was highly important. That families ran

farms, grocery stores, gasoline stations, things of that sort, and that it was a unit of cohesion here in this country. My assignment was to find a farming family that did this and I started the search in Oklahoma and went west looking for them. (Krumgold 1971, 2)

Then as now, film was deemed to be an especially important tool in the propaganda war. Bogart stipulated: "Movies have the ability to get audiences and hold their attention. Seeing a movie is like a prize." Films assemble a "captive audience." "You can do anything you want with them as long as you don't drive them away" (1976, 169). Movies, too, were seen as particularly good resources for domestic use:

> Movies are most easily adaptable for domestic use in the U.S. and can win favorable publicity for USIA. They effectively convey information and are accepted as authentic, showing people how to do things and how to improve their lot. They may be used to expound foreign policy with high credibility (unless the audience is so unsophisticated that it takes the theme literally, in which case the abstractions that a western audience would readily understand must be spelled out). They are the best substitute for word-of-mouth persuasion—and the purpose of USIA films is "attitude formation, not information." (1976, 169)

Seen in the light of the USIA's operating norms, it is understandable that Krumgold's film version of *And Now, Miguel* would find its way into the Cold War propaganda machine. By emphasizing a respect for difference and soft-pedaling racial strife, *Miguel* becomes an effective tool for both domestic and international audiences.

Just as in the film, Gabriel Chávez was called up by the Selective Service in 1952 at the height of the Korean War. Like other rural nuevomexicanos, Chávez anticipated that he would be drafted and serve in the military. He recalls, "It was during the Korean War situation and, of course, the draft was still in effect. When I finished from high school, of course—we all did in those days—we got a call from the draft. And it had always been my understanding and my intention that I would end up being drafted and going in" (Chávez interview). Gabriel's thoughts about serving in the military were premised on what was the traditional expectation in his family and the nuevomexicano community at large regarding service to country. Young men from across the region had served in every conflict since the Civil War, and the memory of World War II and the mobilization of New Mexico's 200 Coast Artillery to the Philippines was very much alive in the years after World War II. Chávez remembers, "Now the Second World War, that brought a lot of the action especially in the Pacific, and I forget what the military unit was, but they were National Guard people from New Mexico, especially northern New Mexico, Taos, Mora, ended up in Bataan" (Chávez interview).

After reporting for his physical examination and being found suitable for induction into military service, Gabriel received an ROTC student deferment and with the advice of the county agent, Ernesto Gutiérrez, he enrolled as an undergraduate at New Mexico State University in the fall of 1953, earning a B.A. in Agricultural Sciences in 1956. Younger brother Miguel was called up some years later, entered the military, and was stationed in Germany in the late 1950s. While he was at New Mexico State University, a series of coincidences led Gabriel Chávez to participate in the distribution of *And Now, Miguel* at a time when the film was being screened by USIS in foreign missions across the globe. Chávez's participation was especially valued in putting the film before audiences in Latin America. Gabriel Chávez recounts how he ended up becoming a goodwill ambassador for the U.S. State Department, visiting every country in South and Central America:

> I ended up in the Department of State somehow. . . . And I don't know if the people who were there already knew about me. I don't think they did, I think they just put two and two together because the movie itself had become quite important and quite popular in foreign countries. So, I suppose somebody decided this is a good opportunity to take this guy and run him through Latin America doing something, showing the movie, presenting the book. (Chávez interview)

Amazingly, for some eighteen months, Gabriel Chávez crisscrossed Latin America with his old friend, Ernesto Gutiérrez, who Chávez remembers running some of the aid programs for the U.S. government. "He took me, again, under his wing and he took me all over the place. Twice he did that, I went down there twice" (Chávez interview). The pair visited the

Altiplano of Bolivia and Peru and the Cochibamba region of the Bolivia. A Spanish-language version of the film was screened mostly for youth clubs and agricultural associations in the rural areas where it was thought *And Now, Miguel* would go over well. Gabriel Chávez recalls:

And the reason I say Bolivia and Peru and all that is because there were sheep-raising people up there, still are, sheep and goats, vicuñas and llamas, and all that. It wasn't . . . and the reason I remember those things is because I would go up in the Altiplano, out in the country, you know, where it seemed there was nothing, like a barren desert, but then at some point somebody would blow one of those horns that they have to call the people to come and in a few hours people started showing up, walking down the mountain, riding their donkeys, or whatever. Before I knew it I had an audience of hundreds of people. But it was very interesting because I would speak and I would show the movie and the people would never speak . . . would never say anything. When it was all over they just turned around and went home. (Chávez interview)

At these screenings, Gabriel Chávez would speak to the assembled public in Spanish about life in the United States, about his home and family life in northern New Mexico. Not all screenings were as inconclusive as the encounters with the agricultural peoples of the Andean highlands. Gabriel Chávez recalls how screenings before university and urban audiences often faced boisterous denunciations of U.S. foreign policy and the work of diplomatic missions in Latin America:

Now that was totally different, you know, because university students, especially the Latin American students, are pretty vocal for the most part. And in those days the Cold War was going on. There was a lot of Communist activity in those places. So I would get accosted with a lot of that stuff too. I had to learn. My inexperience quickly got drained out of me and I had to start watching out for myself in a lot of those areas. And of course the State Department knowing that this was happening they gave me a lot of training in those areas, how to handle things like that, you know. (Chávez interview)

In one memorable in-country visit, Gabriel Chávez met members of the anti-Batista movement in Cuba led by Fidel Castro, who had just emerged from prison along with his brother Raul, still a member of Juventud Socialist at the University of Havana. Chávez remembers, "At that time they were good guys. They were fighting Batista, a dictator that the United States did not relish and eventually ended up helping Castro throw him out of office" (Chávez interview).

It is also the case that Chicanos and Chicanas of a certain age remember seeing this film as part of their middle school and high school studies in towns and cities across New Mexico, a matter that raises a second question: How and why was the film screened domestically? Cold War hysteria of the kind that led to the blacklisting of *Salt of the Earth* also produced a sharp contest for social control of the U.S. domestic populations in the postwar years. As these two films demonstrate, Mexican Americans were not exempt from the fray; to the contrary, *Salt's* story of labor militancy put them squarely in the middle of the arena. Scripted for "showing people how to do things," *And Now, Miguel* certainly fits the bill for showing a contrasting view of the participation of Mexican Americans in the United States. Ironically and despite the competing ideologies that produced the visual examples considered here, both rest on the bedrock notion that interpolates Mexican Americans into the American imagination as a group of people who are the salt of the earth.

5

Red Sky at Morning,
a Borderlands Interlude

Governor David F. Cargo, a Republican who began his first term in office in January 1967, was largely responsible for the creation of the New Mexico Film Commission in 1970. Cargo had long been an advocate of selling New Mexico as an ideal location for Hollywood to make movies, and the Film Commission provided numerous inducements to filmmakers. Exotica, worn to a nub by the mid-1960s, might still supply some enchantment, but the economic incentives (tax breaks, the availability of cheap extras, low hotel costs, New Mexico's status as close to that of a third-world country) were the real drawing card that state government extended to Hollywood moguls.

Among those striking film deals in New Mexico were the producers of *Red Sky at Morning.*[1] Moviemakers were drawn to the Richard Bradford novel of the same name for its appealing mix of adolescent desire, wartime uncertainty, and a setting so distinct from the rest of America as to appear foreign. *Red Sky* thus seemed the perfect project to film in New Mexico, with much to say about life in the heart of the Southwest Borderlands and about how Anglos and Chicanos view one another as neighbors.

A controversy arose around the proposed inclusion in the film of a Penitente procession, similar to those photographed by Charles Lummis decades earlier. And yet Penitentes are referenced only once in Bradford's novel, when Joshua Arnold is seeking to rehire Amadeo and Excilda Montoya and is required to visit the couple in the mountain village of Río Conejo, a town lying north of Santa Fe. After dinner at the Montoyas' home, Josh goes for a walk with their daughter Victoria, his high school classmate. They walk by a low adobe structure that sits at one end of the family farm. The building strikes Josh as distinctive and odd. When he asks about it, Vicky tells him it is a morada used by the Penitentes. Josh asks if her father is a Penitente. She replies that he has never been a member, that the morada is inactive, and that it is used as a storehouse and meat locker where her father hangs venison sides and rabbit carcasses (Bradford 1999, 138). Nevertheless, despite this brief mention in the novel and the filmmakers' idea to add Penitente ritual to the screenplay, not even the word "Penitente" is uttered in the film. The filmmakers' retreat in this regard had the unexpected effect of returning *Red Sky at Morning* to its principal theme, a critique of the southern racial hierarchy into which Josh Arnold was born. To put it bluntly, *Red Sky* is about the ways in which whiteness and the social privilege it accords are challenged in New Mexico.

Red Sky at Morning, Richard Bradford's first novel, appeared in 1968 and received favorable reviews that compared it to *The Catcher in the Rye* and *To Kill a Mockingbird*, two classic examples of the American bildungsroman. Bradford, a graduate of Tulane University, had come to New Mexico in 1956 and would end up spending his adult life in Santa Fe, working as a technical and staff writer and editor for state and federal agencies before his literary career interrupted his professional life. Anyone who reads the novel and views the film will note how the dialogue of Bradford's characters is reproduced nearly verbatim in the film. This should come as no surprise, however, since publication of the novel also led Bradford to a job as a screenwriter for Universal Studios. Bradford's first assignment at Universal was working as an advisor on the screenplay of *Red Sky at Morning* as well as on the actual filming, which allowed him a high degree of artistic control.

Aside from the collapse of the novel's first three chapters on the Arnolds' life in Mobile into a four-minute opening scene, the film generally follows the structure of the novel. Like Bradford himself, Josh grows up alternately in Mobile and Santa Fe. The story is set during the year that Josh's father, Frank, the owner of a shipbuilding company in Mobile, is compelled by patriotism to sign up for military duty in the navy. This year Frank's decision to have his family wait out the war in New Mexico will make it clearly different from Josh's sojourns in past summers. This time Josh will not be a temporary visitor but will reside in New Mexico and come to know the place first-hand. Early on it becomes apparent that this particular summer will be decisive for Josh and its consequences will be permanent. For one thing, it means that Josh's schooling will be in Santa Fe among the locals. His mother, Ann, dreads and abhors the family's move, a sentiment underscored in virtually every line she utters.

Corazón Sagrado: Safe Harbor/Quaint Refuge

In the film, as the Arnolds near their journey's end, Frank Arnold pulls off the road at a spot where it has become habitual for him to take in the breathtaking view of Corazón Sagrado, the fictional name Bradford gives to Santa Fe, a place set off in the story as both foreign and yet familiar. The scene opens with an unencumbered wide-angle vista of Santa Fe and the mountains beyond it (one that's hard to find today). The scene of Santa Fe is aligned to the following description in the novel:

> Ahead of us, stretching to the foot of the mountain range was a great pasture that sloped gently upward, a carpet for a million sheep whose clusters speckled the plain for—I measured it roughly, years later—a thousand square miles. As we topped the plateau, and my father stopped the car to let the engine cool off from the climb, a boy with a herd of sheep took off his broad-brimmed hat and waved it at us. My father said, "My God." (1999, 22)

The shot of the Sangre de Cristos inspires awe. The iconic visual trope of the West as a bold and mythic landscape allows the imagination to take in the scale and scope of this place. Indeed, *Red Sky at Morning*'s opening wide-angle vista could appear in any western that employs landscape to preface its story. While viewers might just as easily be gazing on Jackson Hole, Wyoming; Monument Valley, Arizona; Moab, Utah; or Flagstaff, Arizona, what distinguishes the scene in *Red Sky at Morning* from some point off in the distance is the appearance of the Mexican boy tending a flock of sheep. It is an image that deliberately announces that the viewer is at the border of a very particular locale. Bradford's choice of the animal herder as a living symbol of transgressing a cultural divide was by no means novel or original; rather, as Curtis Marez has shown, figures of pastoral Mexican laborers—farmers, goat herders, wood haulers replete with burros—were staples of the "image repertoire" created and propagated by New Mexico's famous art colonies since the 1930s. Marez notes, "Representations of Mexican labor from the famous tourist centers and artists colonies of New Mexico generally pathologized rebellious Mexicans and pastoralized docile ones" (2004, 108). In this sense, Bradford was simply following what had become the obsessive habit of relocated cultural interpreters to render the land and people of the region in decidedly paternalistic fashion.

These representations of docility were so pervasive that it is no surprise that the lowly pack animal, the Mexican burro, would become the most widely popularized and disseminated iconic representation of the Borderlands, with the image of the lowly goat or sheep herder not far behind. Bradford inherited these symbols and repackaged them into his novel. Quite predictably, both the burro and the herder make their appearance in Bradford's filmed saga. The burro, the more pervasive of the images, was in the opinion of Curtis Marez the ultimate tourist trope:

> During the 1920s and 1930s, artists and producers of mass culture in New Mexico were seemingly obsessed with burros. As we shall see, starting roughly in the last decade of the nineteenth century, burros became the favorite photographic subject, while in the twentieth century they became the staple of picture postcards. Postcards from the first third of the century often focus on burros bearing all sorts of burdens, but especially wood for sale. Singly and in bunches, with human drivers or by themselves, wood-laden burros were photographed, drawn and painted for hundreds, perhaps thousands of picture postcards. And despite the disdain of the art colonists for "standardized" mass culture, they embraced imagery that by 1900 was already a well-established staple of the tourist kitsch. (2004, 112–113)

And indeed, as we come to learn, the boy is always there, standing as an essential prop marking this encounter with ethnic difference. For Curtis Marez the associations with the pastoral are also racialized. He goes on to note the art colonists' "conservative programs for preserving a 'traditional' way of life that centrally include paternalistic forms of servitude that have been historically associated with images of the hacienda and the plantation. Indeed, the barefoot, straw-hat-wearing Mexican boy with his burro recalls the similarly attired plantation 'pickaninny'" (116).

In the novel, Joshua thinks back to his father's ritual stop and the unerring exchange between the sheep herder boy and the Arnolds: "The same boy or another like him would be standing among his sheep as they drove over the top. Dad would point and ask, 'Corazón Sagrado?' He knew it was the right road, but he would always ask, 'Sí claro,' the boy would say. 'Vayn-tay my-lace.' Twenty miles" (34). The film delivers the exchange in the following compact dialogue, ending in Ann Arnold's disparagement of the encounter:

ANN: Every year, almost on this very spot your father asks the same question.

FRANK: I like to. I like to hear the answer.

ANN: Same question, same sheep, same boy.

FRANK: The boy's always different.

ANN: How can you tell?

It is important to note that neither the text nor the film presents its story at the distance of the vista or the wide-angle shot, as the scene above implies. To be sure, several vistas punctuate the film at strategic moments, attesting to the fact that director James Goldstone was not above following the trend of using the natural wonders of New Mexico as a backdrop for his film. The oft-heard adage, "Just turn on the camera and point," is certainly at work here, but Bradford's story is as much about the social and cultural dimensions as it is about landscape and, importantly, about intra-ethnic relationships produced by New Mexico as a place. Thus, a second introduction to Corazón Sagrado happens at street level. In this scene the Arnolds circle the Santa Fe plaza in their sedan as the local sheriff directs the occasional car amid the traffic of burros carrying loads of wood through the town square. We are made privy to the exchange the Arnolds carry on in their car:

FRANK: Sagrado.

ANN: The war hasn't improved it.

FRANK: You want the benefits of war, I hear there is something going on over at Los Alamos. I hear they're making the front end of horses and sending them to Washington for final assembly.

Several markers of the local as foreign appear in this view of Corazón Sagrado; for one thing the commercial center "Main Street" in Sagrado is a plaza, that is, a uniquely Latin American spatial assignment of public space. Conspicuously, there are more wood haulers and burros in Sagrado than automobiles. Curtis Marez's work on the border burro as iconic representation reminds us that this scene of Santa Fe's plaza is anachronistic, since by the time World War II began the New Mexican wood seller and his burro had been replaced by the New Mexican wood seller and his pickup truck. It is the legacy of representation, as Marez notes, that made such images remain ubiquitous and ever-present: "If in 1930s New Mexico the wood vender and his burro were fast disappearing, in other words his image continued to promote the kinds of neocolonial service relationships that helped to make Santa Fe and Taos such attractive destinations for artists and tourists alike" (117).

In this scene, Procopio "Chamaco" Trujillo, the sheriff, appears on the scene and reverses assumptions about who the residents of Sagrado are. As consumers of the novel and film come to find out, all local authority rests with Chamaco Trujillo. Even while framed in long shot, the sheriff at the center of the plaza is obviously meant to be read as a mestizo figure. Bearded and donning a wide-brimmed sombrero, he evinces the look of a Mexican vaquero. In the novel Sagrado's ethnic difference is clearly marked in the Arnolds' first encounter with the town's chief law enforcement officer. Bradford highlights the meeting by emphasizing the sheriff's broken English. As the Arnolds are enjoying a picnic lunch on the plaza, Trujillo approaches them and begins to ask questions:

"Tourists?" he asked. "From out of estate?"

"Yes," Dad said.

"It's my juty to inform you that it's agains' the regulations to sit or stand on the grass in the plaza."

"Sorry," Dad said, "we didn't know." He began to gather up the food.

"No, no," the man continued. "Jew don' have to move. Enjoy the lonch. It's only my juty to tell you. There ain' no penalty for it. Hell, Mayor Chavez, he eats his lonch here every day. That your little boy?"

"That's right. His name is Joshua."

"Oh, Josué," the man said, pronouncing it Ho-sway. "Me, I'm Procopio Trujillo. They call me Chamaco. I'm the shariff." He took his hat off, and we shook hands. "Jew from around sea level?"

"Mobile, Alabama." (23)

Red Sky at Morning's exploration of ethnic group relationships in the local context requires the presentation of multiple personas and characters, and in this way the film affords mainstream America a rare opportunity to come in contact with some subtleties in Mexican American culture. In fact, *Red Sky at Morning* portrays difference, as can be heard in Chamaco Trujillo's inflected speech, but it is among the very first Hollywood feature films to break with rote stereotypical representation of Latinos as greasers, bandits, vamps, or spitfires. It does this by accurately drawing on local types and personalities and by avoiding the tendencies of earlier Hollywood films to front-load the dramatic charge of their stories with ethnic antagonisms. As direct as it sounds, Josh's struggle to find himself in his new place puts him in situations where he finds good and bad in each corner of tri-ethnic Corazón Sagrado. The film's fuller rendering of cultural, social, and racial difference keeps it from landing in the trap of equating people of color with social deviance and cultural pathology, as had been the case in earlier film periods, where the heroic role always fell to the white protagonist and debauchery fell to the cultural or racial other.[2] Thus, even though the film is meant to present Josh's struggle, it unwittingly opens up a new field of representation by providing contrasting characters who represent local Mexican American society.

Social problem films in the 1950s like *The Ring* (1953) and *Giant* (1956) had exposed the racial discrimination that had come from the suppression of the history of Mexican Americans, but these films did not place their protagonists in an uncomfortable storyline where whites find themselves occupying the role of upstarts and immigrants, where they are foreign to the local, and where they must adapt and follow the dictates of the local if only to get along.[3] If *Red Sky at Morning* does not completely unseat white privilege, it does go a fair way down the road to unsettling it. The point is made explicit when Josh's new friend, Steenie Moreno (Desi Arnaz Jr.), points out a new reality for Josh on the first day of classes at Sagrado High School: "See the minority group around here is you Anglos. The Indians are the good guys."

Giant: Casting Mexican Americans into the Narrative of Nation

If by virtue of rendering multiple Chicano characters, *Red Sky at Morning* is required to operate on something other than the binary of heroic whites and stereotypical Mexicans, we can rightly ask who or what takes up the role of the antagonist in the film. Before taking up this matter, let me recall *Giant*, a much earlier film and one that Chicano film critics agree began the process of dismantling southern apathies and attitudes about race by considering how these attitudes were first foisted onto Mexican Americans in Texas, and later onto mexicanos in other parts of the West. Cultural critic José Limón argues that amid the tepid indictments of race that Hollywood managed to offer up in the 1950s (except for the independently produced *Salt of the Earth*), *Giant* by comparison seems a radical alternative. Texas poet Tino Villanueva's collection *Scenes from the Movie Giant* (1993) shapes another critical understanding of the film and the society that it represents. New Mexico, as in all things it seems, would have to wait nearly a full two decades before its own particular and peculiar brand of Chicanismo would be served up in a nationally distributed film, albeit to audiences smaller than those garnered by the big-screen event that *Giant* became in 1956. For Limón, *Giant* is among the very first films to bring to national audiences a view of Mexican Americans in American life. Limón appreciates *Giant* for "how precisely sophisticated, as opposed to naïve, it [*Giant*] was in ensuring that the audience knew that Mexican Americans had a real active presence in American life but did not yet have a full and continuous appearance in the American narrative" (1998, 123).

Based on the Edna Ferber novel of the same name, *Giant* is the story of how Texas grew. The film's sheer length (three and a half hours) and epic scale made for just the kind of titanic moviegoing experience that Hollywood was delivering to eager audiences in the 1950s. Set in the period before World War II and in the first years of the postwar era, *Giant* tells of the success of Jordan "Bick" Benedict and how his family (read Texas) built its wealth in the grand tradition of Texas cattle ranching, which is to say on the back of mexicano land grants and with the jump start provided by mexicano-owned starter herds.

As the film opens, Jordan Benedict (Rock Hudson) is on a trip to Virginia to buy a horse, and while in the South he meets his future bride, southern belle Leslie Lynnton (Elizabeth Taylor). In José Limón's estimation, the marriage of Jordan to Leslie is not coincidental but rather an occasion for reaffirming the historical ties between Texas and the South (1998, 119). If so, it is surprising that despite this shared background it is Leslie, a southerner, who voices Texas's dirty little secret on the silver screen. A woman of unusual character and intellect, Leslie, who has been reading up on Texas history, blurts out over dinner, "We really stole Texas, didn't we, Mr. Benedict? I mean, away from Mexico." To which Jordan Benedict can only respond: "You catching me a bit early to start joking, Miss Leslie."

As the story proceeds we come to learn that Texas's future is deeply implicated in its past, for if *Giant* begins as the epic story of how Texas grew, it now becomes the story of how Texas must now "grow up" under the intensifying forces of modernity, a condition that José Limón argues requires it to throw off its southern agrarian past, a past, excepting Leslie Benedict's progressive views, that includes African American slaveholding and a war of aggression against a host Mexican province.

Bick Benedict's nemesis is Jett Rink (James Dean), a "poor relation" of the Benedicts who discovers oil on a small plot of land adjacent to Reata, the Benedict spread. With the discovery of oil on his land, Rink becomes as wealthy and influential in the postwar economy of Texas as the Benedicts have been in prior decades. A contemporary reading that would look for class solidarity in the figure of Jett Rink falters. Although Rink has lived under the thumb of Bick Benedict, having been reduced to the status of a sharecropper who must live alongside Reata's Mexican tenant farmers, contrary to what one might expect, once he acquires wealth and is free of Bick Benedict's grip he continues to express the most recalcitrant views on race and on the Mexican-origin population of Texas. Indeed, *Giant* vexes the expected comportment of most of its major characters. Just as we are frustrated by the figure of Jett Rink, so too expectations of Leslie Benedict, as I have already noted, are likewise crossed, a condition that bears contrasting to the comportment of another southern belle, Ann Arnold of *Red Sky at Morning*.

It is the South and its deep historical involvement in racial hierarchies and the separation of the races that provides the undercurrent of both *Red Sky at Morning* and *Giant*. *Giant's* representatives of old money and old power, the Benedicts, must be viewed as deeply complicit in the exploitation of mexicanos in the early history of Texas, for as Limón reminds us:

> The first "Anglos" to enter Texas in the 1820s were predominantly Southerners, and Southerners continued to come to Texas, and other

regions of the West, after the Civil War, as they sought land and better opportunities than the war-ravaged South could offer. Within this group, Southern entrepreneurs fomented and dominated the economic development of Texas and the West as a whole, especially in California, although the Southerners in general were more likely to settle in Texas and the Territory of New Mexico. This economic development, however, went hand in hand with the social and political subordination and racial estrangement of the small remaining Mexican populations in Texas and other parts of the West, in particular, the loss of landholdings as a result of racist economic pressures from the new arrivals (often financed by Northern and British capital) and the economic exploitation of Mexican-Americans and others as cheap labor in a rapidly modernizing political economy. (1998, 15)

Perhaps the most important message *Giant* telegraphed to U.S. audiences is that Texas, like the Benedicts, was being pulled along in the 1950s to a new day. As Limón points out, "Significantly it is the Anglo who must experience a move from hostility to ambivalence to at least grudging acceptance that a new social arrangement is underway" (1998, 121). More than any other feature of life in the Borderlands, *Giant* tests the South's taboos on race mixing and intermarriage when Bick and Leslie's son, Jordy Benedict, has the audacity to marry Juana Guerra, a Mexican woman and the daughter of a Mexican doctor who serves the local Mexican American community. In bringing forth the subject of interracial marriage, *Giant* was indeed ahead of its time, even as it fails to condemn segregation and Jim Crow in outright terms, something that was still an everyday occurrence in Texas of the 1950s. Bick Benedict experiences the greatest amount of growth in this regard, for not only must he accept the marriage of Jordy to Juana, he experiences how racism touches his own offspring, his grandson Jordy Jr., who is half Mexican and half Anglo.

Giant's signature moment, the diner scene, has become a kind of synecdoche for the film and a tableau upon which interracial taboos of the 1950s are exposed. The scene unfolds as the Benedicts (Bick, Leslie, Juana, and Juana's son Jordy Jr.) stop at a local diner on a return trip to Reata. As they enter they witness the rough treatment of an elderly Mexican couple whom Sarge, the owner, is about to eject from the restaurant.

Bick interjects, "I'd sure appreciate it if you were a little more polite to these people." Sarge grudgingly condescends to serve the Benedicts, but not without first taking note of Juana and her mixed-race son. "That there papoose down there, his name Benedict too?" he digs. The confrontation explodes into a full-scale brawl as "The Yellow Rose of Texas" plays on the jukebox and patrons in the small diner duck for cover. In the end, Sarge whips Bick Benedict, a circumstance made pregnant with significance when Sarge pulls down a sign that hangs on the wall and tosses it on Bick's limp body. Poet Tino Villanueva's brilliant interrogations of the scene offer testimony of his own "third eye experience" of the film:

> Sarge stands alone now, with all the atoms of his power
> Still wanting to beat the air, stands in glory like a
> Law that stands for other laws. It remains with me:
> that a victory is not over until you turn it into words;
> That a victor of his kind must legitimize his fists
> Always, so he rips from the wall a sign, like a writ
> Revealed tossed down to the stained chest of Rock Hudson.
> And what he said unto him, he said like a pulpit preacher
> Who knows the unfriendly parts of the Bible,
> After all, Sarge is not a Christian name. The camera
> Zooms in:
> WE RESERVE
> THE RIGHT
> TO REFUSE SERVICE
> TO ANYONE
> In the dream-work of the scene, as it is in memory, or
> In a pattern with a beginning and an end only to begin
> Again, timing is everything. Dissolve and the music ends. (1993, 38)

Several plot lines converge in the fight scene: Bick's defense of the elderly Mexicans symbolizes a defense of his own family. What begins as a paternalistic defense of a docile elderly couple by a white hero—the typical role of the white protagonist in social problem films—ends as a personal matter.

And it would be proper to ask: In what ways is *Giant* a harbinger of the future of Texas? It is a classic case of the personal becoming political, but the outcome, unfortunately, is that Sarge wins the day, an event that should be taken to mean that while the Benedicts are growing in their newfound racial awareness, the same cannot be said for Texas, nor sadly for the nation in 1956, for Sarge's victory, as Villanueva so intuitively reminds us, "stands in glory like a law that stands for other laws." In Texas, as in many other parts of the country in 1956, Sarge's writ torn from the wall is Jim Crow imbued with the force of law. Thus, the reality of Jim Crow as it functioned in 1956 is something the film cannot simply wish away and overturn, but only depict. Should we need to be reminded that such was the case, consider that Limón and Villanueva, now respected Chicano academics, were required by law to see *Giant* in segregated theaters as young men growing up in Texas. Sarge's writ would only lose its racial sting in Texas and in the nation with the legal undoing of Jim Crow that came with the enactment of the Civil Rights Act of 1964.

Still, *Giant* is, as Limón suggests, a radical departure from race depictions of Mexicans and Chicanos in the 1950s. If indeed there is no outright denouncement of racism and Jim Crow as an exclusionary system, on an entirely different front *Giant* bounds beyond all the limiting conventions of the period, most especially those governing the depiction of ethnic minorities and the representation of miscegenation in American cinema. It is as visual contestation to Jim Crow that *Giant* is most progressive. The film's close-up shots of Jordy Jr. and of Juana right after Sarge's disparaging "papoose question" dismantles the hypocrisy of Hollywood film codes that up to this time had assiduously stuck to the unwritten rule (not a writ, but a cultural code, a true hegemony) that the mestizo body, particularly in the form of a child of mixed ancestry, should not be depicted on the screen lest it offend the sensibilities of the still race-conscious, race-blinded, "white middle of America." In offering the American public the smiling face of Jordy Jr. at the diner and later in a final scene where the child shares a crib with an Anglo child, *Giant* did what no other film had done before: break the color line by toppling the taboo in American film that the offspring of an interracial union should not be represented. Again, it is Villanueva who intuits the significance of this part of *Giant* as he remembers sitting at the Holiday Theater in San Marcos one afternoon, where, in the poet's words, "What the screen released through darkness was too much for a single afternoon" (1993). Indeed, *Giant* does release great symbolism and promise in its final scene of a mestizo and white child sharing some approaching, although not fully articulated, future.

Like *Giant*, *Red Sky at Morning* confronts matters of race, the South, Jim Crow, and social arrangements with old and new racial patterns that must be determined between Anglos and mexicanos, or in this case, nuevomexicanos. As a point of contrast, consider the conflicting ideas held by the two southern women of the films, Leslie Benedict's sympathetic and embracing gestures toward the Mexicans versus the open contempt and disdain that Ann Arnold heaps on the Mexican help, the Montoyas of Río Conejo.

Apprenticeship on Race; or, Where Enchantment Trumps Jim Crow

In the novel, though not in the film, much is made of Josh Arnold's own peculiar "mixed heritage." It is not a small matter that Josh is the son of a Connecticut marine architect, come to live and work in Mobile, and of a genteel southern mother. His background is the source of a great deal of Josh's consternation about who he is and about how he should conduct himself in the world. The novel describes Ann Arnold as the kind of woman that "young men brought punch to and opened windows for" (12). Accustomed to southern gentility and customs regarding service and civility, Ann Arnold would grow into a woman who could feel at ease only in the South, or so husband Frank reports: "Well I suppose she gets jumpy when she's someplace else. She said once that almost anywhere in the South—Natchez, Baton Rouge, or Savannah, anywhere—she could find a Devereaux or a Dabney headstone in the cemetery and feel right at home" (18). Against this life, Sagrado represents nothing less than banishment for Ann, who must now put up with a pair of indomitable "servants" and a diet of fiery chile-based dishes that only serve to remind her of rustic surroundings. In the novel, Excilda Montoya, who cooks for her, quickly picks up on Ann Arnold's maladjustment:

> "I know what's the matter with her," Excilda said. "She doesn't like
> it here and she's drinking all that wine so she can forget she's in
> Sagrado instead of back in Alabama. She doesn't like this dry air,
> and she's not going to like the snow when it gets heavy. She's not

used to being without her husband. She doesn't like the food I cook, even though everybody says I'm one of the best cooks in the county. She doesn't even like this," she said, indicating the *posole*, which was great.

"And," she continued, "I don't think she likes Catholics." (69)

Ann Arnold's discontent carries over well in the film, helped along by Claire Bloom's effective portrayal of a wispy, sullen, displaced southern belle. On the day the Arnolds arrive at their home in Sagrado, and when Frank reminds her that it will soon be time to renegotiate the terms of employment with the Montoyas, Ann remarks, "Yes, I know the Montoyas, the most unsatisfactory *servants* I ever had" (my emphasis). Later it becomes evident that Ann's contempt for the Montoyas is more than personal antipathy; it is a view hardened by southern racial dictates on the treatment of the help back in Mobile. Frank, on the other hand, comes off as open and in touch with the New Mexican surroundings and as someone better inclined to accept the locals, a tendency that explains his decision to move the family out to New Mexico. In one earlier scene, he explains his motives to Josh:

FRANK: I suppose you're wondering why I settled her out here before I have to report.

JOSH: For her health, you said.

FRANK: That's a big part of it. I also wanted her away from all of that back there, the Dabneys and the Devereauxs and the cousins once and twice removed. I also wanted you away. All that back there, that's old. Of course this is old too, I know, but somehow it's different. [He turns to take in the full view of the landscape.] It's new every morning. You damn well better stay in school this year.

JOSH: You really want me to try for Harvard. Mother keeps talking about Alabama.

FRANK: Oh, hell, all you need to get in there is a couple of affidavits you're white.

However, the southern racial hegemony embodied in Ann Arnold is not the sole antagonistic force operating in *Red Sky at Morning*, though it is surely something that troubles young Josh. It is equally erroneous to conclude that a southern racial autocracy could hold sway in Hispano strongholds like Santa Fe with the coming of southerners. Jim Crow of the kind referenced in *Giant* could be found in southeastern New Mexico, a region even today identified as "little Texas" and an area where "Sarge's writ" had within my memory the same chilling and intimidating effect it had in Texas proper. But north-central New Mexico, that part of the state characterized by a historic Hispano/mexicano presence, had never allowed Jim Crow to take root, and when attempts were made to do so in the 1920s they were roundly and decisively rebuffed.[4]

Frank's comment above is instructive in this regard, for it reveals something about what operates as de facto social truth in this "new place." On the one hand, New Mexico is different from Mobile and the Texas of *Giant*; on the other, for Frank it is something less real, less tangible, something that can only be brought to mind by the camera's sweep of the land and his remark: "Of course this is old too, I know, but somehow it's different. It's new every morning." Despite Frank's rather starry-eyed view of New Mexico as "different and new," this will not turn out to be Josh's experience of Sagrado. Rather, he will have to make his way through the racial minefields laid in place by generations of Anglo-Hispano-Indian interaction, something that never quite squares with the quaint refuge motif, that is, the spot where Frank's imagination-machine of New Mexico gets stuck in gear.

Generally speaking, at issue in *Red Sky at Morning* is ignorance of the "other," a theme that settles like a counterweight at the center of the story. By the time *Red Sky at Morning* was made into a film, a substantial body of literature stood as testimony to an entire era of Anglo American examinations and assessments of the Hispano as other in New Mexico and the Borderlands, a project which came to be known as Southwestern regionalist literature and which took hold in New Mexico in the years between the world wars. It was not, however, a movement posited on the kind of objective inquiry that would acknowledge the shortcomings of outsiders' attempts to know the other. It was a presumptuous project, one that assumed to know all about Hispanos and about what was good for them and what their future was to be. That project, writes Charles Montgomery, would turn on very selective views of the "other," especially and whenever these views could be used to promote "the perfect antidote to American standardization," a place to find just the kind of solace that the Arnolds seek in Sagrado:

The most celebrated writing of the period represented a flight from critical politics writ large, from "present-day political, economic or sociological problems" and into a reassuring preindustrial past. The apolitical orientation is particularly striking in the literary depictions of rural Hispanos. In the nineteenth century assorted soldiers, missionaries, and travel writers described *los paisanos* as unsuited for citizenship in the American republic. After the Great War, treatments of *los paisanos* became more sympathetic but less anchored to expectations of industrial and social progress. With some notable exceptions, prominent literary works portrayed Hispano villagers as the bearers of folk wisdom, a people who knew enough to keep their distance from a cold and sterile world. Finding sustenance in warm agrarian traditions, they confronted their future by turning to their past. (2002, 191–192)

For several decades the exotic romanticism of Southwestern regionalism built on lore and local color stood as the master narrative for New Mexico. The discourse proved to be so totalizing that in Charles Montgomery's view it effectively masked "the suspicious marks of inequality and social trauma" that were apparent to anyone who was willing to see "Indians or Hispanos in relation to the Anglo-dominated economy" (203). Against this backdrop, the publication of *Red Sky at Morning* in 1968 appears if not as a radical departure from the earlier discourse, at least as a kind of heresy set against the masterworks of J. Frank Dobie, Harvey Fergusson, and Mary Austin. It begins through its open, albeit mild, admission that Josh Arnold (read Richard Bradford) is the outsider who has a thing or two to learn from the locals. Subtle though this may be, the novel's shift in perception makes it possible for the locals, in this case the Chicanos of Sagrado, to establish a viewpoint that had been noticeably overlooked by the earlier regionalist persuasion.

The film is coterminous with the increasing attention that Chicanos and Chicanas were receiving in Movement-inspired documentaries. These early works along with more frequent screenings of *Salt of the Earth* on college campuses throughout the 1970s would in time change the poetics of Latino film representations in documentary, ethnographic, and commercial films, but in 1972 these were still nascent endeavors and Hollywood still called the shots (many observers argue that this is still the case).[5]

In the 1970s, Hollywood repackaged its balding, decades-old, rancid Mexican film types as part of its repackaging of the cowboy film now done up as the Italian or spaghetti western for the tastes of contemporary audiences. Film scholar Gary Keller argues that not only did Hollywood reacquaint a younger generation of filmgoers with a host of already despicable *bandidos* and *cantineras* in these films, but also that it in fact intensified the villainy of these characters. Keller sees the Hispanic image in the 1980s as regressing as a result of the tendency to add graphic and gratuitous violence to the spaghetti western. Keller also maintains that the gritty, often sadistic realism of these new westerns was helped along by the relaxation and decline of the Hollywood Production Code, which accompanied worldwide efforts to break down censorship and conventionalism in film.[6] In Keller's words, "One of these trends, well represented by the Spaghetti Western, was the increasing prominence of nudity (both with respect to the number of films and the extremity of the phenomena), interracial sex, rape and other sexually related crimes and acts of violence, extreme acts of cruelty or sadism, offensive or 'dirty' language, and so on" (1994, 102). Unfortunately, in this decade ethnic minorities were too often cast in the role of the depraved other.

Red Sky at Morning by comparison appears almost wholesome in its depiction of Chicanos and Chicanas. While a spirit of denouncement does not drive the film, neither does it entirely peg Raza characters to a type. The film also brings forth a story where white privilege is not massaged by white largesse (the standard operating procedure in most social problem films) but rather by the agency of the mexicanos themselves, something that happens when the latter group assumes the role of guide who must tutor Anglos in the ways of local culture. An example of this agency carries over from the novel, as we have seen in Excilda Montoya's diagnostic profile of her moody employer Ann.

Almost from the beginning of the film we see nuevomexicano agency at work, as in a scene where Frank must enter into elaborate negotiations with Amadeo Montoya as a pre-condition that guarantees the Montoyas will continue to work for the Arnolds. As Amadeo, Frank, and Josh have lunch and several glasses of wine, much is made of renegotiating the terms of employment. After Amadeo's conditions are met (having less to do with salary than with establishing a climate of mutual respect between employee and employer), a ritual toast is made by which an old and powerful form of social hierarchy known as the *patrón* system is supposedly retired:

FRANK: Salud.

AMADEO: *Salud, patrón.*

FRANK: Don't call me patrón, those days are over.

AMADEO: You're damn right!

This pact of mutual respect will later be threatened when a distant cousin, Jimbob Buel, arrives in Sagrado for an extended visit. Immediately upon arriving, Jimbob, who shares Ann's propensity to want to correct all that he finds wrong with Sagrado and with the Mexican help, begins to ride the Montoyas:

JIMBOB BUEL: Amadeo. Don't you know anything about horticulture? You should put much more of that animal fertilizer on the fruit trees.

AMADEO (*AFTER A PAUSE*): *Señor, usted se parece a un caballo y huele como una puta.* (Laughter.)

JIMBOB: See, he agrees with me.

AMADEO: Josué, you better tell him what I said.

JIMBOB: It's not necessary, what he said was obvious.

JOSH: What he said is that you look like a horse and smell like a whore.

JIMBOB: Well, the man was smiling.

ANN: He didn't say anything like that.

JIMBOB: Well, even Amadeo wouldn't presume. He knows we'd have to dismiss him.

Amadeo's retort is an example of *el respingo* (literally, to rear up), or, as might be said in other cultures, to "sass back." Ann and Jimbob's very ignorance of what was said intensifies Amadeo's rebuff. The exchange is humorous, of course, but it is deeply instructive, since as irony it reveals who is truly acting with presumption. A scene or two later, Ann and Josh will haggle, with Ann suggesting that Amadeo's defiance is the cause of a collapse that lands Jimbob in the hospital:

ANN: You've been very rude to Jimbob since he came. He's in the hospital. I don't know what's happened to you. That's not the way you were brought up.

JOSH: How I was brought up? What about him? You know, I'm surprised Amadeo didn't put him in the hospital, the way Jimbob treats him.

ANN: Amadeo seems to be forgetting that he is a servant and not a member of the family. Stable society is a society in which everybody knows their place.

Later, when Josh manages to convince Amadeo and Excilda to come back to work, Amadeo makes it absolutely clear that he will not put up with any more of Jimbob's derision: "If I come back, what about that *piojo* [louse] Jimbob? I don't take no more orders from him. Some of the things he said to me . . . I should have killed him."

The thicker story of interethnic relations in Santa Fe happens at the level of Josh's interactions with his classmates at Sagrado High School, who are predominantly Mexican American. The first day of school, Josh meets Steenie Moreno, a senior who is half Mexican and half white. Steenie schools him on local identity politics, imparting knowledge that will help Josh to get along in the local community. Steenie's primer on interethnic protocol in Sagrado goes like this:

STEENIE: I'm Agustin Jesús Manuel Aquiles Moreno. Everyone calls me Steenie.

JOSH: Joshua Arnold. Josh.

STEENIE: Are you going out for athletics?

JOSH: Maybe so, if I can get used to this high country. It's all sky and no air. My nose bleeds every day.

STEENIE: Ah, it will stop when you're out of blood. Where you from?

JOSH: Mobile, Alabama.

STEENIE: See that kid over there? (*We see a black student running across the campus.*) You gonna lynch him?

JOSH (*AFFECTING A SOUTHERN ACCENT*): Well not unless he tries to marry my sister.

STEENIE (*CONCERNED*): Well, we don't want any racial trouble around here, so don't call him a Negro. He thinks he's an Anglo. I admit he's awfully dark to be white but that's the way it goes. See, around here you have to learn our little customs and folkways or it's your ass.

JOSH: Nice.

STEENIE: See, we only recognize four kinds of people in Sagrado: Anglos, Indians, and Natives. So you have any objection to your sister marrying an Anglo?

JOSH: Well to tell you the truth, I don't even have a sister. Anglos, Indians, and Natives—that's only three kinds.

STEENIE: Well, I'm the fourth kind. My father is a native and my mother's a Greek. So that makes me an itanglo or an anglota. You can take your choice. The best of both worlds, or the worst. Oh, so you've seen the girl over there with the knockers (a *Chicana leaning forward in a loose blouse*).

JOSH: She really stands out.

STEENIE: She's got memory trouble. Don't think of her as a Mexican. Her name is Viola López, refer to her as a Native, that is unless you're comparing her to an Indian, then she is white.

JOSH: What about the Negro, the colored . . . ?

STENIE: I told you he's an Anglo, unless you're comparing him to an Indian, then he's white.

JOSH: What does that make me?

STEENIE: The same thing.

JOSH: I better give this some thought.

STEENIE: Yeah. See the minority group around here is you Anglos. The Indians are the good guys.

It is important to recognize that Steenie's identity speech is not a Hollywood contrivance. As Charles Montgomery reminds us, ethnic identification in New Mexico moves on a historical axis. I quote Montgomery at length to lend space to this scholar's first-hand experience, including an exchange from his own school days in Santa Fe:

In the twentieth century, as Indians became a people largely of the farming village and the reservation, segregated for the most part from New Mexico's larger towns, businesses and political parties, Hispanos and Anglos shared control of the state's political economy. Brought together by the pursuit of wealth, they often worked in close proximity yet rarely stood in side-by-side accord. They remained divided by language, custom, religion, perceived physical differences, and decades of suspicion. To get along they established formal means of sharing power and, perhaps more important, unspoken rules of daily interaction.

One such rule involved the naming of Hispanos. Twenty-five years ago, when I was in a Santa Fe grade school, I already knew that Anglos always referred to their Spanish-speaking classmates and their families as *Spanish*. *Chicano* was a derisive term, very often a fighting word. *Mexican* was wholly taboo, a slur term no self-respecting Anglo, not even a child, would utter in public. Even in the heyday of the Chicano Movement, the belief that Spanish-speaking people were culturally Spanish, certainly not Mexican or Indian, was never in question. (2002, xii)

Josh does not have the time to sort through Steenie's advice before he is immediately confronted with a kind of pop quiz on interethnic and intercultural tensions in Sagrado. Moments after parting ways with Steenie, Josh runs into his first "Native" in the person of Chango López (Pepe Serna), a tough-talking pachuco classmate who tells Josh in no uncertain terms: "I'm goin to bash your ass," as he delivers a knee to his groin and struts away. A second encounter will come when Josh, Steenie, and Marcia—the female member of this buddy group who will eventually pair up with Josh—meet Chango and his sister Viola at the fork of two dusty Santa Fe dirt roads. Here is another opportunity for Chango to deliver a chorus to his earlier "warm" greeting: "Hello, you *pendejo*, bastard. If I didn't have my sister with me, I'd bash your ass." I take these belligerent outbursts as evidence of Montgomery's "decades of suspicion" motive. Josh is at a loss to understand Chango's deference to his sister when Marcia intervenes: "Chango, you give me a pain in the butt." He responds, "Don't talk dirty, not in front of my sizzter," even though he has just told Steenie, "Just stuff it up your *culo*. I got you too. I'm going to put on my boots and estomp the shet outta you."

Josh's next encounter with pachucos happens as he is ambling through the back streets of Santa Fe. As he turns a corner, he finds Chango sitting on a guardrail pointing across the way. Chango threatens: "I'm going to estomp on you a little beet, but first I want you to meet a friend of mine. This is Lindo Velarde. He likes to estomp on Anglos almost as much as me." Sensing that he is about to get his "ass bashed," Josh manages to push the pair over the guardrail, which starts a frantic foot chase through the back streets of Sagrado. This youthful goading, ill advised as it is, nonetheless reflects the interethnic competition that characterizes public life in Sagrado, and while it is the pachucos who instigate hostility and conflict, these acts do not end up reinforcing a stereotypical portrait of Chicano youth in the film, nor do they lionize the pachuco lifestyle as in the case of the *pachucada* that Luis Valdez celebrates in the 1981 film *Zoot Suit*. In *Red Sky at Morning* the stereotyping of pachucos cannot stand, since audiences come to learn that there are indeed different types of pachucos just as there are different kinds of mexicanos in Sagrado. Lindo Velarde, as the audience will come to see, is by far the more dangerous of the pair, chasing Josh down the back streets of Sagrado.

Another run-in with Chango and Lindo happens one Saturday night when Josh and Steenie decide to date the Cloyd twins, Velva Mae and Velery Ann. After a movie and a drive, the boys take the girls to lover's lane where they park to neck, only to have Chango and Lindo arrive. A confrontation, scuffle, and fight ensue. As things escalate, Chango pulls Lindo off Josh, allowing him just enough time to make it back into the safety of his car and drive away. The action is suspended when Lindo turns on Chango and threatens to stab him with a switchblade. From the cars to the music to the angle of the cameras, the whole of this scene is reminiscent of Luis Valdez's staging of the Sleepy Lagoon rumble in *Zoot Suit*.

The Monday following the brawl, Chamaco Trujillo shows up and pulls Josh out of class for a talk. Chamaco questions Josh about his run-in with Lindo, and it is from Chamaco that we learn what has happened since Saturday night:

CHAMACO: You know a boy name Lindo Velarde?

JOSH: Just enough to run from.

CHAMACO: Well, generally he goes around sticking a knife in people's tires. This time he stuck it in a friend of his, Maximiliano Lopez.

JOSH: Chango?

CHAMACO: No, no . . . he got him in the guts and in the liver. Oh, you know where Lindo is?

JOSH: I don't even know where he lives.

CHAMACO: We've been to his house. His father told us to take a flying . . .
jump at the moon. We know he is hiding out somewhere. You know
his mother says he is *loco*. Oh and to be *loco*. Me, I just hope I don't
have to shoot him. You're a good friend of Chango Lopez?

JOSH: I'm not exactly a friend of his, but I'm sorry he got a knife in him.

CHAMACO: Chango's tough, but he ain't as much trouble as a lot of boys.
You're sure you're not good friends. No . . . he keeps saying I want to
talk to Josué Arnold about this, and he won't tell me, just you.

After school Josh, Marcia, and Steenie pay a visit to Chango, who is recovering in a hospital. They enter the hospital room as Viola is saying goodbye to her brother. Chango remarks, "That Viola she's a saint. All the time growing she'd be bringing birds home and fixing their wings. I'd be out kicking dogs." Josh notices that Chango's hardened pachuco image and speech have dissolved. Chango even says "please" at one point. Chango warns Josh that Lindo has sworn to "finish the job" on him and that he should be careful. We soon find out that Viola is not the saint her brother considers her to be. That is, we learn that while she may have initially been moved by Christian charity to help Lindo, who is hiding out in an abandoned shack deep in a Sagrado neighborhood, she is vulnerable to his sexual advances, or so the scene where Lindo fondles her breast and leads her off to his hideout implies. Some days later a distraught Viola shows up at Sagrado High, the obvious victim of Lindo's battering. From Viola, Josh learns that Lindo (his clear antagonist) is up in the mountain village of La Cima, where the locals are protecting him. La Cima is revealed to be a remote and strange place that shuns outsiders, even if they are other Chicanos, and so the stage is set for a final confrontation with Lindo and a cadre of "real others" or, in this case, "extreme others," *la plebe*, the people of La Cima.

Cordoning Off Enchantment:
The Hispano Village as the "Real Other"

There is a curious bipolarity in *Red Sky at Morning*, one by which Corazón Sagrado (Santa Fe) is walled off from the rural villages that surround it. Sagrado appears as an urban enclave more hospitable to Anglos than the upland villages to the north. Indeed, there were no visible and sizable

numbers of Anglos living in rural northern New Mexico prior to the "hippie invasion" of the 1960s, largely owing to the fact that Hispano village
self-sufficiency, riddled with poverty, offered little inducement for folks
of any background to make a living. It was to the villages that bohemian
artists and writers of the 1930s and 1940s turned in their search for an
alternative to machine-driven industrialization and the life there that they
ended up exalting and idealizing.[7] But these folks were not as bold as their
hippie successors, who actually moved in with the villagers in the late
1960s. A handful of social scientists starting from the Depression era, however, had described the villages as poverty-ridden, places where idleness,
ignorance, superstition, and a deep suspicion of foreigners pervaded daily
interactions. *Red Sky at Morning* lapses back to representations of Hispano
villages that were well established in earlier works of Southwestern literary
regionalism to present the villages as exotic, remote, and pristine. In truth,
the remarkable beauty of the *río arriba* could and did often act as a cover
that made it difficult to assess the harsh economic conditions that faced
the impoverished residents of New Mexico's upland villages.

Truchas, New Mexico, a village some forty minutes north of Santa Fe and
the setting in the film for La Cima (the Crest), proves an interesting example
of *Red Sky*'s schizoid view of nuevomexicanos. In both the novel and the film,
La Cima calls forth the mystery and drama of the unknown and of a habitat unfamiliar to Anglos. Truchas's distinctive location, perched halfway
up the western flank of the Sangre de Cristo range and at the base of two
majestic mountain peaks, made it a place of remarkable natural beauty
where legions of tourists had stopped to take in breathtaking views, often
without the slightest regard for the people of Truchas, for how they lived,
or for what they thought. Charles Montgomery offers this sobering account
of Truchas, taken from a prewar economic survey of the region:

> A 1935 study of Truchas measured how much the stunningly beau-
> tiful mountain village, set high against the snowcapped peaks,
> belied its residents' daily struggle. Living in houses that averaged
> fewer than three rooms, the town's one thousand residents who
> still owned property (fifty-four families did not) farmed on plots of
> less than four acres. With only one reliable well in the village, most
> used the main irrigation ditch for drinking and washing. Sickened

by typhoid, which ran rampant across northern New Mexico during
the decade, residents were forced to travel more than thirty miles for
medical attention. Nor did their diets do them much good. Because
milk and beans were scarce, they lived mostly on white flour, which
left the children chronically underweight. (2002, 166)

Bradford's imaginary view of La Cima is, of course, wildly impressionistic. When Josh, Amadeo, and Victoria Montoya drive up to the town to
see what can only be called a surrealistic wedding ritual in the village,
Bradford writes:

> Ahead of us, across a steep gorge, was La Cima, perched like an
> eagle's nest on a bluff, the white peaks shining behind it. A thou-
> sand tiny fires made the village glow, and the wind from the moun-
> tains brought the sweet smell of pine and piñon smoke to us.
>   "It's beautiful," I said, and it was. Two hundred years seemed to
> disappear, and we were back in the days of the viceroys and the
> Apaches. Only the truck's motor and the roar of the heater kept us
> in the twentieth century. (1990, 176)

Josh's sojourn to La Cima to see the ritual of "el santo oso" is described
as a regression in time to a place even further marked by difference and
exoticism than anything he has experienced in Sagrado. Josh's guides,
Amadeo and Victoria, tell him "these La Cima people are funny," and as
evidence they point out that they speak an archaic form of Spanish. The
cimeños (my term) are so suspicious of outsiders that when a university
professor writing a book on their language came to the village, they burst
into his rented house and burned all his books and papers. And La Cima
people don't like the police meddling in their affairs, or so Victoria Montoya tells it: "The cops don't go up there unless they have to, and they
don't like to do it. If somebody gets killed, the people like to handle it
themselves. Sometimes the man that did the killing gets killed too and
sometimes he doesn't. They figure it's none of the cops' business" (175).
All of the mystery and foreboding of La Cima expressed in the Montoyas'
anecdotes is compressed into a few lines of dialogue in the film, which
come at the point where Josh and Marcia are talking about going up to the
mountain village. Excilda exclaims:

EXCILDA: Ay Dios Santo! Why do Anglos always go where they are not wanted?

AMADEO: She's right. People who go to La Cima, they have no brains. I'll take you.

The village scenes in *Red Sky at Morning* were all filmed on location in Truchas, New Mexico. They are remarkable for their rendering of the sheer natural beauty of the setting, of course, but also because the use of the village and the local inhabitants in them comes as close to an ethnographic encounter as *Red Sky at Morning* will ever be. In fact, *Red Sky at Morning's* footage of the winding road up to and through Truchas records nearly the exact views of the village that appear in *The Lash of the Penitentes*. The major omission in *Red Sky at Morning* is the Penitente *calvario*, a Truchas landmark that still stands at the southern entrance of the village, a marker made famous by countless Southwestern photographs and a Georgia O'Keeffe painting. Going to Truchas and not shooting its Penitente calvario strikes one as tantamount to filming an aerial survey of St. Louis and failing to include its famed Gateway Arch. The omission, I believe, confirms the success of the Penitente protest discussed earlier. In its stead, the camera lingers on a state highway road marker of La Cima (population 402) that has been sprayed with a graffiti tag that reads "Chinga a todos," which the filmmakers politely translate as "Screw all." The sign, like the Penitente cross in *The Lash of the Penitentes,* is a tribal marker meant to warn against unwanted incursions by outsiders.

Josh will find himself in La Cima at two moments in the film. His first visit piques by his curiosity about the strange ways of the people of La Cima and comes when Amadeo agrees to drive Josh and Marcia up to La Cima so that they can see a traditional *corrida de gallo*, a rooster pull, as it is staged in New Mexican villages for feast days and wedding celebrations. The ritual is one in which men make daring running passes on horseback at a rooster buried to its neck in the ground to determine who is the most skilled and able rider. The first horseman to grab the bird and hold on to it is declared the winner. The film's *corrida de gallo* is a response to the thwarted plan to film a Penitente ceremony at this point in the story. The *corrida's* color and excitement not only had dramatic effect, but added a touch of ethnographic truth that generally does not appear in Hollywood films. This latter point is important because Bradford's novel provides no such ethnographic accuracy. Curiously, Bradford crafted a completely fanciful and imagined ritual called "el oso santo" in the novel. Bradford's "oso santo" ritual is set at night and involves a weird ritual dance in which the villagers drag a chained black bear to the center of the village square and then bring out a visibly pregnant village girl wearing "a pair of canvas gloves" and "a crown made of wreathed evergreens" (180). As the ritual progresses the pregnant woman is made to straddle the bear and ride on its back. Bradford's ceremony is so fantastic and out of character for anything even remotely related to celebrations in the villages that the rooster pull inserted into the film ironically provides a more accurate ethnographic accounting of village celebrations. We can only conjecture as to why Bradford conceived of "el oso santo" to stand in for a village practice. Perhaps, like Josh, Bradford simply had no real knowledge of the deep culture of the villages. Perhaps he already anticipated the backlash that could come from identifying some quasi-religious activity in the villages that would offend the religious sensibilities of the Penitentes or the villagers more generally. His "oso santo" ceremony seems an attempt to secularize a ritual, to denurture it by avoiding any reference to an actual folk ritual.

The novel and film do coincide at the point where Josh, the outsider, determines that the female object of the ritual is in need of his protection. The pregnant girl of "el oso santo" and the "prize" to the winner of the rooster pull is, in both instances, Viola López. Josh has convinced himself that Viola is participating in the village ritual against her will, and when he attempts to pull Viola away from the crowd of village celebrants, he ends up getting beaten across the back with rawhide whips. The villagers' histrionics further underscore the idea that they are given to tribal savagery and blind anger.

La Cima's *corrida de gallo*, from the time Amadeo parks his rattletrap 1948 Dodge pick up at a viewing spot along a village street to the moment when Josh leaps out of Amadeo's truck to save Viola, runs all of some two and a half minutes; still, it is important as a moment in which the contours of a New Mexican village are glimpsed. Though the filmmakers may only have thought of Truchas as a backdrop, if one looks carefully one sees that here is an instance where the director, James Goldstone, did little more than point his cameras at this New Mexican arcadia. The truth of locale,

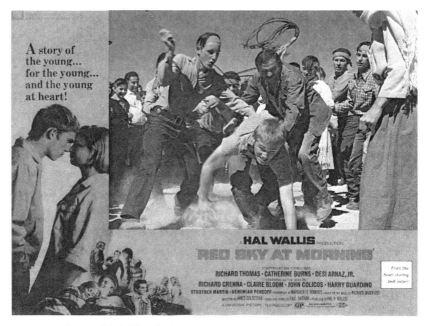

FIG. 11. Josh Arnold (Richard Thomas) removed from La Corrida de Gallo by La Cima townsfolk. *Red Sky at Morning* lobby card (author's collection).

sans undue cosmetic doctoring, brings forth some measure of ethnographic realism that is rare in American commercial cinema. In the scene, La Cima (Truchas) is bedecked as for a festival as scores of bona fide Truchas residents converge on the center of the village and line both sides of Truchas's dirt roads, where colorful paper streamers wave from village *portales* and rooftops. The camera pans across Truchas's famed snowcapped peaks as villagers and horsemen set themselves in place for the start of the *corrida*. Suddenly a pistol shot sends eight riders off on a mad dash for a rooster buried at the end of road. The camera flashes on the doomed bird and two young boys peer out from the line of villagers to get better looks at the riders as they bear down on the prize. The scene is filled with the brown faces of northern New Mexican extras; as folk historian Enrique Lamadrid notes regarding *Los Comanches*, a related equestrian tradition, the riders were not actors but men from neighboring villages who were engaged to stage a *corrida*, something that was a dying tradition by this time.[8] Here, *Red Sky at Morning* shares something with *The Lash of the Penitentes*, which also put northern New Mexican villagers in the gaze of the camera. La Cima's villagers, it appears, were asked to show up at the filming in their daily attire, the attire of rural farm people everywhere, a minor detail but one that spares them from undue distortion. Truchas, too, is for the most part presented in its everyday appearance, chinks and all. Its main street, unpaved and hilly, serves as the racecourse for the *corrida*, and the impartial gaze of the camera takes in Truchas's tin-roofed adobes in various stages of repair. All this rings true to those of us who know the region, and if there is a virtue to this it is that finally the people appear, real and intact, if only for the two and a half minutes that Hollywood required as touchstone of cultural authenticity upon which to set the film.

Josh's second visit to La Cima comes when he is prodded by Chango Lopez to give him a ride to the village to avenge Lindo Velarde's beating of his sister Viola. Chango and Josh arrive just moments ahead of the sheriff, who, informed of Lindo's whereabouts, is on his way to arrest him. The action moves swiftly as Chango runs door to door and from one person to the next, asking, "Dónde está Lindo Velarde? Buscamos a Lindo Velarde." A few frames later, Lindo appears around the corner of an adobe house and strides to the middle of the road in gunslinger fashion and says, "Orale, Chango. I was expecting your sister. She likes me." An enraged Chango charges Lindo, but a villager who has been chopping wood, apparently uninterested in what is taking place, suddenly decks Chango with a blow to the back that lays him out in the street. When Josh tries to go to him, two other village men hold him back as Chamaco Trujillo pulls up in a car, walks up to the men holding Josh, and tells them in Spanish to let him go. Chamaco faces Lindo Velarde and says, "OK, Lindo, it's time to go into town," but as he does, he makes the mistake of turning his back, believing Lindo would not dare attack him. Instead, Lindo flicks open a switchblade and charges the sheriff from behind. Josh, kneeling beside his fallen buddy, alerts Chamaco and, rising up, knocks Lindo momentarily off balance. Lindo manages to swipe Chamaco across the forehead, causing a superficial wound that bleeds profusely. As Lindo reels back, Josh trips him again and he stumbles, giving Chamaco enough time to matter-of-factly pad his forehead with a handkerchief, draw out his revolver, and shoot Lindo in the leg.

This final confrontation ends Josh's entrance into the realm of the other, or what *Red Sky at Morning* has staged as his foray into the realm of the "extreme other." It is important to ask at this point: Just exactly where is the "extreme other," the one that La Cima is supposed to represent? Tourist literature and narratives of Penitente hunting from the 1930s and 1940s had built expectations about that other, suggesting that "in towns like Tomé, Chimayó and Placitas, where the effects of time and Yankee civilization have scarcely been felt, the life of these people goes on much as it did a century ago" (qtd. in Montgomery 2002, 162). *Red Sky at Morning*, on the other hand, is not really about locating the charms of time arrested or about traditions preserved. Lindo Velarde is not a representative of Old World charms; he is closer to what social workers in the 1940s would call a social delinquent, maladjusted to modern society. If *Red Sky at Morning* falls short in its rendering of the "real other," it is because it proposes to explain Lindo, the "criminal pachuco," as the product of his environment, that is, the village of La Cima. By having the people of La Cima harbor a fugitive of the law, by having them abet and assist him in his lawlessness, the film equates Lindo with the outlandish, clannish, and unlawful ways of La Cima. In point of fact, while a great many Mexican American youth in New Mexico were taken with the style of the tough-talking pachucos, from the perspective of the villagers, pachucos were the city cousins of the rural poor. To them it was abundantly clear that the symptoms of cultural maladjustment and disaffection could be observed in the outlandish behavior of pachucos and pachucas. Rather than harbor their antics, the villagers who were for the most part engaged in ranching or agricultural pursuits had neither the time nor patience for them. Villagers would have been more apt to reprimand wayward *plebe*, referring them in the worst cases to the local Hermano Mayor, for they saw la pachucada as tantrum of youth. Such rebellion they believed would wear away with age and wisdom as these young people took up the plow as earlier generations of village men had done. But by presenting Chango, Viola, and the Montoyas as somehow different than the people of La Cima, *Red Sky at Morning* subscribes to the notion that malevolent intent hides in precisely those places where Anglo influence is not present. Since it is logical to expect that Chango, Viola, and the Montoyas would be organically connected to the village and to village patterns, *Red Sky* creates an artificial boundary in its depiction of New Mexico's ethnic communities that splits them into unnatural camps. Despite its best efforts to understand the other, the film reconstructs a binary that suggests that some nuevomexicanos are foreign while other nuevomexicanos are "really foreign," a depiction that renders the latter category as distinct, distant, and just as inscrutable as New Mexicans had been in any of the worst film representations of earlier decades.

In the end, *Red Sky at Morning* reinforces the divide between Anglos and nuevomexicanos by making cultural and class affiliations the measure of Anglo acceptance and favor, for even though Josh and Frank Arnold's Mexican American acquaintances are not of the rico class like those who had befriended Yankee newcomers to New Mexico in the nineteenth century, they are by virtue of living in Corazón Sagrado, rightly or not, viewed as "the friendlies," whereas all other Chicanos, especially those still deeply attached to the villages and the ways of the past, remain "the hostiles." Keeping true in some ways to the New Mexico case where, as I have suggested, "enchantment trumps Jim Crow," *Red Sky at Morning* divides New Mexico's ethnic communities along the lines of cultural difference, a point that carries over in some ways into the production values of the film. While it is true that the New Mexico Film Commission played a hand in curtailing the filmmakers' attempt to heighten sensationalism by using the Penitentes, it nonetheless keeps the reality of interethnic struggle at a distance. It does this by continually centering and recentering the two white teenagers, Josh and Marcia, and making them the axis of story. This is troubling since in the novel Bradford makes a great deal more of the budding friendship between Victoria Montoya and Josh. They are schoolmates who share similar schooling experiences, the inference being that they might some day pair up as a couple. Production Code or no, the film version of *Red Sky at Morning* simply excises Victoria from its storyline and thus dismisses the one opportunity in Bradford's story that could rethink Hollywood conventions about gender and the white hero. Unlike *Giant*, which challenged the racialized convention concerning interracialism, *Red Sky at Morning* falls back on the Hollywood writ that prescribed that Anglos be the central protagonists. A competing love interest from a brown villager, it seems, was simply too complicating a tension to introduce here.

Older Truchas residents are still likely to remember the day the film crews came to their town, the day they were paid a few dollars to act as they would have at one of their own village festivals, the day Truchas and La Jicarita Peaks basked in real and celluloid sunshine, the day they could see themselves in their own habitat, and the day in which they "estomped on Josh Arnold a little beet" for being, just as the script called for, a perfect pain in the ass, an *entremetido*, a busybody. If Richard Bradford was insisting on providing his readers with an examination of the theme of learning from new surroundings, he too must have found that Hollywood dictums compromised his viewpoint. In the final frames of the film, Josh voices a romantic and nostalgic elegy for his youthful years in Corazón Sagrado:

MARCIA: Sagrado has gotta change too, wait and see.

JOSH: I hope it stays what it is.

STEENIE: What is it?

JOSH: A place to hide, from each other, from cities, from people hating each other, killing each other.

Josh's dialogue finds its way to the film through the work of the Southwestern regionalists who, Suzanne Forrest reminds us, had come to New Mexico seeking their own solace from the affairs of the world: "Others, a small and diverse group, thought they had found an Eden, unexpectedly, in the remote and starkly beautiful state of New Mexico with its two large agrarian populations—Hispanic and Indian—just emerging into the industrialized world of the twentieth century" (1989, 45). Late in the twentieth century, Hollywood and U.S. society generally would still refuse to look beyond the stark beauty of landscape. Things might have continued on this way were it not for the social organizing known as the Chicano movement, whose demands for better filmic representations finally required filmmakers in New Mexico to do more than just turn on their cameras and point.

Things offscreen had also changed by the 1970s. As this case shows, by this time the protests of the Penitente brotherhood would have a measure of influence in determining the project outcome. On July 18, 1970, Hermano Supremo M. Santos Meléndez wrote to Governor Cargo expressing objections to the staging of Penitente ritual activity in the film, as had been reported in local news coverage. Cargo responded a few days later, "I am presently reviewing 'Red Sky at Morning,' and I would like to discuss this matter with you personally. I certainly don't want any filming done that would put the Penitentes in a bad light" (Melendez personal papers). Following a meeting with leaders of the Brotherhood in Santa Fe, Governor

Cargo sent an unsigned note to the production company urging them to change their plans:

Dear Bill,

In regard to the letter from Mr. Santos Meléndez, I would appreciate very much your consideration of a substantial change in the script involving the Penitentes. The section of the script is definitely not authentic material, and in my opinion would cause undue embarrassment to this group of people. In the past the Penitentes have suffered a great deal through misconceptions of their various rituals.

I have remained very close with the Penitentes, and believe that to use the segment of the script involved as it is written would bring undue hurt and humiliation to the people involved.

This is the first time I have become involved in any script planned for New Mexico, but in this particular case I feel compelled to ask your cooperation. I look forward to working with you over the next several weeks, and certainly remain at ready to assist you in any way possible.

Sincerely,
David F. Cargo
Governor

In the end, *Red Sky at Morning* was completed on location in Santa Fe. A *corrida de gallo* (rooster pull) replaced of the staging of Penitente ritual. The compromise signaled that for the moment sacred drama and ritual was off-limits to filmmakers, detouring for a time the patterned way of inscribing remoteness and difference in New Mexico village landscape and humanscape.

6

The King Tiger Awakens the Sleeping Giant of the Southwest

Geographically, South America is as big as China and the United States put together. That's why they call it the sleeping giant. Even though it is great, it is made up of a new breed of people from the mixing of Indian and Spanish blood according to Law 2, Title 1, Book 6 of the Laws of the Indies which have been frozen and hidden.
—Reies López Tijerina, 1969

Land loss has historically been the latent grievance of the nuevomexicano. Therefore it comes as no surprise that the Chicano movement of the 1960s, a broad-based social movement aimed at redressing the exclusion of Mexican Americans from educational and employment benefits—and a myriad other social concerns—would become closely identified with Reies López Tijerina's struggle to regain lands that had once belonged to New Mexican Spanish-speaking communities.

Tijerina's land grant movement and the issues it raised would in time spawn the most radical reconsideration of the Chicano experience in the Borderlands since the U.S. takeover in 1848. Its impact would be felt in a number of social and educational quarters and its effects would extend far beyond the dramatic period of direct action and confrontation (1965–1967) that put Tijerina and his movement in the national spotlight.

Well before Tijerina came to prominence, and before the American public ever saw Tijerina's face on television or in movie newsreels, the voice, if not the face of the "King Tiger," as the *Saturday Evening Post* dubbed him, was familiar to most nuevomexicanos. In the years prior to his famous Tierra Amarilla courthouse raid in June 1967, Tijerina, the fiery and outspoken leader of the Alianza Federal de Mercedes (the Federal Alliance of Land Grants), had managed to organize nuevomexicano land grant heirs and other allies without ever coming to the attention of the Anglo-dominated political and governmental institutions in New Mexico. It was only when Tijerina's movement threatened to upset the social and political status quo that governed interethnic relations in much of the Southwest that public concern came to focus on him. After Tijerina, the safe and commonplace notions of multiculturalism and regional interethnic harmony in the Borderlands were shattered as the hidden transcript of a history of conflict in the region emerged with new force.

Knowledge of the land grants as a public policy question accelerated dramatically when Tijerina took to the airways on April 1, 1965, and began to broadcast "La Voz de la Justicia" (The voice of justice), a program that aired daily on KABQ, Albuquerque's premier Spanish-language radio station at the time. In his autobiography, Tijerina describes the importance of this program to his movement: "It was a station of 5,000 watts. Every morning at 10 AM I would speak to our community. This was the best media to reach the community about the issue of land. Soon word began to spread about the radio program. Hundreds upon hundreds of heirs who had not heard of the Alianza began calling and writing to join the Alianza. This daily radio program resulted in the greatest weapon that I had ever used. Our community had never before felt that power in New Mexico" (2000, 57–58).

Tijerina typically began his daily broadcasts with a scathing indictment of Anglo-dominated public institutions in the state of New Mexico. He would then proceed to enumerate Chicano land claims, using the Treaty of Guadalupe-Hidalgo and other historical documentation as the basis of his invectives. In this sense, Tijerina was prophetic.[1] An important feature of Tijerina's broadcasts was the open-line portion of the program where listeners could call in and voice their viewpoint on the issues the program raised. While some listeners attacked Tijerina, labeling him a charlatan or slandering him as a communist or accusing him of duping his followers for his own gain and advancement, others understood that just indignation fueled his angry diatribes.

Despite detractors, Tijerina's movement had strong appeal among vast numbers of everyday New Mexicans. In the beginning, Alianza membership consisted mainly of the older residents from rural communities in northern New Mexico, those that knew the history of the land grab or had been told the story by elders who had lived that history, people who were sometimes referred to by the moniker "manitos." It was only after the Tierra Amarilla courthouse incident that young people joined the cause in visible numbers. Just before the Tierra Amarilla courthouse raid, judicial authorities in New Mexico were pressing the Alianza to turn over records of its membership, lists that reportedly had the names of some 30,000 members (Tijerina 2000, 75).

While Tijerina made strident calls for the redress of land claims, he was ultimately concerned with the protection of the culture and language of Mexican Americans, a people he often referred to as "Indo-Hispanos," employing this hybrid term to more accurately identify the dual heritage of mestizos and mestizas as inheritors of indigenous and Spanish traits. Tijerina often evoked language that put the land question on a par with respecting Chicano culture: "If we can save the land, we can save the culture. If we can save the culture, then we can save our families" (71).

Tijerina's call for the vindication of Chicano culture resonated in many quarters. Even after the period of the direct action that included the takeover of the Echo Amphitheater in Coyote, New Mexico, in June 1966, the raid on the Tierra Amarilla courthouse in 1967, and the burning of National Forest signs in Coyote in 1968, the symbolism of these actions continued to inspire community activists, educators, writers, and filmmakers.

The raid by members of the Alianza Federal de Mercedes on the courthouse in Tierra Amarilla, New Mexico, on June 5, 1967, was an electric moment in the Chicano movement. Mexican Americans across the nation followed the story as it developed with keen interest. It forever changed the way Chicanos would permit themselves to be viewed in the American imagination and, along with other forms of community mobilization, added to the general questioning of the images of Mexicans that circulated in the American media.

The incident at Tierra Amarilla was a case of a plan gone bad. Tijerina and the leadership of the Alianza had hoped to use their constitutional right to make a citizens' arrest of Alfonso Sánchez, the district attorney for the northern half of the state and the person *alianzistas* believed was waging a vindictive, personal campaign aimed at suppressing the land grant movement. When Sánchez ordered the seizure of the Alianza membership records and had the New Mexico state police orchestrate a campaign of intimidation in the Alianza's stronghold communities in the summer of 1967, the stage was set for a confrontation.

In the days before the annual convention of the Alianza, scheduled for June 5, 1967, the state police began to stop cars coming in and out of Coyote, New Mexico, the site of the Alianza convention. The police dragnets led to the arrest of eleven high-ranking members of the Alianza. On June 5, Alianza members gathered in Canjilón to discuss the events of the recent days. They were aware that members of their movement, including Reies's brother Cristobal, were to be arraigned that very afternoon in Tierra Amarilla, the county seat of Rio Arriba County. Believing that Alfonso Sánchez would be present at the arraignment, Reies put the idea of making a citizens' arrest of the district attorney before the membership. Tijerina's followers agreed to take that action, and at around 2 P.M. a group of Alianza members, including Tijerina's daughter Rosa, piled into three cars and swooped down on the courthouse from the nearby mountain village of Canjilón some fifteen miles away (Tijerina 2000, 80). With Reies in the lead, the group rushed the courthouse and proceeded to smoke out Alfonso Sánchez and to arrest him as an enemy of the people of Río Arriba County. But Sánchez had not come to Tierra Amarilla that day, and the intrusion produced chaos that ended in a burst of gunfire inside the courthouse. As the event unfolded, a jailer, Eulogio Salazar, a deputy sheriff, Daniel Rivera, and a state policeman, Nick Saiz, where wounded by the gunfire.

The aftermath of the Tierra Amarilla courthouse raid, by all accounts, produced high drama of the kind most often found in action films. The news of the raid broke almost as it happened due to the work of Larry Calloway, an on-the-ground UPI reporter who happened to be in the courthouse as Tijerina and his raiders entered the building. Sensing trouble, Calloway took refuge in a phone booth and while holding on to the phone began to narrate what was happening to his office back in Albuquerque. Within hours, radio and television stations were interrupting programming with special news bulletins on the situation in northern New Mexico. That same afternoon, after listening to those same reports, Tijerina and several of his closest *valientes* decided to flee into the nearby mountains, having become fugitives from the law. With Governor David Cargo out of state on business, Lt. Governor F. Lee Francis, a native of Laguna Pueblo, mobilized the New Mexico National Guard, and by nightfall the law enforcement establishment in New Mexico was engaged in the largest manhunt in the history of the state. The next several days were tense and chaotic across the whole region.

With the National Guard's arrival, state police, New Mexico mounted police, and other law enforcement agencies surrounded the village of Canjilón, New Mexico. Almost immediately, what had been Tijerina's base of operations took on the appearance of a military outpost in Viet Nam. In his autobiography, Tijerina recalls a surreal moment when he and his loyalists could see the dark green tanks and armored vehicles moving about the countryside from the mesas high above the San Joaquin Land Grant. Tijerina recalls that a sense of doom and finality came upon him and his men as they briefly contemplated leaving the country and making their way to Mexico or Cuba (2000, 85).

At Canjilón and in the surrounding mountain villages, the state police conducted house-to-house searches in pursuit of Tijerina and others known to have been at Tierra Amarilla. The police rounded up men, women, and children. Alianza members were herded into corrals at the ranch of Tobías Leyba. Some individuals were detained in open-air pens for at least twenty-four hours. Tijerina later maintained that his wife, Patsy, then only twenty-one years old, suffered great physical and emotional abuse at the hands of federal marshals while in captivity at Canjilón, and as a result she had a miscarriage.

With Tijerina hiding out in the remote and least accessible sections of the National Forest—areas that were part of the communal lands of the grants claimed by his valientes—and moving about a topography the valientes knew like the back of their hands, the media cast the entire matter in the guise of a revolutionary movement inside the United States. Indeed, a day or two into the manhunt, Tijerina appeared to be setting the agenda, as alianzistas made it known that certain individuals would be selected to visit the "King Tiger" at a mountain hideaway where he was holding audience. Those selected to see Reies were blindfolded and transported by various modes of transportation deep into the mountains. Among them were Peter Nabokov, a writer who published an overnight book on Tijerina, and Clark Knowlton, a university professor who had championed Hispano civil and cultural rights and who at the time was the most informed land grant historian in the country. With frustration building from the inability of the National Guard and state agents to find and capture Tijerina, the parallels to General "Black Jack" Pershing's punitive expedition against Pancho Villa in 1916 became apparent, even to the detail that the man at the head of this operation was Pershing's namesake, General John Pershing Jolly. Five days after the raid on Tierra Amarilla, Tijerina made the decision to leave the mountains and travel to Albuquerque to turn himself in to the authorities there. En route, a gas station attendant at a roadside filling station spotted Tijerina as he emerged from a car to take a drink of water from a hose. The attendant alerted the state police, who apprehended Tijerina a few miles down the road.

"Reies": Citizen Number One of La Nueva Raza

As things were unfolding in New Mexico, noted Chicano filmmaker Moctesuma Esparza, a student at UCLA in 1967, was among the first Chicano organizers to recognize the importance of the Tierra Amarilla incident. In *Chicano,* Esparza recalls, "It was like Emiliano Zapata and Pancho Villa were alive again. And they had gone and claimed their land again. It was like wildfire in the movement when we first heard about it. We heard it like that [*snaps his fingers*]" (1996). Esparza was personally drawn to the land grant movement and attended the national convention of the Alianza in 1968. These were heady times for the young activist, who in a recent interview recalls the large stake Mexican Americans had in this growing social cause:

> I went to the Alianza's Second Annual Conference in Albuquerque, so, I was there. It was big. . . . I remember, kind of an auditorium-barn, huge, gymnasium . . . and there was a whole group of us who came from LA along with members of US which was Ron Karenga's Black nationalist group. We rented a bus and some brown berets and myself, members of UMAS, it wasn't MeCHA then it was still UMAS and . . . we departed from an Episcopalian Church of the Epiphany, Father John Luce, which was kind of our headquarters . . . and we took this bus to Albuquerque. We had heard about it, of course, because it was national news and that along with Cesar Chávez's

fast and the organizing that had been going on in Los Angeles with students, all pushed us in the direction of the awareness of not just a local movement but a national movement for Chicanos, for rights . . . and the Treaty of Guadalupe Hidalgo was a constant reference point to the trampling of our rights, so the fact that Reies was trumpeting those violations of the treaty and the basis of the movement of the Alianza was of land grants resonated a great deal with us, because it provided us with the platform of not being viewed as aliens in our own land. (Esparza interview)

Moctesuma Esparza belongs to the first wave of Chicano filmmakers, a group Chon Noriega has labeled the "Political Generation." Noriega writes that the group included a number of students who joined the Chicano movement as activists and who came to see their role as documenting the ongoing social protest and emergence of the Chicano movement (2000, 101). Citing the importance of the first two film programs in the nation to enroll minority filmmakers, Noriega notes that Esparza, a member of the L.A. Thirteen, a group of Chicano activists who led the L.A. student boycotts in the Los Angeles School District in 1968, became a part of the newly formed Ethno-Communications Program at UCLA. Noriega notes:

But although Chicanos such as [Susan] Racho, [Sylvia] Morales, [?] García and [Moctesuma] Esparza had entered UCLA between 1966 and 1968, it was not until the creation of the Ethno-Communications Program, in 1969, that the film school enrolled "the first group of Third World film students." Eliseo Taylor, a Black professor in film production who brought in Esparza as a "hired gun" to recruit students, design the curriculum, and raise funds, initiated the program. Although he was a history major, not a film student, Esparza drew upon his considerable skills as an organizer within the Chicano student movement. Esparza and twelve other minority students, including Martinez and Garza, formed a multiracial group called the Media Urban Crisis Committee, with "Mother Muccers" as its acronym. The group staged sit-ins and other protests that resulted in the establishment of a pilot program for ethno communications, with Mother Muccers as its first class. (104)

Esparza's first film project was linked to the land grant struggle in New Mexico. In the spring of 1969 he invited Reies Tijerina to speak to a group of students and members of the Chicano community at the Ackerman Ballroom on the UCLA campus. Initially, Esparza was responsible for inviting and coordinating the talk, but perhaps because he was now ensconced in the Ethno-Communications Program, he had the presence of mind to have Tijerina's speech filmed. The filming itself was straightforward and static but nonetheless produced a film document of enormous cultural and historical significance.

The Tijerina piece is also among the earliest examples of first-wave Chicano filmmakers like Esparza working in the mold of what Chicana film critic Rosa Linda Fregoso calls a "documentary impulse," that is, the desire to locate and film the roots of the Chicano experience in the Borderlands. As such, Esparza's is the only unspoiled footage of Tijerina delivering one of his hallmark oral performances. The Tijerina speech also provides a counterweight to an NBC special report that aired on May 6, 1969, with the prejudicial title *Reies Tijerina: The Most Hated Man in New Mexico*. Despite the fact that the NBC report presents a rare view of the deep poverty in which nuevomexicanos lived, *The Most Hated Man* drew a very negative portrait of the land grant leader and his followers.

Esparza's film, titled simply *Tijerina*, was part of the young filmmaker's plan to focus on the emerging leadership of the Chicano movement. In an interview Esparza recalls the urgency that compelled him to start this work:

> Well, we were struggling to find images, heroes and so the only frame of reference that we had, since many of us had grown up hearing about the Mexican Revolution, was Zapata, Villa, and so, here we had someone who took it upon himself to confront the people who were oppressing this movement and took direct action, so yes, that was very positive, yes. I had invited Reies to come to UCLA to give a speech and there was a movie that was made that I helped produce. (Esparza interview)

Esparza's film, an unadorned and straightforward piece of film journalism, begins with an intertitle ahead of the Tijerina speech that announces:

Reies López Tijerina, one of the militant leaders of the Mexican American struggles for justice and equality. His organization *La Alianza Federal de Pueblos Libres* is charging the U.S. government with the violation of the Treaty of Guadalupe-Hidalgo. Through this treaty, which ended the Mexican War of 1846–1848, the United States acquired territory now comprising California, Arizona, Nevada, Utah, and New Mexico. Tijerina claims that although the treaty recognized many existing land grants, both private and communal, many people were subsequently deprived of these lands. (*Tijerina*, 1969)

As the intertitle rolls away, a voice off-camera introduces Tijerina as "citizen number one of *la nueva Raza*." Tijerina strides to the stage flanked by a Brown Beret bodyguard. Taking the podium, Reies clears his throat, takes out a handkerchief from his pocket, wipes his mouth, and thanks the audience for the opportunity to speak about "things that have been hidden for the last one hundred and twenty years." Tijerina becomes animated as he lists the grievances of his people against what he labels an "organized Anglo conspiracy." For the next thirty minutes Tijerina lays bare his case, sharing his particular view of the problems affecting Mexican Americans with a sympathetic audience of students and community members.

The talk is a rather complete repertoire of the metaphors and anecdotes that had become signposts of Tijerina's charismatic and fiery oratory. As was his habit, Tijerina made it a point to remind his listeners that he considered loss of language and culture to be the most oppressive force acting against Chicanos. He does this by telling the parable-like story of the man who clipped the wings of a caged bird:

Ladies and gentlemen, the problems of the Mexican Americans are many. . . . I can't enumerate them all. I cannot mention them all. Before I go any further, I'm speaking in a language that I use 2 percent of my time. I use Spanish 98 percent of my time. I noticed that the Anglo told me you are now free. You are a free man in the land of the free; don't you feel better than under the Spanish Empire, under the Mexican Empire, and the Republic of Mexico? You are free . . . but don't speak Spanish.

I like to compare that freedom to the freedom that a man gave to a bird that he had in a cage. He took this little bird and he said, "I'm going to set you free, free, no longer behind the bars" and he took a pair of scissors and he cut the two wings—"Now go, go." Well, naturally, the bird couldn't fly and the blue-eyed cat came and ate the bird.

So . . . that's my freedom, ladies and gentlemen. For me, to me, the language, which is the accumulated result of the exercised experience of centuries, the language makes up the two wings of the bird. With our language we defend ourselves, the language is the primary element of our identity and there are many crimes, but the greatest crime of all is to rape a culture of its language . . . to tell a culture not to speak its own language. (*Tijerina*, 1969)

The offscreen drama stemming from the rise of Tijerina's land grant movement far outstripped the ability of any film to capture and disseminate it to those who had not lived the moments of its greatest intensity. Esparza's *Tijerina*, like other Chicano film projects of the time, had the virtue of allowing the subject of the living drama, in this case Tijerina and the movement he represented, to have a forum from which to voice the experience of generations. Other non-Chicano media had its own raison d'être, which more often than not was to uphold the status quo.

Tijerina: A Most Hated Man

Such is the case of NBC's investigative report *Reies Tijerina: The Most Hated Man in New Mexico*, a program that aired while Reies Tijerina was on a speaking tour of universities in California. If it did anything at all, *The Most Hated Man* brought before a national audience the litany of economic and cultural grievances that Reies Tijerina had spent a decade articulating in the name of rural nuevomexicanos. Not since George I. Sánchez's *Forgotten People*, published in 1940, had these issues been addressed with such vigor. Footage in *The Most Hated Man* of rural nuevomexicano families hauling drinking water from *acequias* (feeder ditches) and *norias* (shallow wells), and of generations of rural nuevomexicanos living on government food commodities and welfare, lacking adequate health care and hemmed in by Forest Service policies that restricted the grazing of their livestock on public lands, made for a powerful indictment of class and racial inequities among Mexican Americans. In this sense, *The Most Hated Man* lived up to its billing as a "white paper" in the tradition of Edward R. Murrow's post–World War II investigative journalism.

Tom Pettit, the lead reporter for NBC, seemed less sure about what to do with the figure of Tijerina himself. Pettit also was vexed by a set of cultural markers in New Mexico about which he was uninformed and consequently could not understand. Pettit, as had others before him who were unfamiliar with New Mexico, stood camera in hand, unable to fathom the depth of the racial, cultural, and religious politics that informed the land grant cause. When Pettit's knowledge about such matters ran dry, he did what others before him had done; he relied on stock explanations of nuevomexicano cultural and religious mores. Remarkably, some of his material harkened back to Charles Lummis and some of the earliest travel narratives that cast New Mexico as remote, foreign, and different. Pettit drew on tropes that by 1969 had all but been forgotten, and yet when they were unearthed in the context of Tijerina's militancy, they appeared newly minted, fitted to the moment and trotted out before TV viewers as the facts of this case.

The Most Hated Man opens with a Tijerina speech. This time Reies is caught in mid-stride as he delivers an invocation to a seated group of his followers. Reies is fully animated, walking to and fro and gesturing like a man possessed. He shouts: "Reies López Tijerina, the Alianza, the Brown People, the Indo-Hispano, this is the fire that is coming from the volcano which is in the northern part of New Mexico. And as much as the Devil, as much as the enemy, as much as the oppressor would like to have the world believe that I'm a King Tiger, that I'm a militant, that I am a violent man . . . he is mistaken, for I am as violent as Jesus Christ!" The report cuts to a Taos Art Colony painting of a penitent procession as an unidentified voice intones a sacred Penitente *alabado.* Then, the camera pans slowly over a New Mexican *bulto* (a statue in the round) depicting Christ crucified. While not specifically tying the Brotherhood to Tijerina's Alianza Federal de Mercedes, the opening sequence casts New Mexico as a land of violence and fanaticism, hence a place open to the likes of Tijerina. In the opening narration Tom Pettit claims objectivity and authority, but the words of his text harken back to the descriptions left by the vagabond photographer of earlier years: "The mixture of religion and violence is in the blood of New Mexicans. It is home to the Penitente cult with its Good Friday ritual of self-flagellation. Penitentes no longer crucify one of their own but the worship of Death remains one of the strongest emotions in the remote mountain villages of northern New Mexico." The essentialist descriptions of northern New Mexico, particularly of the Spanish-speaking population, pepper the program. Pettit reports: "Reies Tijerina evokes powerful emotions in New Mexico, especially here in the mountainous north where years of isolation and in-breeding have produced a people who are intensely passionate and sometimes violent." To permanently weld the dots into a profile of New Mexico as a land of blood, violence, and moral turpitude, Pettit introduces Tijerina as one "who speaks for the poor of New Mexico and the Southwest whose career has been marked by violence and controversy" (*Most Hated Man*). Pettit tells viewers that Tijerina has been compared to Martin Luther King, Zapata, and even Castro, something that makes him the most hated man in New Mexico. The documentary splices back to Tijerina speaking to the crowd as he delivers his version of the Gospel story of Christ throwing the merchants out of the temple in Jerusalem. "We fight not only for our land, but for our culture and language," Tijerina shouts, "because we believe that the rape of a culture and the language of a people is a greater crime that the rape of a two-year-old child [the camera pans to a small child in the audience who lumbers up on stage]. We don't believe in violence, but Jesus used a whip to drive the false preachers from the temple. We used a whip to clean out the court house of Tierra Amarilla" (*Most Hated Man*). The middle section of the documentary recounts the events at Tierra Amarilla and tells of Tijerina's instant notoriety in the wake of the raid.

It is only at those moments when *The Most Hated Man* stops hating Reies López Tijerina and entertains a discussion of the socioeconomic privation rampant in northern New Mexico that viewers get anything resembling the "white paper" exposé as promised by such investigative programs. Midway through we are introduced to the Pablo Valdez family of Ensenada, New Mexico. The Valdez family lives in a community not far from Tierra Amarilla. Pettit sets up his portraiture of poverty by noting that Rio Arriba County, just south of the Colorado–New Mexico border, is an area "bigger than the entire state of Connecticut." We see Pablo Valdez chopping wood as his wife hangs clothes out to dry on a rickety clothesline on a cold wintry afternoon. Pettit points out that young people from the area typically go off to work in the cities, leaving behind only the very old or very young to eke out a living. A classroom scene showing Elizabeth Valdez, age fourteen, and her younger brother Nelson follows, as Pettit continues: "English is the second language for each new generation of children in Rio Arriba county." Pettit intuits that the children pictured are years behind in English. The second-rate schools, Pettit concludes, are the result of a system of political spoilage that ironically props up a first-rate bus system where contracts go to party loyalists. The footage of the school bus delivering the Valdez children to their home in Ensenada, New Mexico, is especially effective as it provides the backdrop for Pettit to outline the living conditions of typical Rio Arriba County residents.

The Valdez family lives in a three-room house without plumbing, central heating, or a telephone. The family car, a rusting 1957 Chevy station wagon, is essential as the nearest doctor is seventy-five miles away. The camera moves inside the Valdez home as Mrs. Valdez prepares a meal. Cooking, says Pettit, is done on a wood-burning stove "three meals a day for eleven people." As the family sits to eat, the camera lingers on the head of household: "Pablo Valdez is forty-seven, he speaks no English. Even though he is out of work this is a better than average meal, beans, bread, sweet rolls, and spaghetti. No meat, no fresh milk. Mrs. Valdez is forty-three, she has nine living children; two others died as babies. The infant mortality rate in Rio Arriba County is high. Medical facilities are very limited and so are opportunities." The camera takes inventory of the main rooms of the house before moving outside again. "The Valdez family has lived here for generations," Pettit reminds viewers. "Their sense of family loyalty and affection is strong." The camera follows Nelson Valdez as he dips a bucket into a nearby acequia to draw up water for household use. Pettit continues, "The Valdez family gets its drinking water from an irrigation ditch; most families, at least, have a well. Pablo Valdez has no land to leave to his children. He sold it four years ago. Rio Arriba County is fertile territory for the oratory of Reies Tijerina" (*Most Hated Man*).

Pettit churns a volatile mix of violence and emotionalism. His narration weaves together the cult of the *caudillo*, the martyr and religious fanatic, to draw a menacing portrait of Tijerina and of his followers. One is struck by the staying power of these views of the land and people conjured up decades earlier by the vagabond-reporter of an earlier era. *The Most Hated Man* ends by installing martyrdom as a psycho-cultural complex that moves and conditions Tijerina as the leader of the Alianza. Tijerina's own words are used to reshape the legal-political history of land grant fraud in New Mexico into a messianic, cultist, and irrational movement. Sounding like a terrorist car bomber, Tijerina declares, "I'm not afraid to die. I think the danger of the pursuit is beautiful, it's exciting. I only hope that my death will redeem the respect and the culture of my people. For our culture comes first and then the lands. The best choice I could make is to die for my people." Pettit fits the noose around Tijerina and his movement by invoking the language of the vagabond-reporters of yesteryear and concludes, "When a messiah fails, he can succeed only by becoming a martyr. In the old days the Penitentes would pick one of their members and hang him. It was an honor to be sought after" (*Most Hated Man*).

Despite its essentialism and inaccuracies, the impact of the investigative report was widely felt. In his autobiography, Tijerina notes, "I left for California at the beginning of May to speak at various college and universities. I spent eight days on the speaking tour. When I was at San Bernardino, I saw the NBC program 'The Most Hated Man in New Mexico.' The thirty-minute documentary reached into millions of homes. U.S. society was beginning to learn of our cause and struggle" (2000, 131). In its wake, state politicians tried to put a good face on the embarrassment, reeling from a national program that equated New Mexico with the poorest areas of the rural South. Irked by the way *The Most Hated Man* confused and conflated Penitent religious identity with Tijerina's political struggle, the Hermanos Penitentes protested the mischaracterization of the documentary.

The Brotherhood's Concilio Supremo Arzobispal (Archbishop's Supreme Council) raised objections to the use of sacred material and to an unsubstantiated claim that the Penitentes were part of Tijerina's *Alianza*. The Chicano community paper *El Grito del Norte* (Española, New Mexico), following receipt of a letter from M. Santos Meléndez, reported that the Penitentes were considering a lawsuit against NBC for the use of photos and other materials about them "without permission and sincerity" (*El Grito del Norte*, May 19, 1969).

If the reaction from this quarter was vehement, what then did it say about Tijerina's implied or real connection to the Penitentes, and what does this say about the essentialist view expressed by Tom Pettit in his report? In his autobiography, Tijerina notes that when he first arrived in New Mexico in 1958 as an itinerant preacher with no resources to speak of, some of the first people to give him a helping hand were members of the Penitente Brotherhood (2000, 14). Later, Tijerina would come into contact with other members of the Brotherhood and he would confide: "I began to learn the history of the Penitentes and discovered a great deal. They were the few who saved the culture and the history of the settlers of New Mexico that remained. They were also the few who had the strength to resist Anglo influence. They lived with the dream of recovering their land in New Mexico" (28–29).

How, then, are these emphatic testimonials to Penitentes as the keepers of New Mexico culture to be understood in view of the threatened lawsuit the Hermanos announced in *El Grito del Norte*? The answer is that Tijerina did know and associate with several individuals who were or had been members of the Penitente Brotherhood. A few of these individuals remained loyal to the Alianza movement even as it waned in late 1970s. Tijerina, however, never had the endorsement of the entire organization, largely because his rhetoric, which embodied the habits of an itinerant preacher with calls for direct, militant action, were anathema to the Penitentes who steered away from politics and confrontation. But in the last analysis, it was the interpretation that *The Most Hated Man* gave to the association between Tijerina and the Brotherhood that most irritated the rank and file of the Penitentes, a group that was more inclined to predicate its actions on the model of a meek, humble, and sacrificial Christ over that of the punishing Christ of the temple that Tijerina had made into a symbol of his cause.

Despite the inherent drama of the Tierra Amarilla confrontation, no Hollywood film has ever been made in the United States about Tijerina or the Alianza. In the mid-1970s, a group of filmmakers in Mexico did take note of Tijerina's movement and began work on a film about the land grant leader that they entitled *Chicano*. Tijerina and his daughter Rosa were both involved in the filming. Reies had a starring role in the film; Rosa, on the other hand, who had been at the raid, was given a minor role as the wife of one of the raiders (Durán interview).

The Filmic Turn: Depicting Manito Culture
and Documenting *la vida buena y sana*

To date, only a handful of films qualify as being made "by, for, and about" Chicanos, and all of these can be said to have begun with Luis Valdez's 1969 film *I Am Joaquín*. While they are few in number, Chicano and Chicana films have brought forth self-fashioned representations to counter blatant stereotypes and misrepresentations about Mexican Americans in popular media. In New Mexico, where there were considerably fewer opportunities for making films than in California, Chicano filmmaking collectives did not emerge as they had in more urban parts of the Southwest. Nonetheless, the Chicano movement did allow Mexican Americans in more rural areas of the Borderlands to represent themselves and their experience in a variety of ways. It is also at this time that Mexican Americans began to critically examine the impact of film on their identity and on their sense of self-expression. In general, the climate for cultural expression that resulted from Chicano movement politics sensitized some blocs of society (as in the case of *The Most Hated Man*) to the plight of Mexican Americans to some degree. Many in society wanted not only to empower Chicanos/as to represent themselves but also to share in their collaborations. Building from the foundation set by Chicano and Chicana writers and poets, stories informing important aspects of the Chicano experience emerged. In some instances these narratives became part of works of important regional authors like Frank Waters, John Nichols, and others. Literary critics found that as certain mainstream writers invoked the Mexican American experience, they were approximating the style of Mexican American authors like Rudolfo Anaya and Demetria Martínez. Similar interests flowered among documentary filmmakers who began to document numerous examples of traditional folklore and folk life in rural New Mexico and adjacent areas. These documentaries began to examine what it meant to grow up Hispano/Chicano in New Mexico and the Borderlands.

Sensing that there were stories that could be drawn up from the "deep culture" of Indo-Hispano life in New Mexico, Moctesuma Esparza would return there many times throughout the course of his film career in search of Chicano film projects. Esparza's interest in Tijerina's land grant movement and other film subjects that he might find in New Mexico was a natural one:

> What Nuevo México represents is the uninterrupted tenancy of our people in the Southwest, whereas in most of the Southwest, it has been interrupted in significant ways, even though there are those who can say that they are Californianos or those who can say that they are Tejanos and trace their lineage before the United States, their land owning tradition was wiped out and so their connection to that ancient tenancy was compromised in terms of a relationship to land and to being the pioneers and settlers of the country. So that existence of long-term tenancy in Nuevo México uninterrupted provided that platform for us to be able declare to the world that we were not the illegal aliens, undocumented workers, that this was our historical land and that we belonged to it. So that was a very powerful symbol and Reies bringing it up, you know, it was powerful for us in providing more fuel and energy for our movement. (Esparza interview)

In 1978, Moctesuma Esparza joined director Esperanza Vasquez to make the short documentary *Agueda Martínez, Our People, Our Country*. The eighteen-minute piece, shot in Rio Arriba County, took as its focus the life of an elderly Indo-Hispana woman from the farming community of Medenales, New Mexico. Esparza had by this time graduated from film school and had completed *Cinco Vidas* as part of his thesis requirement. *Cinco Vidas*, which presented the lives of five Chicanos and Chicanas living in and around Southern California, won an Emmy in the documentary category. Esparza parlayed his success with *Cinco Vidas* into an agreement with McGraw-Hill to produce more Chicano programming, and thus Esparza again went on a search for suitable subjects that could represent the breadth of Chicano life in both traditional and nontraditional settings. Esparza felt sure that he would find the traditionalist viewpoint in northern New Mexico:

> I wanted to find traditional people and those that were professionals to cover the range of our tenure in the United States and throughout the Southwest and so I wrote a description. I said that

I want to find someone who lived on the land, who was a *curandera* or a *partera*, who grew her own food, who was potentially a weaver and who had owned her land for generations, and so I knew that the only place that I would likely find that person was in northern New Mexico, so having written that description, I then went on a journey to find her. (Esparza interview)

Esparza and Esperanza Vasquez sidestepped the Tijerina firestorm by focusing on the day-to-day sojourn of a woman who was living a quiet yet truly remarkable life on the small parcel of land that was her ancestral inheritance. Esparza's search for a suitable subject was complicated by the internecine cultural politics of northern New Mexico, something he encountered on his initial meeting with an emerging cultural group known as La Academia de la Nueva Raza.

About the time Esparza returned to New Mexico in 1974, the land grant struggle had evolved and morphed into a general awareness in the Chicano community of the importance of cultural and linguistic maintenance, the very kind of thing Tijerina often spoke about. Esparza recalls that La Academia de la Nueva Raza had begun to publish the occasional journal *La Resolana*, something that added to the clout of this small cell of oral and community historians.[2] Esparza recalls:

In 1974, northern New Mexico was quite insular, if you weren't from there you didn't get a wide-open welcome, even though I knew a lot of the folks from there. So I knew enough of them that I ended up with the guys that started Resolana, up in Dixon.

So I went up to them and I told them what I wanted to do and they literally put me through an interrogation. I felt like I was in the Inquisition. Why are you here? ¿Por qué estás haciendo esto? What are your intentions? And I sort of survived it and then after it was all over one of them said, "Listen, go see Regenio Salazar in ah, Española, and he'll know someone, he'll know somebody so you can find what you want." So, after I went through this ordeal, my consolation prize was to be referred to someone else. Those guys were rough. (Esparza interview)

Esparza was undeterred by the antics of these emerging cultural warriors, and after repeated visits to the Saints and Sinners, a bar in Española owned by Salazar, he was directed to the postmistress at Medenales, who as it turned out was Doña Agueda Martínez's daughter.

Esparza seems to believe that more than mere luck directed his steps that day: "[Regenio] sent me out to Medenales and my first vision of Agueda as I was approaching and it was dusk, was that she was standing on the loom and she was weaving." Rosa Linda Fregoso has pointed out that "the formal properties of the film mark *Agueda Martínez* as one of the most eloquently crafted films of the period" (1993, 13). Indeed, the film is a type of auto-ethnographic representation in which Doña Agueda, assisted by the non-interventionist filmmakers Vasquez and Esparza, narrates her own life experiences and daily routines.

Like *The Most Hated Man in New Mexico*, this documentary opens with a voice intoning "Buenos Días, Paloma Blanca," a religious hymn. Doña Agueda begins to narrate and her words, like the hymn, put before the viewer a sense of the sacred. "Era buena vida aquí en Nuevo Mexico," Doña Agueda remarks as the voice of translator-actor Carmen Zapata takes hold and moves the story forward.[3] "It was always a good life here in *Nuevo México*. I come from a people that are very old." The effect is momentary but extremely powerful as the hymn, *Doña* Agueda's speaking voice, and the unobtrusive English narration blend and merge effortlessly in the first minutes of the film. And it is in those same first few minutes that the major motif of the film is announced. The film will be a treatise on the nuevomexicano idea of "la vida buena y sana." One of most common and abiding *dichos* or sayings in northern New Mexico, "Vivir la vida buena y sana," translates as "To live a good and healthy life." While the good and healthy life mantra of northern New Mexico appears trite, worn thin by overuse, it merits consideration here precisely since its universal application in the region suggests that the tenets that lie beneath this philosophical maxim run deep in *Manito* culture. It is an especially key trope to contemplate against the examination of the film representations that precede *Agueda Martínez*, since it establishes an intuitive understanding of the depth and charge associated with living in balance and harmony with the earth. It should be noted that the Spanish word "sana" means both "healthy" and "sane." It is the *sane* connotation, of course, which is most interesting in the context and against the gamut of film depictions that have purported to translate *Manito* culture to others. *Sane* refers to the soundness of mind and body that suggests a concern with the whole individual, and it expounds the view that a successful life is one lived in balance and harmony with others and that accords high value and high regard to a set of ennobling standards of behavior and comportment.

Agueda Martínez readily and openly acknowledges this important community standard, and thus the film brings forth a compact illustration of this aspiration as it follows Doña Agueda, a person who epitomizes living *la vida buena y sana*. The camera follows Doña Agueda in the repetition of her daily activities. We see her as she sweeps her patio, draws water from her well, chops and gathers wood for her stove. It is the old woman's narration that is most effective in providing the viewer with an encounter with Manito "deep culture," and to the dimensions of "the good and sane life."

Mis abuelitos fueron rancheros. "My grandparents were ranchers. My father's parents were animal-breeders. My mother's father was a poor man, but yet he had a large family and with honest work he supported all of his children," Doña Agueda recounts. Married at eighteen, Agueda was left to her own resources when her husband was incapacitated by a crippling illness early in the marriage. Doña Agueda recalls how she had to learn to weave to add to the family income. The camera, which up to this point has followed Doña Agueda as she does her tasks, now lingers in the front room, pausing over old family photos of brides and grooms, soldiers and first communion candidates. "I have a large family, I have eight children and sixty-seven grandchildren and I have forty-five great-grandchildren, so there are over one hundred people from my blood." As though trying to keep pace, the camera follows Doña Agueda as she dons her bonnet and heads out across the fields of her ranch.

Doña Agueda tells of her deep identification with her land and to the customs of her forebears. As she explains her daily habit of hauling water from the well and bringing wood for heat she asks, "The wood stove is less expensive and it provides a warmth for one's health that is better than gas. How couldn't the life we had be better than what we have nowadays? I still have the beliefs of my parents, in everything." Equally remarkable as Doña Agueda at seventy-seven years of age is the fact that her community is able to retain a communal agricultural lifestyle amid the massive social changes that had been under way in New Mexico since at least the turn of the last century. Agueda Martínez proudly asserts that she makes her living from harvesting the crops her farm ranch produces and by weaving her zarapes in the winter. While only eighteen minutes in length, *Agueda Martínez* is remarkably compact and whole in its reproduction of the details of Doña Agueda's story. As Rosa Linda Fregoso has pointed out, the work is masterfully structured: "The film reproduces the movement of the day, beginning with sunrise and ending with the setting sun. The visual orchestration is laid over another marker of time, the cycle of the seasons. Indeed, the cinematic representation is designed in cyclical fashion, opening with springtime (Agueda's craft of harvesting [*sic*]) and closing with winter (Agueda's craft of weaving)" (1993, 14). Equally important is the distillation of several hours of oral conversation into a concise and powerful voiceover that accompanies the visual frame of the film. In short order, Doña Agueda references her distant Navajo forebears and speaks of the diaspora of family members to other parts to the West. She notes the invasive nature of modern society, which she detects in her grandchildren's "bewitchment" with television and their straying from traditional Catholic practices. She tells of her attachment to traditional ways as she hauls water from the well, chops wood, and refuses the convenience of a gas stove inside her home. Amazingly, the film still provides Doña Agueda with time to speak of food preparation, of her role in the upbringing of her grandchildren, and of the symbolism found in her weavings.

The film closes with Doña Agueda's eloquent *testimonio* of a life of fortitude and self-sufficiency, one of humble but noble purpose. In a final sequence, she is at her loom just as Esparza and Vasquez first encountered her and as she speaks about weaving, her life's passion: "There are times I weave until twelve o'clock at night, as the saying goes from sun up to sunset. I don't get tired, work doesn't tire me. I'll stop weaving when I can't move any more, until then you'll find me dancing on the loom." In the final shots we find Doña Agueda out in the fields of her rancho, as the cycle of another harvest returns: "How can the land not be blessed? I shall never sell my land in my lifetime. They may sell it when I have gone to the grave but not in my lifetime will I sell my ranch, because the land is my life and my children's too. *La tierra es la única que da vida.* The land is the only thing that gives life and when one goes back it eats you up. As the saying goes, I am of earth and earth I will be."

Agueda Martínez is among the first films to align the landscape and humanscape of northern New Mexico's rural Indo-Hispano communities, following what Fregoso has called the "documentary impulse" of early Chicano cinema. Fregoso includes *Agueda Martínez* among a set of early Chicano films, which she qualifies as "*actos* of imaginative re-discovery." Fregoso considers *Agueda Martinez* to be a fundamental step in the filmic turn in the representation of Chicanos in the media: "The efforts to recover history are intimately connected to the re-invention of an alternate notion of Chicano identity. Given that Chicanos and Chicanas were depicted as 'others' according to the perverse logic of the discourse of racism, each of these films labors to dismantle the dominant system of representation" (1993, 2).

Nuevo México as Humanscape:
Performing the Drama of Land Grievance

Moctesuma Esparza's assertion bears repeating: "What Nuevo México represents is the uninterrupted tenancy of our people in the Southwest." Here is an assertion that takes on special meaning in light of the Chicano-themed film depictions that grew out of the militancy of the land grant movement. As is the case for *Agueda Martínez*, ideas of great consequence are tied up in the question of land tenancy in New Mexico. Tijerina's admonition, "We fight not only for our land, but for our culture and language," is also worth recalling here, since unequivocally Chicano-themed films and documentaries shot in New Mexico after 1967, especially those made by Chicanos or as collaborations, would to some measure be bound up in the complexities of land, culture, language, and ethnic identity.

"*Un Milagro,*" *Another* Salt of the Earth

For Moctesuma Esparza such complications would lead him to his next major collaboration, a project that would bring the 1974 "cult novel" *The Milagro Beanfield War* to the big screen. The story of this Chicano-themed film begins with the author, John Treadwell Nichols, and his thirty-plus years of identification with New Mexico, in particular with the rural Indo-Chicano population of northern New Mexico. Nichols first came to New Mexico in the summer of 1969. Not one to deny his left-leaning socialist politics, he often launches into invectives against exploitative capitalism. Half in earnest, he has remarked, "I was drawn to New Mexico because I thought it would make a good place to overthrow the capitalist system" (Nichols 2000c, 2). If one thing encapsulates Nichols's brand of politics, it is his participation and defense of the local through grass-roots activism. For Nichols, the resistant and resilient form of regional culture that he found in New Mexico represented a kind of antidote to globalization and domination by world capitalism. Nichols writes, "New Mexico may be funky, and poor, and brutal, but there's a spirit here, raw and beautiful, that transcends much of the rest of America" (2000c, 10).[4] Arriving in New Mexico in the wake of a period of direct action and confrontation, Nichols was immediately drawn to the resistant politics of Native American and Chicano communities:

> I chose to live in Taos because I was inspired by the Pueblo's struggle to win back their fifty thousand acres of Blue Lake land. I also sensed there would be spillover in the county from Reies Tijerina's land grant movement that might result in some spirited progressive advances if the fates were kind to us. Too, Taos at the time was festering through a Hippy-Chicano War that pitted old-time values against new age woo woo-ju ju. Confrontations like these can't help but expand knowledge of the overall situation and politicize the citizenry. (2)

As a writer, Nichols has had only moderate financial success and his earnings have waxed and waned on several occasions. Over a twenty-year span Nichols has published over twelve books, and with the exception of a couple of peak years in which his writing brought him some respectable royalties, he readily acknowledges that none of his books has ever paid back an advance (2000b, 128). Nichols remains sober about the financial gain of his books: "And today, even though nine or ten of my titles remain in print, the combined royalties for any given year don't amount to more than $3,000" (129).

Nichols infuses his writing with a wry brand of self-deprecating humor to create a narrative style that is a mix of biting humor and serious commentary on social reality. Satire, irony, and humor drive *The Milagro Beanfield War*. These are stylistic elements that find their way into several more of his essays on writing as a social activist, living in one of the poorest areas of the United States, and surviving personal and political catastrophes. In two of his more acerbic works, *Armageddon and New Mexico: Writing for Fun and Profit in the Poorest State in America* and "Night of the Living Bean

Field: How an Unsuccessful Cult Novel Became an Unsuccessful Cult Film in Only Fourteen Years, Eleven Nervous Breakdowns, and $20 Million," He talks at length about the evolution of the *Milagro Beanfield* film project. He expresses frustration, awe, and incredulity concerning the process of turning a novel into a film. In "Night of the Living Bean Field," he confesses that making *Milagro* into a movie was one of the hardest things he did in his life (2000b, 133).

Nichols looks upon the whole experience as an endless and ghoulish nightmare that began in 1973, the year he sold the novel and a time when he was flat broke. Nichols was paid $10,000, which he recalls as "an incredible fortune to me in those days" (133). The money didn't change things much and publication of the novel, Nichols says, was only the beginning of his woes. First off, there was the matter of some scathing early reviews. Nichols recalls:

> The novel was published in 1974 to a resounding shrug. The *New York Times* lambasted it, and local newspaper mogul Mark Acuff, editor of the infamous *New Mexico Independent*, called the book a "bomb" and "a shallow insult" to all of us. A Santa Fe scribe, Tom Mayer, writing for *The Rio Grande Sun* in Española, accused me of creating a world "utterly without moral subtlety," functioning with a literary design that is "too obvious, too calculated and polemical, and not one character escapes symbolic function to achieve the status of a person you know, let alone care about."
>
> Next day the *Los Angeles Times* called me a "second-string sports reporter" and terminated their review by saying I had written a "book that takes hours to read, a moment to forget." (133–134)

In spite of this, *Milagro* did manage to garner the attention of a couple of respectable film producers who took out an option on the book the first year it was in print, a development that renewed Nichols's optimism, at least until the option deal went belly-up. This less-than-auspicious start may have prompted Nichols to write:

> So *Milagro* had a couple of strikes against it when Bob Christiansen and Rick Rosenberg took out an option in 1973. What sort of strikes? Let me count the ways:

Its length.

Its subject matter.

Its politics.

Its numerous characters.

Its ethnic composition.

Its lack of structure.

Its filthy language.

Its support of Spanish culture and tradition.

   (In a country where thirty-seven states have passed English-only laws, this story had a foreign—well, Spanish—word in the title. My agent wanted that word *out*. My publisher wanted that word *out*. For a long time, the film people wanted that word *out*.) (136)

The novel, some 629 pages, is a long read and while its plot is uncomplicated, the novel is dense in its presentation of characters and its inclusion of a great many episodes drawn from Nichols's years of living in Taos County. His own assessment of how ill suited the book was for Hollywood is telling:

Perhaps, before I delve into the celluloid shenanigans of shallow, racist, childish, chauvinist, anti-communist, money grubbing, egomaniacal, fascist Hollywood, I should at least give you a basic synopsis of my profound, tolerant, adult, feminist, pro-communist, money-scoring, humble, self-effacing, compassionate novel—in case any of you have not been able to read it yet.

Milagro begins with a nineteenth-century lunatic digging a hole to China, trying to find his lost dog. It ends with a Vista volunteer having his lights punched out after riding a vicious Shetland pony during a fiesta celebrating the fact that not all the horses in China can stop disempowered people from harvesting the fruits of their own labors if they are really hungry for a bean burrito. In between, a vast and jumbled assortment of characters catch trout illegally, fornicate in runaway VW buses, butcher mice, fire dumdum bullets at undercover police agents, kill crows with their bare hands, drive bulldozers over the Rio Grande Gorge, commit adultery, play boogie-woogie piano with just one arm, adopt orphan robins, slaughter skunks, rip up parking tickets, chuck pebbles at tourists, almost rape inquiring reporters, snowshoe around the high mountains in midwinter, and declare war against the U.S. Forest Service, the New Mexico state engineer, the governor and his lackeys, the banking system of America, all realtors and resort developers within a five-hundred-square mile area and the president of the United States.

In short, the novel, like anyone who has ever tried to explain New Mexico to an outsider, tends to ramble. Like our state, the novel is big, it is bold, and it mostly empty spaces.

That tendency is not real cinematic. Basically your average movie has two main characters, two supporting roles, and a fairly tight plot. (135–136)

Nichols's tongue-in-cheek synopsis of *Milagro* emphasizes the twin mainstays of the novel: the work is episodic and it is a satirical treatment of the foibles of life in the poorest state in the nation. While grand in scope, *Milagro* is in fact an anti-epic, a parody of novels holding to a very serious tone and tenor that accompanies great, transformational moments in the history of peoples. In this, and in *Magic Journey* (1978) and *Nirvana Blues* (1981)—his New Mexico trilogy—Nichols casts about for ways to explain New Mexico to outsiders. In *Milagro*, Nichols bifurcates his purpose, delivering his politics amid the episodic to-and-fro of high jinks and hilarity. In the end, *Milagro* is effective in sending two messages about New Mexico to readers: it's a poor place, but in the face of this poverty its people (Indo-Hispanos in this case) laugh at and with their condition.

A decade after publication, *Milagro* was still embroiled in option purchases. Nichols rejected most offers out of personal loyalty to Christiansen and Rosenberg or out of the feeling that other buyers were driven by profit alone and lacked any social integrity. Throughout, Nichols remained committed to the idea that *Milagro* should be at least half as good a movie as *Salt of the Earth* (2000c, 12).

In the early 1980s Moctesuma Esparza became the fifth in a line of prospective buyers vying to option *Milagro* and take it to the screen. Nichols recalls that at first meeting he took a liking to Esparza: "We met for a beer in the Albuquerque Sheraton Old Town and I liked him a lot. The one piece of his work I saw was a short documentary on a Medenales weaver, Agueda Martinez, which I found quite beautiful. Plus Mocte had been arrested during the Chicano movement days of the 1960s in L.A. To my thinking, pretty good credentials. Integrity" (141).

Moctesuma Esparza had been tracking *Milagro* as a result of a grant he received from the National Council of La Raza to make a series of movies based on Chicano culture and literature. It was at about this time that Esparza acquired the rights to *With Pistol in His Hand* by Américo Paredes and *Pocho* by José Villarreal. Esparza's interest in *Milagro* reflected his commitment to develop Chicano-Latino films as a way to improve the film portrayal of people of Mexican ancestry living in the United States:

> I was looking to capture our culture as represented in the literature, that would represent who we were as a people and *The Milagro Beanfield War*, although not written by a Latino, I think is an extraordinary piece of work that captures this both picaresque and very committed relationship to land and to the lifeblood of land which is water, and to that culture that it has supported and that lives on today, still in some communities of Nuevo México. So that's what attracted me to the film and that's why I wanted to frame for you how it came to be that I did both those movies. It came out of this collaboration with the National Council of La Raza. (Esparza interview)

After landing the option, Esparza got a call from Robert Redford, who also had maintained a long-term interest in *Milagro*. The call led to a joint venture agreement and an invitation to take the project to the Sundance Film Institute to begin work on a script of the film. The collaboration kept Nichols involved in developing the script and treatment until Universal Studios agreed to fund the production of the movie in May 1986, a decision that brought into view the full predicament of taking the story back to its source: northern New Mexico. Bringing the film project to northern New Mexico filled Nichols with trepidation of the kind that only someone committed to the sovereignty of New Mexico village life can know. Nichols says he called Redford to ask that he consider filming the movie on the back lot of Universal Studios so as to avoid stirring up local animosity for the project. Redford answered succinctly: "No, he wanted it to be in northern New Mexico, for authenticity" (2000b, 143). As Nichols recalls, "Redford picked Chimayó as the perfect bucolic village for his picture. But Chimayó told him to go screw himself. So Bob decided to choose a more insane path and he made a deal with the small, tough, proud, insular mountain town of Truchas. I couldn't believe it. I envisioned an all-out race war in the boondocks, and me the guy to blame" (143–144). Truchas, the setting for *Red Sky at Morning* and the gateway scene for *The Lash of the Penitentes*, would once again fall under Hollywood's gaze. Redford too succumbed to the town's rugged beauty and started his cameras rolling there in August 1986.

Like *Red Sky at Morning*, *Milagro* opens with a vista shot of the Sangre de Cristo mountain range. Into the magnificence of the landscape, Redford inserts the silhouette of a dead cottonwood tree set against the ridgeline of Truchas Peak. The silhouette is superimposed over the vista shot and recedes from the foreground as the rouge-tinged, snowcapped peaks in the distance light up at daybreak and become a visual reminder of how the land has decayed and is abandoned. The symbolism continues as the camera pans the dust-strewn streets of Milagro. A dust devil, known locally as a *remolino*, works its way across the village, and from the vortex emerges a Mexican angel, sporting an accordion, a sombrero, and huaraches. The angel, meant to be read as the spirit of Milagro, dances out and bounds forth to make his rounds through the town.

As Nichols had surmised, a chief concern for the *Milagro* film project would be to find a way to reduce the number of characters in the novel into six or so major figures to carry the story. The spirit of Milagro, a figure played by Robert Carricart, was one way to bring out what critics had described as Nichols's inclination to employ magic realism after the fashion of Gabriel García Marquez, Carlos Fuentes, or Isabel Allende, to conjoin the sense of the ordinary with elements of the fantastic or otherworldly. In the novel, Nichols builds a sense of the uncanny into the stories and anecdotes that villagers tell about one another. The film, on the other hand, required the story to be tailored along the classic lines of protagonists and antagonists. Following some well-trodden Hollywood situational premises, the film sets the town of Milagro, represented by Joe Mondragón (Chick Vennera), Ruby Archuleta (Sonia Braga), Sheriff Bernabé Montoya (Ruben Blades), sociology student Herbie Platt (Daniel Stern), Charlie Bloom (John Heard), and Amarante Córdova (Carlos Riquelme) against the forces of development and exploitation, represented by Ladd Devine (Richard Bradford),[5] Kyril Montana (Christopher Walken), and an assorted group of lackeys, both native and nonnative, who carry out Devine's plan to turn the town into a resort development that threatens the traditional way of life practiced by the town's predominantly Mexican American community.

The film's inciting incident comes when Joe Mondragón, angry over not being hired to work on the Devine project, drives out to his father's abandoned agricultural field to sulk. In anger he accidentally kicks open a head gate on the nearby acequia, which causes water to course over the long neglected furrows of his field. In a poignant moment, Joe, about to shut off the water, reaches down into the muddy rivulets to cup the flowing water in his hands. The camera lingers on this single moment just long enough to communicate the idea that water is a sacred and living thing. This is one place where the film successfully translates the cultural meaning and the reverence northern New Mexicans have traditionally had for water and nature.

The pretext for conflict in the film is the act of discharging water for agricultural purposes. Whether by accident or intent, Mondragón's act becomes a threat to Devine's master plan to build a major resort in Milagro. Devine's plan calls for Joe's field to be the thirteenth fairway of a new pro golf course. The town's rumor mill is pushed into gear by Joe's neighbor, Amarante Córdova, who circulates the news of the unsanctioned irrigation to all interested parties. The ensuing rumor builds to a confrontation that will pit Hispano farmers against greedy developers and inept state regulators. Water as the basis of a dispute over natural resources and the future of New Mexico's upland village communities has a history as deep and as troubled as the land grants themselves. It is that history that inspires Nichols's tale of resistance and regeneration among rural Chicanos. In speaking of the importance of water and the ditch irrigation systems that ensure its flow to communities in northern New Mexico, researcher José Rivera points out the fragility of maintaining the old watercourses in the face of increasing development:

> Since the early 1960s, however, high water markets and demographic forces behind them such as population growth, immigration, and land development pressures have placed these fragile *acequia* communities at great risk. No one disputes that emerging water markets, if left unchecked, would sever water from traditional

agricultural uses in the region and cause economic stress to rural
villages. Water laws in New Mexico, as in most western states,
adhere to the doctrine of prior appropriation and the principle
of severability, where water can be transferred to alternative beneficial uses. Like other property commodities, water rights can be
bought and sold in the open market. Less well known, however, are
the broader impacts on the regional and state economies that can
result if these historic *acequia* villages literally dry up. (1998, xviii)

If *The Milagro Beanfield War* is about real and contentious issues like
land, water, and the displacement of Chicanos from their ancestral villages, it is also about how the autonomy and individuality of these places
give form to intercultural encounters of various kinds. On this level it is
also very much about Nichols's attempt, as I have already noted, to explain
rural New Mexico, particularly its Indo-Hispanos, to those unfamiliar with
the people of the region.

In this sense, *Milagro* shares something with *Red Sky at Morning* in that it
plays off the idea of newcomers being at a disadvantage and on the outside of
the collective relationship that local residents maintain to place, homeland,
and community. Two figures in *Milagro* share a kinship with Josh Arnold in
Red Sky. One is Charlie Bloom, a left-leaning activist lawyer in the middle of
a long, self-imposed exile from New York who came to live in Milagro six
years earlier. Bloom identifies with the plight of the rural Chicanos and publishes a local alternative paper called *La Voz del Pueblo* in which community
concerns are aired. The other figure is Herbie Platt (Herbie Goldfarb in the
novel), a Ph.D. candidate in sociology from NYU who sets foot in Milagro
for the first time in the role of a Vista volunteer sent to help the rural communities of northern New Mexico as he simultaneously does research for a
dissertation on "indigenous communities." Charlie and Herbie clearly represent aspects of Nichols's personal story of coming to New Mexico. Charlie
voices Nichols's politics and activism in the story, whereas Herbie illustrates
Nichols's first awkward years of apprenticeship in New Mexico. Herbie, a
younger embodiment of Nichols, is the know-it-all kind of fellow that Nichols confesses he was when he first arrived in 1969:

When I graduated from college thirty-eight years ago, I had to start
over, as you most certainly will, learning everything from scratch. My

formal education had prepared me to succeed in our culture, but not to really understand the planet or sympathize with it in a compassionate manner. I knew very little about love or work or the tragedy of environment and people under attack by material development. You could say I was probably like most of you: a real sábelotodo, compréndelonada [a know-it-all who understands nothing]. (Nichols 2000a)

Nichols, like Charlie Bloom, stayed around and listened to the culture long enough to learn that the locals even had a saying for this peculiar kind of psychic aliment. As Nichols went on to say to the graduating class at the University of New Mexico in 2000, Hispanic villagers referred to such upstarts as "sábelotodos, entiéndele nadas" (literally, "know-it-alls who understand nothing"), a barb they most often direct at Anglo outsiders purporting to have the right solutions and best interests of the communities at heart. It is Herbie Platt who bears the "know-it-all" tag, not because he is particularly arrogant or bombastic, but because his academic credentials as an NYU sociologist and his urban savvy carry absolutely no weight in Milagro, USA. Herbie's arrival provides an amusing example of this insider/outsider contrast. In the film, Herbie climbs down from a battered yellow school bus that has deposited the visibly bewildered and travel-weary young scholar in the middle of the Milagro's town plaza. Herbie's first encounter with local culture happens when he blurts out to a villager walking briskly across the plaza: "Excuse me, can you tell me where I can find Mr. Cantú?" Sizing him up, the villager responds, "Sammy Cantú, Billy Cantú, Melitón Cantú, Felipe Cantú, Amarante Cantú, Eloy Cantú, Chemo Cantú, which one?" And while Herbie reaches into his pocket to check the name, contrary to common courtesy the villager simply walks away, leaving Herbie in a tizzy of befuddlement. Herbie backs away and narrowly avoids being knocked down by a bandana-adorned *cholo* with mad-dog sunglasses piloting a lowered Chevy Impala. Sensing his misstep, Herbie walks over to the driver's side and blurts out, "Sorry, excuse me," to which the driver of the low rider retorts in a deadpan voice, "O.K.," and throttles his low, rumbling Chevy forward.

When Herbie eventually does find the mayor of Milagro, Sammy Cantú, it is a meeting bereft of any gala, open-arms reception he might have imagined. The encounter goes like this:

HERBIE: Uh, Mr. Cantú? Hi. Herbie Platt. Department of Sociology, NYU. Did anybody tell you about me?

CANTÚ: Yeah.

HERBIE: OK. Herbert Platt, Department of Sociology. I'm doing research. I'm writing a thesis.

CANTÚ: Yeah. Oh.

HERBIE: I'm supposed to be here six months; I've got a grant to stay here. Ah, nobody told you I was coming, uh?

CANTÚ: Well nobody told me. That doesn't mean nobody told nobody. Maybe somebody told somebody, but they didn't tell me.

HERBIE: Uh, OK, I don't have a place to stay?

CANTÚ: What, we're going to have to get you a house?

HERBIE: Well no, no . . . but I need a place to stay. Hey, I'm not looking for a handout here. I'm gonna work, I'm planning on working. Look, I want to help out around here, maybe . . . teach.

CANTÚ: Look, if we don't know it already, chances are we are not interested in knowing it.

HERBIE: Well . . . what am I supposed to do?

CANTÚ: Join the army.

If these scenes do anything about the larger need to dismantle typecast representations of the Chicanos in film, it is in the way they momentarily evaporate the "mi casa es su casa" image of docility and servility so deeply engrained in first encounters on film between Hispanics and Anglos.[6] Here, too, they add a complexity to both sides of these encounters. Sammy Cantú's "Join the army" line exemplifies the complexities of this encounter. What moviegoers might first take as a hostile outburst is a moment in which class and racial connotations surface. The mayor employs language that among the working class in America is a kind of mantra that says, "Grow up, go out, and do something that is useful to everyone," and this is to say that throughout the preceding dialogue Cantú's sense of things has hardened and condensed around the idea that "Milagro folks are burned out on do-gooders and they are busy carrying on with their lives such as they are." At moments like these, the film keeps true to John Nichols's intention to side with "the wretched of the earth" and specifically with folk that he has claimed were great teachers to a self-described "sábelotodo, entiéndele nada." Nichols remarks, "These friends of mine have a remarkable sense of humor. They are full of chistes, chispa, chisme, chile verde; amistad, orgullo, coraje y alma. . . . These neighbors are the indefatigable majority on earth, and they gave me my novels and the other books I've published and all the films I've worked on. In short, they gave me my real education and taught me the shape of existence around the globe and where I belong forever" (2000a).

The main plot of *The Milagro Beanfield War* continues amid these characterizations. Herbie will, after a time, be apprenticed to Milagro's oldest and wisest resident, Amarante Córdova, who, in the fashion of living *la vida buena y sana,* is neighborly and patient with Herbie. He teaches him the deep values that come from living in community. This bonding is so strong that when Amarante is nearly killed chasing away one of Ladd Devine's henchmen and hijacking a Devine bulldozer and tumbling down the Rio Grande gorge, it is Herbie who takes the fall of the old man most to heart.

Several more Nichols characters come forth amid the escalating tension that has been produced by Joe Mondragón's illegal irrigation of his bean field. Three of the most important are Kyril Montana, an ex-narco state cop sent up from Santa Fe to infiltrate Milagro and to keep the local population on edge; Bernabé Montoya, whom Nichols describes as "forty-three years old and the bumbling sheriff of Milagro" (1974, 158), and Ruby Archuleta, a feisty independent mountain woman whose strength and determination is modeled after Esperanza Quintero in *Salt of the Earth.* Nichols's long description of Ruby in the novel is meant to convey the awe and admiration Ruby inspires in her neighbors:

> An aura of mystery and of knowledge surrounded Ruby Archuleta, and so of course the average Milagro citizen both envied and resented her, both loved her and hated her guts, thought she must be a Communist, refused to have his automotive or plumbing needs catered to by anyone else. . . . and nobody knew Ruby very well although everyone had known her all their lives.
>
> Actually, there was nothing that peculiar about the Body Shop and Pipe Queen (as some jokers occasionally called her). Awake, each morning at five, Ruby dressed in a work shirt, weathered jeans, and cowboy boots, cooked breakfast for the men, tied her long hair

up in a red-checkered bandana, and marched outside to start over-hauling cars or organizing plumbing jobs. She cut pipe and welded metal joints, installed shocks and stripped down engines—you name it. (1974, 89)

It is through these three characters that the festering issue of land, water, and community displacement gains dramatic traction in the film. Ruby assumes the role of leader of the Milagro resisters as she entreats Joe to continue watering his field, and then calls upon Charlie Bloom to address a protest meeting of the townspeople that she organizes. Kyril Montana sets about to disrupt any and all efforts at community empowerment by running a covert action campaign to intimidate Joe Mondragón, discredit Charlie and Ruby, and get Bernabé Montoya to clamp down on all community dissidents. For his part, Bernabé Montoya must work to keep a delicate peace in a situation that promises to explode into another chapter of the festering land grant struggle in the north or a rash of National Forest sign burnings.

Another Milagro, *Another* Salt of the Earth

On several occasions, John Nichols expressed the hope that *The Milagro Beanfield War* might come to be seen as another *Salt of the Earth*. In his address to newly minted university graduates, he paid tribute to the men and women who made *Salt* by underscoring the common humanity and creative power of the laboring classes:

> But they make the world work, and they labor so hard on behalf of everyone. They create and harvest the energy we all thrive on. They live at Taos Pueblo, in Truchas, or the South Valley of Albuquerque, and on the llano near Tucumcari. They speak Spanish, Tiwa, Diné, good old boy Gabacho. They make all kinds of vital music and years ago in Silver City, they even made a movie called *Salt of the Earth* that I wish everybody here could see as a graduation present. (2000a)

Following the many reworkings of the script, Nichols observes, "I was praying for the movie to turn out at least half as powerful as that 1954 classic film about a miners' strike near Silver City, *Salt of the Earth*" (2000c, 12). Two moments in *Milagro* hark back to *Salt*. The first and more pivotal is the community meeting that Ruby Archuleta presides over in the village church. The scene builds slowly, which allows the theme of community bonding to develop. The assembled townsfolk waiting to hear from Ruby and Charlie duplicates the scene of miners and miners' wives in the union hall in *Salt* embarking upon the contentious decision of whether or not to continue the Empire Strike. Both films introduce audiences to the divisiveness that plays into community decision making as various members of the community rise up to take a stand on whether to resist or bow down to the institutions and forces that impinge on their way of life. As described in an earlier chapter, the union hall scene in *Salt* is the moment when the Chicanas of Zinc Town take power for themselves and when Esperanza Quintero frees herself of self-doubt. *Milagro* brings forth a powerful and animated figure in the character of Ruby Archuleta, who, like Esperanza in *Salt*, becomes the conscience of the community. In what is the longest soliloquy of the *Milagro* script, Ruby speaks eloquently and with conviction about the need to act for the common good of Milagro and the people of the north. In opening the meeting she reminds everyone:

RUBY: My friends, my cousins. Do you remember when we were not rich, but when our poverty was different, not a thing to be ashamed of. . . . There was a time when our children stayed home and raised their children in Milagro. Think about that. We could become a town of old men and old women. We are a family and I love you very much. But I must tell you, sometimes when I wake up in Milagro, I want to cry. I think about Ladd Devine and the development and I know, if it comes, it means the end for most of us. I've spent too much of my time watching bad things happen to my people, but if we want to fight the recreation area we have to understand it. I know it is very complicated, that's why I asked our friend Charlie Bloom to talk to us and explain things.

Charlie's speech, by contrast, is short and minimal. He speaks of how the tax base in Milagro will skyrocket with the new development, how the only jobs Milagro residents will qualify for will be menial labor and how in the end they will not be able to afford to live in Milagro. The community meeting ends in a near riot as Milagro residents take to recriminating with one another, as a passel of those already benefiting from the system (National Forest rangers, the mayor, storeowners, etc.) clash with those who are disenfranchised (underemployed youth, disempowered elderly, traditional farmers). For all the disruption, the scene echoes *Salt of the Earth*'s call for unity and community autonomy as it evokes the power that can come from shared governance in the voicing of community concerns. The community meeting ends in a raucous spate of charges and counter-charges, but it is clear from the interaction that the resolve of the community is to fight the developers.

The other *Salt* moment is *Milagro*'s final scene. Here, those who were sensitized by the community meeting gather collectively in support of Joe Mondragón's right to take water from the community ditch and to water his land. Milagro residents join as one community to celebrate the show-down that foils Kyril Montana's plan to arrest Joe. That scene begins with Joe returning to Milagro after evading Kyril Montana, who has chased him into a mountain ravine (with the help of a Devine foreman, Horsethief Shorty) in the nearby mountains. An ecstatic Joe invites those who have been waiting for him to join him at his bean field to help harvest his first crop. News of Joe's safe return and of the impending celebration circulates far and wide, and soon a parade of cars and pickups filled with Milagro villagers circles through the village, growing as it snakes its way to the bean field. The caravan of madly honking cars and trucks filled with jubilant people of all ages reproduces the actual scene that transpired in the summer of 1966 when Reies López Tijerina and his valientes entered the Echo Amphitheater Camp Ground in Rio Arriba County, arrested the park rangers, and claimed the area as part of the San Joaquin land grant.

At the bean field, Milagro residents begin to dance and embrace as they fill their baskets with beans and take time to thank Joe for standing up for his convictions. But the village celebration is cut short when Kyril Montana and a fleet of state police cruisers, sirens blaring, track Joe there. Kyril takes Joe prisoner and is about to haul him away despite legal protests from Charlie Bloom. The confrontation suddenly turns deadly serious as several village men haul out a slew of hunting rifles from their pickups and block Montana and the state troopers. Here is the long anticipated ugly incident that the governor and other public officials had sought to avoid all along, and, just when it seems the story has reached its darkest hour, in steps Bernabé Montoya to break the impasse. Stumbling, literally, in between the two armed groups, Bernabé brings news that Amarante Córdova's condition has improved and that the octogenarian is out of harm's way and, importantly, that he has decided not to press charges against Joe in the accidental shooting that wounded him. As the situation is defused, the governor reaches Kyril Montana by police mobile phone and orders him to abort his arrest of Mondragón and pull back to Santa Fe. Having won the showdown and turned back Kyril and the state forces of economic oppression, Joe, the villagers, and now Bernabé Montoya return to celebrating.

The scene follows the logic of the final scene in *Salt of the Earth*, where dozens of miners and their families mass to prevent the local sheriff from serving an eviction notice on one of the union families. In both films, community members celebrate a momentary, symbolic victory over oppressive social forces. In *Milagro*, the village celebration takes on the trappings of New Mexican *fandango*, a community dance animated by troubadour Cipriano Vigil and former New Mexico Lt. Governor Roberto Mondragón. As folks at the bean field twirl and swing to a set of festive and raucous *rancheras*, popular in northern New Mexico communities, it is Charlie Bloom who dampens the mood when Ruby Archuleta gleefully reports:

RUBY: Look at all these signatures.

CHARLIE: Yeah. They're gonna wake up with a hangover tomorrow and come begging and crying to you to take their names off that list.

Ruby understands that the victory is momentary and that it is important in the moment and as it has happened. She responds: "But right now, at this moment. Isn't wonderful?" It is not insignificant that immediately following this, Bernabé Montoya takes the clipboard from Ruby's hand and signs the petition to halt the Devine development. As in *Salt*, the moment is used to supplant apathy and powerlessness, leaving the audience with the hope that unity and solidarity can change even the bleakest situations. The bean field scene is brought to a close with a kind of community singing of "De Colores," a song that became ubiquitous and synonymous with the activism inspired by Cesar Chávez's United Farm Workers movement in California. For a generation of Chicanos, "De Colores" was the anthem of unity and common struggle. Original land grant documents record how Spanish-Mexican *amercedarios* (grantees) took possession of land by doing unexpected things, like pulling up the weeds of a new homestead, firing muskets in the air, and rolling and tossing rocks from one place to another. In this scene, Joe's neighbors and friends take possession of the land again by pulling up the crop of beans and bean stalks, frolicking in the fields, and firing their hunting rifles into the sky.

The Proxemics of Location

The decision to shoot *Milagro* on location in Truchas, New Mexico, created a number of political ripples that were of concern to John Nichols. By the 1980s concerns about how and where *Milagro* would be filmed signaled that more was being made of the politics of representation than of the social politics that had birthed the land grant activism of an earlier generation. The grievances of Mexican Americans in New Mexico were indeed beginning to change. For one thing, northern New Mexico, characterized as "insular and proud" just a decade before, was no longer insular. The antipoverty programs of the 1960s, coupled with the counterculture revolution of the same decade, penetrated the veil of poverty and insularity that Richard Bradford had described in his novel a decade before. This is despite the fact that Reies López Tijerina had become a cause and that John Nichols had romanticized him as the powder keg of revolution at the end of the 1960s. By the 1980s, one was more likely to find some former hippie running town council meetings in Taos or Santa Fe and standing at least as good a chance of being elected to local offices as the sons and daughters of old time *parcientes* or *amercedarios* in those same communities.

There was one minor skirmish in the arena of *realpolitik* early in the filming of *Milagro*, when Tijerina, the "King Tiger," threatened a lawsuit against Universal Pictures for making his life story into a film. Nichols recalls:

> One morning I saw my face, Robert Redford's picture, and Reies Tijerina's handsome mug in *The New Mexican* and the *Albuquerque Journal.* Tijerina was suing *Milagro* for stealing the story of his life. When I read the article's fine print, I saw that Robert Redford, Universal, David Ward, Moctesuma Esparza and a couple of producers were being sued, but not me. A Universal executive was quoted asking, "Why are they suing *us?* They should be suing John Nichols. *He's* the

guy that wrote the book." Hollywood, the most compassionate shark
on earth. (2000b, 145)

Clearly, there *is* more in the novel that, loosely construed, connects the
Milagro story to the Tijerina story. There are moments when Nichols
describes Charlie Bloom's defense of César Pacheco, a local land grant
heir, part-time plumber, and militant activist from one of the surrounding
communities, and where Bloom's speeches (as at the community meeting) elucidate some deep sociological currents that affect the northern
communities. There are also occasions when Bloom lays out the villagers'
grievances against the National Forest Service, the impact of conservancy
districts, tourism, the out-migration of the native population for economic
reasons, and so forth. But, indeed, Tijerina's claim that the *Milagro* film
charted his life or incidents generated by the Alianza is specious and far-
reaching, for all the representations in *Milagro*, as should be clear by this
point, are more caricature than historical.

The list of irritations that came with the filming of *Milagro* reflected
more ordinary and prosaic concerns that fed the local press. As Nichols
recalls, "Every day, if Redford so much as sneezed, The *New Mexican* and
the *Albuquerque Journal* gave it front-page, forty-eight-point headlines"
(2000b, 144). The rejection by Chimayó residents to become the set for
Milagro garnered lots of local press, but, significantly, nothing more happened. Residents in northern communities did not come out and blow up
bridges to keep film crews from filming the sacred corners of their villages.
Residents of the once proud and insular north were now more concerned
about the traffic tie-ups between Santa Fe and Truchas caused by the reckless driving of film crew vehicles and the toxic waste they dumped in Truchas area creeks. It is also telling that the Chicano community as a whole
was not particularly invested in Tijerina's claim that Redford and Universal
Pictures had stolen his story; rather, it was concerned about the politics
of portrayal of Latinos in the film. Thus the political militancy and direct
action tactics of the Chicano movement had by this time changed and the
terrain of contestation by the early 1980s was centered in the arena of cultural representation.

Cultural and political activists did have a legitimate gripe with the
film, since Redford had given over the lead roles to non-Chicanos. Redford

FIG. 12. Miguel Gandert, "¡Qué Milagro! Sundance on the Plaza, 1988." Robert Redford greets fans in Santa Fe. Used by permission of the photographer.

picked Ruben Blades, a Panamanian songwriter and bandleader, to play the role of Bernabé Montoya. Sonia Braga, the Brazilian bombshell who did not speak Spanish or English, was given the role of Ruby Archuleta, and Chick Vennera, an Italian American with bad Spanish pronunciation, was cast as Joe Mondragón. According to Nichols, emotions on this point were further inflamed when Redford shunned Chicano actors Edward James Olmos and Cheech Marin for parts in the film.

Moctesuma Esparza confirms the notion that casting was an area of disagreement he had with Redford:

> I had a big part in the actual manufacturing of the movie, in that I handled the casting. I brought in all the actors. I spent six months videotaping every single Latino actor I could find and I brought all these videotapes to Bob. From those we selected 90 percent of the cast. I knew Carlos Requilme, his work, you know having watched Mexican movies as a young boy, and so, sought him out and Bob again was completely enamored of him. And, the one area where we had a disagreement was in the casting of Joe. (Esparza interview)

Esparza goes on to describe how he urged Redford to cast Cheech Marin to play Mondragón: "There was actually a moment there that lasted three days that Cheech was going to play the role. Redford agreed that he was the guy and Redford then changed his mind and I had the unfortunate duty of telling Cheech that he didn't have a role anymore. Cheech didn't talk to me for quite a few days after that, he was pissed off at me" (Esparza interview).

Moctesuma Esparza takes solace in the idea that many roles in *Milagro* did go to Latinos and Chicanos and, if taken as a barometer of Chicano participation, the final bean field scene does show the high participation of Truchas and northern New Mexican residents. Six hundred and fifty or so of them also showed up at a special benefit showing of *Milagro* in Santa Fe on March 19, 1988 (Nichols 2000b, 148). The participation of the locals in *Milagro* raises another point of comparison with *Salt of the Earth*. In this case, the stakes were not nearly as high as in the case of *Salt*, where miners and their families put their jobs and futures on the line to make the film. In the case of *Milagro*, as in the case of *Red Sky at Morning* before it, Truchas residents and their shining town on the mountainside did "represent" and to this extent they shaped and gave form to what can appropriately be called a decidedly Chicano-themed story.

7

Filming Bernalillo

Post–Civil Rights Chicano Film Subjects

Danny Lyon arrived in New Mexico around the same time John Nichols was making his way to Taos. Like Nichols, Lyon emigrated from New York after having spent ten years working as a staff photographer for the Student Non-Violent Coordinating Committee (SNCC). His time at SNCC involved Lyon in a number of major actions in the civil rights movement in the South. As with other disaffected, college-educated Americans of this period, Lyon's left-leaning cultural and political views kept him involved in emerging social movements. Recalling those years, Lyon writes: "The South rolled out in front of me—highways and cotton fields, shotgun houses with screened porches, and nineteenth-century towns built around small squares. I loved it almost as much as I loved the movement. And the truth is the two were inseparable. Putting aside my history books in the libraries of great universities, I had the rare privilege to see history firsthand" (1999, 24).

Lyon's first trip to New Mexico had a very clear aim. He wanted to learn about some hippie-counterculture residents who had managed to establish a commune in Placitas, New Mexico, folks who were becoming known for their innovative geodesic dome community. Despite his contacts there, Lyon chose to live in Bernalillo, a town lying astride the Rio Grande some six miles down the mountain from Placitas. Lyon's decision would have a deep impact on his creative outlook. His neighbors in Bernalillo were mainly farmers and working-class Hispanos, and he chose to make them the subjects of his films. Bernalillo, the county seat of Sandoval

County, was approximately 92 percent Mexican American: it was largely a Spanish-speaking community that had earned the reputation of being a poor stepchild to Albuquerque, the state's only real urban center at the time. Bernalillo's neighbors were the Keresan-speaking Pueblo Indians from Santa Ana Pueblo on the north and Tiwa-speaking Sandía Pueblo tribal members on the south.

New Mexico's small towns effected a transformation in most counter-culture exiles who wandered through in the late 1960s, and Danny Lyon was no exception. "This place changed my life," he said, and he went on to tell just how different everyday life in Bernalillo was from anything he had experienced elsewhere in the United States: "You know what I liked about this place, the people didn't speak English in the Post Office. Mr. Ortiz was the postman and you'd go in there, routinely, and just like there are today—there'd be older gentlemen chatting away in Spanish. Wow, I thought, I'm not in America. This place gave me a community and it's still there and it's great" (Lyon interview).

Like Herbie Platt, John Nichols's alter ego *in The Milagro Beanfield War*, Lyon also went through a cultural apprenticeship in which he slowly learned the ways of his neighbors. Early on, Ezequiel Domínguez, a long-time resident of Bernalillo, befriended him. This initial contact was not entirely by chance but grew out of the informal network developed by the activist community that was converging on New Mexico in those years. At the time, Domínguez was active in Reies López Tijerina's Alianza Federal de Mercedes. Activists like John Nichols, Betita Martínez (a former editor at HarperCollins who had done civil rights work with Lyon), and others found common cause with the activities of the Alianza's militant land grant members. Even before Lyon hit New Mexico, someone brought up Domínguez, telling Lyon, "If you're out in Bernalillo, go see Ezequiel."

Domínguez initiated Lyon into New Mexico localisms in both cultural and political ways. Even before Lyon was fully settled into his new community, he was asked to get involved in an antidevelopment campaign that was attempting to block the construction of Sun Country Estates, which was intended to be the largest mobile home park in the nation and slated for the outskirts of Bernalillo. Lyon was cajoled into writing a position statement for the antigrowth people and was soon immersed in the collective action that required him to attend public meetings with the Sandoval

County Commission. With Lyon's help the plan to develop the mobile park was defeated.

At about this same time, he began to detach himself from his work as a documentary photographer and began to pursue a newfound interest in filmmaking. He still continued to involve himself in book projects and museum shows featuring his still photography. He recalls "going forth, photography would step aside and the next ten or fifteen years I devoted to film in Bernalillo."

Over the next twenty-five years, Lyon would produce a set of evocative films that recorded the comings and goings of his Bernalillo neighbors. The films, *Llanito* (1972), *Little Boy* (1978), *Willie* (1983), and *Murderers* (2002), are, to one measure or another, interdependent filmic documents of the same town.

"Like Bugs under a Microscope"

Lyon's decision to shoot *Llanito* was not a deeply studied aesthetic turn. Rather, it appears to have been prompted by a much more elemental consideration: Lyon's emotional and psychic need to understand his adopted town and his new neighbors. By Lyon's own admission, *Llanito* is not his most polished work: "It's funny, but we're talking about my second film. I've made a dozen films but this is one of the simplest, the crudest, and we usually don't talk about it" (Lyon interview). What seemed at first glance a relatively straightforward aim would become a protracted search, given the complicated ethnic, religious, and historical makeup of the region and the vexing cultural, sociological, and political realities of Bernalillo.

As a first film, *Llanito*'s virtues are also its weaknesses. Lyon admits the film was raw and crude and does not mask the fact that he was experimenting a good deal with film as a new medium. Writing in 1997, Jan-Christopher Horak adduces that Lyon's lack of polish saved his work from a worse fate: "Lyon's amateur film aesthetic consciously removes him from the polished forms of traditional documentaries, which maintains a pretense of objectivity through their narrative construction, even while making their ideological agendas invisible" (197).

Llanito, for reasons I will soon go into, gives the impression that one day Lyon simply took up his camera, walked out of his house in north

Bernalillo, and quixotically began to film the barrio and his immediate neighbors as they moved about in their homes or tended to their fields. Horak observes, "He began *Llanito* by filming his neighbors with a 16mm camera and soon discovered a world apart: Spanish speaking, and therefore cut off from the English-speaking middle class, mainstream, struggling, poor, but proud" (200).

Giving Bernalillo a Foundational Narrative

The fifty-four-minute movie, shot in black and white, presents twelve extended sequences sandwiched between an opening and a closing segment. Lyon formally introduces audiences to Bernalillo with wide-angle footage of the Rio Grande valley shot from atop the mesa above San Felipe Pueblo. The film begins with the camera following a hawk as the bird circles above a line of *alamogordos*, the ubiquitous native cottonwoods that forest both banks of the Río Grande. The camera tracks the black bird and pans across the desert until it takes in a full view of the village of Bernalillo.

Viewers learn that Ramón Luján, a next-door neighbor, trusted guide, and mentor to Lyon, is standing next to him as he films. Lyon recalls being drawn to Luján, a man who had spent a good part of his adulthood working as a shepherd in western New Mexico. Curtis Marez has called this pattern of employment "livestock sharecropping." While working on lands owned by large ranching concerns, Luján would have amassed a great deal of practical knowledge about the land and animal husbandry, but his lot would not have been easy, nor would his employment have done much to ease his poverty.[1] Despite differences in class and education, Lyon was drawn to Luján. There was something in him that reminded Lyon of his own father, a German immigrant and medical doctor back in New York. But on this day Ramón Luján is present to narrate his own very personal and unscripted version of the founding of Bernalillo, a town that had long billed itself as the "City of Coronado." Luján starts his story in a brocaded English as he describes Francisco Vásquez de Coronado's 1540 *entrada* into the upper Rio Grande valley. "Coronado is Spanish, really, really Spanish," he insists and then, off-camera, he continues:

> He comes from Spain and he bring the soldiers and comes up here
> to fight with the Indians—it's just Indians over here, just Indians.

And they put fire around the Pueblo and they start to burn, to burn
that Pueblo, the Indians go out, the chiefs go out and they told Coronado, "Please don't kill the Indians." Well, and Coronado he say, "I
don't kill these Indians for my soldiers . . . they need some, they
need some, some pussy," you know, and the Indians say "All right"
and "You have to bring single girls for each soldier," and the chief
say "All right." That's what they call the blood, you know, the Spanish and the Indians, and that's what belongs here, the Spanish and
the Indian. (*Llanito*, 1972)

As Ramón Luján concludes his story the camera follows the glint of the five
o'clock Atchison, Topeka, and Santa Fe Super Chief speeding south toward
Albuquerque. The shot from high atop the mesa renders the glint of the
train moving down a straightaway as a thin lance, a directional arrow, pointing toward the town that will be the focus of the remainder of the film.

Llanito's sepia footage is exuberant even with its rushed pans of the
landscape, its episodic structure, and Lyon's absolute refusal to edit out
the grit of Bernalillo's underclass. All these make *Llanito* a magnificent
example of "observational cinema" (MacDougall 1995). While Lyon rejects
the idea that he was making ethnographic films, his process follows Mac-
Dougall's call for working with "an uncritical faith in the camera's power
to capture, not the images of events, but the events themselves" (1995,
123). Whether Lyon was cognizant of it or not, at a basic level, he was
engaged in some form of research filming. Indeed, his films function as
a tool of inquiry, following a method cultural anthropologists have vari-
ously labeled "direct cinema," "research filming," "observational cinema,"
or simply "the filming of naturally occurring phenomena" (Sorenson and
Jablonko 1995). Most of Lyon's films, and certainly *Llanito*, do not employ
voiceover narration, and they are devoid of the formal elements found in
the documentary as a genre. The only speech in the film comes from the
subjects speaking for themselves, as is the case with Ramón Luján's foundational narrative.

The sequences following Lyon and Luján's mesa-top exposé are the
derivatives of what Sorenson and Jablonko call "opportunistic sampling,"
a procedure that involves "a photographer filming opportunistically[;] he
flows with the events of the day and cues them at some personal level,

suddenly noticing that 'something' is about to happen and following such events intuitively, without a worked-out plan" (1995, 149). Colin Young acknowledges the close relationship of observational cinema to cinéma vérité and concedes that some degree of opportunism marks any film sampling. Young stresses the idea that "in observational cinema the camera is not used randomly but in fact the opposite—very purposefully and self-consciously" (1995, 108).

In MacDougall's opinion, observational cinema trades on the fallacy of producing omniscient observation, whereby the unavoidable outtake or what viewers ultimately don't see is masked by the power of the medium to "create a world" through the use of a few direct and unfiltered images. In all his films, Lyon is able project a fullness of representation by assigning the role of observer and witness to the audience inasmuch as Lyon's camera is able to document and thus preserve events long past. Here is a quality that makes each screening a (re)witnessing of occurrences that have long faded from individual memory.

In this way *Llanito* provides me with a number of third-eye experiences. The first of these comes in the segments of *Llanito* that were filmed on January 5 and 6, 1971. I know the exact dates of the filming because these days were part of a singular, regional weather event in New Mexico—one of the hardest cold spells to hit the Borderlands in modern times. It was so singular, in fact, as to fix it on meteorological charts as the coldest recorded temperatures in the upper Rio Grande Valley. Seeing scenes of Bernalillo covered in snow and hearing local radio reports of plummeting temperatures (40 degrees below zero, for example, in nearby Cuba, New Mexico) stirred a memory in me that I had long forgotten. I was a high school senior on Christmas break when those three bone-chilling days hit north-central New Mexico and virtually shut down Albuquerque. In Albuquerque, temperatures dropped to −13 degrees at night, making it cold enough for frost to build up on the inside walls of some of our neighbors' houses and causing the oil in the crankshafts of cars to turn to lumpy globs. The first cars to give out were those with car batteries supplied by Ace Auto, the local auto parts store serving the barrio. The store's motto was "Bueno, barato y bonito" (good quality, cheap, and pretty). My "third eye" experience of *Llanito* transported me back to days spent jumpstarting and push-starting our neighbors' cars and installing a light bulb in the crawlspace of our frame house to keep our family dog from freezing to death. Screening *Llanito*, I was transfixed by the scenes of Bernalillo covered in snow at the base of the Sandia Mountains, not because they verified my own adolescent years, but because they feature people not unlike myself going through life in a Chicano manner and causing me to ruminate on how most of us in New Mexico coped with the twin whammies of constant poverty and tundra-like weather—"bueno, barato y bonito," indeed.

Los traviesos

Bernalillo became Lyon's Montmartre, a place to work from, and though it was devoid of fellow travelers, Lyon contends, "The focus of everything that matters in America happens in this little obscure town that no one cares about" (Lyon interview). His "opportunistic sampling" begins when, with camera in hand, Lyon accompanies a group of five or six pre-adolescent Chicano boys as they fool around on the train tracks and climb up a dirt embankment leading up to the town cemetery. No standard documentary cues provide viewers with a context for understanding the worth of this mundane action. Viewers must watch and listen carefully to determine who these kids are and what they are up to.

Traditional Chicano culture makes subtle distinctions in marking changes in the formation, development, and behavior of young people as they grow. In Bernalillo in 1970 and still today among those who recall these cultural measures, the schema goes like this: young people in general occupy the category of *la plebe* (literally plebeians); the youngest of them are most often referred to as *la plebecita*. Moderately unruly children, those whose natural curiosity and disposition to explore their surroundings, often without adult supervision and with the propensity to get themselves in fixes of one sort or another, are given the moniker *los traviesos*. By and large this group is populated by pre-adolescent boys, although young girls can be equally *traviesas*. Teenagers, especially those who begin to deviate widely from expected norms of comportment and exhibit the inclination to engage in behavior that can cause lasting harm to themselves or others (heavy drinking, drug use, insubordination, fighting, altercations, theft, petty crimes, etc.), are labeled *atroces* or, sometimes, *plebe atroz*. The onus at this stage is on the bifurcation of choice and decision making that *atroces* come up against. The uncertainty of what will happen to them frequently provides the torque in the conversation of *la gente madura*, the adults and elders who ponder how these unruly young people will modify and regulate their risky behavior and take up adult responsibilities and decorum. Will they refrain from doing harm to themselves or others? Will they embrace *respeto* as a community norm and conform to the expectation of the esteemed seniors in the community? The alternative is to continue in a pattern of incorrigible actions that are the cause of pain and consternation. Concern is expressed over young people who in the best of cases will become an economic burden and in the worst will fall deeper into habitual destructive or even criminal behavior. The tags for chronic delinquents often proliferate and none are positive. They are alternatively referred to as *sin vergüenzas, léperos, locos*, or *malvados*.

Unwittingly, without the benefit of knowing this typology, Lyon's Bernalillo films provide a window on each of these three stages of Chicano youth development. In addition, Lyon quite unintentionally tracks some Bernalillo and Santa Ana residents who belong in the *gente madura* category, people like Ramón Luján in Bernalillo and Sophie Sánchez at Santa Ana Pueblo. These people represent some of the community's reputable adults, men and women who have experienced the vicissitudes of youth and have adjusted into fairly stable patterns of living. Many credit their religious upbringing for ushering them into responsible adulthood. Naturally, *la gente madura* make it their business to pass these values on comportment to younger people, and when given the chance they will advise and reprimand the errant behavior of juniors.

As *Llanito* begins, Lyon places his viewers in the predicament of figuring out what some Bernalillo traviesos are up to. Lyon, camera in hand, follows them to see what they find so interesting about Our Lady of Sorrows Cemetery. As the kids amble around the graves, they code-switch from Spanish to English among themselves. Although uncharacteristic of most American twelve-year-olds, though not surprising in Chicanos of this generation, they speak openly about their dead *vecinos* or neighbors. Willie Jaramillo, who will reappear in later Lyon films, is the most verbal and talkative. It's Willie who explains things, points out to his buddies (Lyon too) that "this part is only babies," and reads off a recent gravestone "Beloved son"; then, as if he were visualizing the dead man, he continues, "I saw him at the funeral." Lyon will get back to these traviesos by filming them on other days, in other settings and situations, but this sequence is important for understanding the close proxemics Lyon manages to develop with selected people and sites in and around Bernalillo.

A tricultural social arrangement typified life in Bernalillo in the 1970s, a kind of pragmatic pluralism, some of which is still in evidence today. The particular shape of triethic Bernalillo, as Lyon came to know it, included the town's large Hispano-mestizo population concentrated in Bernalillo's core neighborhoods. Dominant in size though only moderately significant in economic power, Hispanos held working-class occupations as ranchers, tradespeople, insurance agents, stockers and clerks in grocery stores, and state, county, and municipal employees. While many Hispanos would have been working-class wage earners, it would have also been the case that some portion of them could be found on some form of public assistance. Native Americans from Sandia Pueblo and Santa Ana Pueblo, the town's adjacent neighbors, would be residing in their ancestral villages and tending to their own agricultural lands. Indians were set apart socially and culturally and represented a transitory population who visited Bernalillo on their own timetable—to buy goods, to deal with county governmental agencies, to sell their produce and wares, and occasionally to mingle socially with Chicanos. The third community forming the social contours of the valley are Anglos or people routinely referred to as Anglos by Indians and Hispanos. Lyon himself, while Jewish, would not have seen himself as Anglo and yet, ironically, would have been seen as a WASP by his neighbors unaccustomed to having whites as neighbors in their town. Anglos were a decided minority in Bernalillo and only a small percentage of Anglo families actually chose to live in the town, although they may have owned businesses or held prestige jobs in the professions or as government bureaucrats.

Lyon introduces us to some Anglo residents of Bernalillo in *Llanito*, although not to the powerbrokers or decision makers constituting this socially, politically, and economically dominant group. In the sequence following *los traviesos*, Lyon is aboard the Sandia Peak Tram on a day trip with a group of patients and their caretakers from Saint Joseph's Manor, a home for mentally challenged children and adults. Here is another instance where, as MacDougall reminds us, the camera places the audience "in the role of witnesses to events." The patients are oblivious to the camera, behaving as though the filmmaker is not present. MacDougall theorizes that this is the standard effect that comes from a filmmaker having spent enough time with subjects to put them at ease such that they move to a point where they lose interest in the camera. In fact, MacDougall believes that these moments produce a more natural course of behavior than might be had in the presence of an ordinary observer. He explains, "A man with a camera has an obvious job to do. His subjects understand this and leave him to it. He remains occupied, half-hidden behind his machine, satisfied to be left alone" (1995, 119).

As the tram travels up the east face of the Sandia Mountains, passengers listen to an informational recording that describes the ascent of what is billed as the second longest aerial tram ride in North America, with clear spans between cable towers that are more than a mile long. It is a spectacular ride. The camera tracks the shadow of the tramcar zooming over the rugged landscape below. The voice of a tour guide informs us that we are on a "vertical ascent of 4,000 feet, from 6,000 at the base of the ride to 10,400" at ride's end on Sandia Crest. Passengers are informed that the Rio Grande valley below, that is, Bernalillo and adjacent areas, has been inhabited for 20,000 years. The narration caters to tourists seeking to experience the natural and cultural adventure of the Southwest, all this sightseeing enhanced by the equally wondrous technological marvel of the aerial tram ride itself. Tourists and travelers are encouraged to feel good about this unique encounter with the region's natural beauty and its ancient and advanced civilizations. Yet, by juxtaposition, Lyon takes issue with the logic of an ever-advancing, ever-improving progression of history. Lyon, in fact, thumbs his nose at this very idea by showcasing the residents of Saint Joseph's Manor—a group of discarded or warehoused human beings whose very presence inserts a troubling counter-experience to the notion of progress in modern America.

Llanito strategically cuts away from the tram ride and places viewers in front of several Pueblo Indian men who have gathered outside an adobe house to perform some Keresan dances. And while their songs are powerful, these men are not participating in traditional, that is, structured and tribally prescribed ritual. They are an informal group gathering and socializing with beer and wine. The footage is difficult to watch: viewers are introduced to a moment of bruised nostalgia for traditional ceremony as these men enact the lost balance of tribal dance and song. *Llanito* does not provide further visual or narrative explanations for what this scene signifies; however, Jan-Christopher Horak sees the scene as providing a powerful visual counterpoint to the naturalized sense of "white, middle-class America" as being the only subject worthy of film's gaze. Speaking of the scene in which Native American song and dance is performed, Horak concludes, "More important, though, is the sense of unity and strength that these narratives provide. Indeed, their history has survived in oral traditions, despite official neglect, because it has functioned and been used by its narrators as an oppositional force" (1997, 201).

The film moves through a rapid succession of crosscuts among the various groups Lyon has previously introduced in the film. Each sequence is best described as a day spent with various Bernalillo residents. Thus one day includes the scene of a group of school girls and boys (*los traviesos* among them) out on the yard of their elementary school right behind Saint Joseph's Manor—the camera itself has caught their attention and the kids act out, pressing up on a wire fence, pushing and shoving to get in on the filming. Across the fence some of the Saint Joseph Manor residents are engulfed by the schoolchildren who press in around them. On another day, Lyon takes us inside a bar room full of Mexicans, Indians, and Anglos drinking and shooting pool at Bernalillo's famous Silva's Cantina.

The scenes in the second half of *Llanito* become fuller samplings of Bernalillo folk, a quality enhanced through an intensification of the camera's "invisibility and omniscience" that, as MacDougall reminds us, reaches the point where "the self-effacement of the filmmaker begins to efface the limitations of his physicality" (1995, 120). A testament to Lyon's capacity to go unnoticed, to render himself nearly invisible in the second half of *Llanito*, is the intensity of the personal disclosure that comes forth from the subjects as they go about their everyday lives.

Several encounters in *Llanito* demonstrate the propensity of film subjects to talk unabashedly and in situations that occur in private and personal arenas of church and home: exactly those areas of experience often closed off from the exterior social world. One such encounter involves Joe Hagerty, a young man in his mid-twenties and a resident of Saint Joseph's Manor. Inside his living quarters Lyon films a staged but deeply intense and psychologically rich encounter with Joe as he performs an impromptu, outwardly parodic, mock sermon on the Passion of Christ. The scene is jarring in several ways. The first is the near invisibility of the camera in a room set up as a makeshift church, where a dresser filled with statues of saints and a crucifix serves as an altar. Joe has invited, perhaps enlisted, some patients in the institution to play the part of his dutiful congregants. Joe begins to preach. He emotes in a disquieting falsetto that pierces out a series of impromptu invocations. He begins, "Good day everybody, this is the day that the Lord has made. Let's be glad and rejoice in it." The scene is a *One Flew over the Cuckoo's Nest* kind of moment. Here Joe urges the inmates not to run amok but to mimic the local priest, complete with gestures and liturgical formulas, which he delivers in a series of non-sequiturs. Gesturing and thumbing the beads of a rosary, the young man intones:

> This is the cross of Jesus. He was nailed to a cross and died for our sins.
> What is sin? Sin is when we do some wrong.
> God made some nice things: he made the clouds, the sun, the stars and the moon. He created things out of nothing, just like that.
> He was born on Christmas day, died on Good Friday and rose on Easter Sunday. They cursed him, called him names: "Crucify him, crucify him."
> How would you like to be nailed to a cross?
> Praise the Lord, don't be scared of noth'ng. (*Llanito*, 1972)

Lyon's emphasis on the everyday comings and goings of his Bernalillo neighbors no doubt accounts for the fact that his films contain none of the better-known forms and occasions of the nuevomexicano vernacular ritual cycle: matachines, pastores, Holy Week ceremonies, the very things, as I have shown in earlier chapters, that moved earlier generations of film-makers to make movies about Borderlands subjects. Joe Hagerty's sermon is the closest Lyon comes to making a connection with the area's popular religiosity. Although highly filtered and disjointed, Hagerty's speech brims with the gestalt of Christ's Passion and is infused with the ritual of Catholic liturgy, a testament to its presence even among the most marginal of Bernalillo residents. More surprising yet is Lyon's blank-slate viewpoint in the face of what Joe Hagerty mimics. Recalling it, Lyon explains, "It's an amazing scene. First of all, I'm Jewish, I don't spend much time in churches and the story of the passion of Christ is not one I had heard often. But, I knew Joe was an amazing guy and he told me that he wanted to be a priest and I knew he lived in this little room. It was his idea and he wanted to do it. The only instruction I gave him was that I was going to come in the room and he would start" (Lyon interview). We cannot, of course, know whether this kind of indeterminacy actually caused Lyon to be more unobtrusive, more discreet, and more invisible in this particular encounter.

The Deer Hunter: *Santa Ana Style*

When I asked Lyon about his contact with Alamo Zucal Sanchez, a Santa Ana Pueblo man, Lyon shrugged it off, attributing it to his proclivity to poke around the community, behavior that in retrospect was only possible thirty-plus years ago when the film was made. A bemused Lyon recalls, "You know, of all the scenes I shot in *Llanito* I got thrown out of. . . . In other words, you get some rights and you push further, further, and further and eventually some one says, 'Hey what's that guy doing in our house?' And so, one day I showed up at Andrew and John Sanchez's house and there was a sign someone wrote saying, 'Hippie stay out!'"

The sequence that led to Lyon being barred from the Sanchez house begins inside Silva's Bar in the center of Bernalillo in a scene were Alamo is playing pool and carrying on with a group of mostly Hispanic patrons. The scene itself is an unfiltered look at the ambience of a working-class cantina, complete with Antonio Aguilar *corridos* blaring from the jukebox and customers screeching out *gritos* in the segues to the songs. At some point the camera follows Alamo outside, where he begins to hitch a ride to the Pueblo. The scene cuts away to Alamo standing in front of a deer head mounted on the wall inside the family home on the Pueblo. He alternately holds up a bow and arrow and a .22 rifle as he code-switches between English and Keresan and rambles through the exploits of his being an able and sure hunter:

> I was in New Zealand, New Guinea. Who was the one who was going
> to beat the war? We won the game, the Philippines . . . all the way.
> I'm the man that put the . . . what you call it? . . . the gun to them. I'm
> brave enough to show . . . this American Indian. That's why nobody

shot me. I won't even say anything about it. I am proud of my own country . . . trucker and everything . . . that's all I've got to say. (*Llanito*, 1972)

Alamo's speech shifts when Sophie, his mother, comes in and finds Alamo instructing a nephew on how to be a good hunter. Sophie Sanchez, a woman in her seventies and the person who directs the affairs of this household, is clearly upset with the shenanigans she sees going on. She begins to chastise Alamo: "He tells everybody . . . he even tells his friends . . . but he don't tell anybody that he has been drinking and I have to support him too." The conversation goes to matters of a personal, familial, and kinship nature. We learn that Sophie has not been happy with her son's conduct since his return from service. She especially abhors his drinking. Alamo counters that she sold his cattle while he was gone and that she favors Bob, his brother. Sophie says Bob is responsible and trustworthy: "He goes after the wood and does things around here, but you don't even help your brother when he goes to Llanito to sell beans and chili, but you don't even hoe or irrigate." To deflect the berating, Alamo pipes up, "When I was a deer hunter . . . ," only to have Sophie break in, "Ah, you never did even go hunting deer. He never did hunt nothing. Why do you have to tell lies to your friends?" Then mimicking him, "'Look how much I did,' but he never did went out, never" (*Llanito*, 1972). Alamo relinquishes the point, walks away, and lies down on a bed where he continues to talk, though now only to himself and to Lyon's camera. The scene closes with Alamo exhibiting symptoms that can only be described as those experienced by post-traumatic stress victims. His speech trails off. "How many soldiers did you kill in Viet Nam . . . in New Zealand? After that I was in Japan. When I was in Japan, I was a buck sergeant. When I came back I was a PFC. . . . When I got discharged . . . I made buck sergeant" (*Llanito*, 1972).

The scene has unintended effects. For one thing, it contains the point in the film where Mrs. Sanchez pulls the wrap off the hidden camera with the filmmaker present in her home. Though elderly, Mrs. Sanchez has not yet melted into an unawareness of the filming, nor is she about to relinquish authority in her home to a wayward son and an unannounced visitor-friend. The intrusion, it appears, exacerbates the situation above the daily struggles of battling with her son's drinking. It is the unannounced presence of the filming that bothers Mrs. Sanchez the most and thus she questions, "Why do you have to tell lies to your friends?"—a not-too-veiled reference to Danny Lyon filming Alamo. The sensitive nature of this footage no doubt explains the "Hippie stay out" sign that Lyon found on a subsequent visit to the Sanchez home.

There are other moments in which, to borrow a term from Edward T. Hall, "the proxemics" between subjects and filmmaker draw up tight and then rupture and tear the narratology of *Llanito*. For Hall, "proxemics" in research filming is about "how people regulate themselves in space and how they move through space" (qtd. in Collier 1995). In many instances this shifting, as happens in the scene at the Sanchez home, ruptures the compact established by subjects and filmmaker, and the artifice of the filming becomes visible for a brief time. We see this again when Willie Jaramillo, one of the traviesos, goes over to the filmmaker's house to hang out. Lyon films Willie as he walks across the snow-filled fields and makes his way up the path to the filmmaker's house. It is one of those bitter cold days in January 1971. Willie is clad in tennis shoes, jeans, a short-sleeve shirt, and some workman's gloves, yet he appears unaffected by the cold. Once inside, Lyon films the boy as he watches *Dark Shadows*, a favorite "new format" soap opera that was popular in the early 1970s. Lyon's tendency to cut away to melodramas and top-forty radio is especially contrapunctual here. Horak notes, "In *Llanito* Willie talks about the dead he has known, while *Dark Shadows* can be seen on a portable television, juxtaposing the real horror of his life with the media's fake horror" (203). Willie is absorbed in watching the program, but he gets up occasionally to warm himself by the wood stove. His disclosure strikes us as out of character for a boy of twelve or thirteen and it is heartbreaking to hear him talk about the dark shadows in his own life. He says, "I already took nine weeks of drug education. . . . If you take some of those drugs you can't get rid of them, you have to take them all the time." Willie pauses and goes on. "My cousin died of a heroin overdose . . . Jilks, his name was." Lyon asks, "How old was he?" Willie continues, "About twenty-eight. First his brother died, Neal, and then him, two weeks later. And then my grandma. She had sugar diabetes for thirty-five years. He was going to go take a shot of heroin in Albuquerque, him and Alex and they shot him, killed him."

Suddenly Willie turns away from speaking about the recent deaths in his family and changes the subject as he surveys some of Lyon's still photographs hanging on a wall. "Do they pay you for doing that?" Willie asks. "They said that you might be just a spy or something and tell, you know, report, how they live and all that . . ." (*Llanito*, 1972). Willie's question is prompted by his travieso curiosity, and it marks the place in the proxemics of *Llanito* that rips apart the veil of film as artifice. The obliqueness of observational cinema is ripped away and real time, real space, and a self-reflexive viewpoint permeate the exchange. While Lyon does not appear on camera, his presence is unmasked through the innocent turn of perspective, a rare moment indeed in which the subject of filming brings into question the purpose of the filmmaking, but also inquires into the right of the filmmaker to work in this community. Twelve years later in the film *Willie*, Jaramillo again reminds Lyon of the difference between filming and being filmed as he blurts out, "This is my life we're talking about. My life and I got a life to live" (*Willie*, 1983).

Other samples of life in Bernalillo are interspersed throughout *Llanito*. Lyon recalls, "I filmed three separate groups of people, and the only thing the characters had in common was that they lived within a few miles of each other and occasionally crossed paths" (1999, 70). One day the film follows them going out to the acequias or irrigation ditches where they spend an afternoon spearing fish with a pitchfork. Another day, the camera accompanies them when they stop in at Lovato's Drug Store after school. The younger kids drink Cokes and mix in with a few high school kids as the jukebox blares R & B tunes. A group of fidgeting girls sit together on the opposite side of the soda shop. Another day Lyon is invited to Julio Luján's wedding at Our Lady of Sorrows Parish. There is the opportunity to record the formality of *la gente madura* in the full display of their Catholicism. Joe Hagerty watches as photos of the wedding party are being snapped in front of the church and boldly calls out, "I hope they have a happy death too!" Another time Lyon is with Ramón Luján on a wood-hauling trip up on the mesa.

A powerful moment comes when Ramón visits his brother Elfego's farm in the midst of the January freeze. Elfego is elderly, visibly poor, dressed in tattered, worn out clothes. He is frail. He has lost the use of one arm, but he must still chop and bring in his own firewood to keep the room where he is living warm. Ramón and Lyon have come to take Elfego, but he does not want to leave his ranch to go into town. Ramón speaks only Spanish with his brother but switches to English, acknowledging the presence of the camera and Lyon. He first reports how Elfego's ranchito outside the village was the place where the family raised many different kinds of crops in earlier times. He then tells Lyon that Elfego likely does not want to leave his house for fear a thief will come in and rob him of his possessions. Ramón, at first, takes the tack of counseling his brother to close off the house and stay in the room with a stove and make sure he has enough wood on hand to stoke the fire through the night. Elfego nods in agreement. Then Ramón takes another tack and begins to rib and joke with his older brother, suggesting that maybe his reason for holding out is that he doesn't want to part with his money: "I don't know maybe he has some *dinero* . . . maybe he has some money, I don't know." The segment ends as Ramón manages to convince his brother to go into town. It is evening; the sun and temperature are dropping. Ramón calls out to Lyon to stop his filming, "OK it's time to go. We better go." Ramón assumes his role of *hombre maduro,* advising all present that this mission is complete and all must make it back to better shelter.

In an interview, Lyon recalls how a special premiere screening of *Llanito* was arranged at the University of New Mexico in the mid-1970s. The screening brought together a good-sized audience. Since the film included portions of the Luján-Montoya wedding, he invited members of the two families to attend. The film was not altogether warmly received. Some of the photographers and filmmakers with academic credentials pointed out that *Llanito* was technically amateurish, poorly edited, and included a great deal of unsteady camerawork. But the comment that stuck most with Lyon came from a Chicano professor who chided him for treating the *raza* subjects "like bugs under a microscope." Lyon was disheartened on some level but was not dissuaded and did not give up on his film projects.

Llanito begins and ends with material that underlies the racial, ethnic, and social makeup of Bernalillo. Whether purposeful or not, Lyon's opening and closing scenes deal with the matter of the valley being cohabited by nuevomexicanos and Indians, and thus the film is pregnant with the significance of what this social condition means and how others, particularly outsiders, see it. That said, what I appreciate most about *Llanito* is how it makes visible the culture and society of small-town and rural New Mexico from some thirty years ago. Mine is a third-eye experience of *Llanito* found in the way the film brings back to my mind's eye a similar set of events that I lived through, now distant and blurred in my own memory. Thus, as MacDougall suggests, the images are "a piece of evidence, like a potsherd" and "a reflection of thought" (1995, 122). Like the traviesos in *Llanito*, I too hung out at the ditches as a child growing up in Mora, New Mexico. I recall (can even now insert myself among their number) how we used to press up against the wire fence that bounded our dirt schoolyard, bouncing off the wires like boxers in the ring. More astounding is that when my family relocated to Albuquerque, I spent my summers working at the Good Shepherd Manor in north Albuquerque, a facility run by the Brothers of the Good Shepherd who also administered Saint Joseph's Manor, and I recall the special character of this kind of institution, including the unconventional quirks and personalities of the residents. But there is more: *Llanito* provides a way to renew my understanding of experiences that I personally did not live but that somehow I need to slot into the continuum of a reality that extends beyond the edges of my private, blurry recall of growing up in the upper Rio Grande Valley.

The closing sequence in *Llanito* exemplifies Sorenson and Jablonko's admonition to the research filmmaker to "seize opportunities," a trait that Lyon hones in his first Bernalillo film. It comes as Alamo Zucal Sanchez is walking back toward Santa Ana Pueblo, crossing the road behind Ramón Luján's goat and chicken pens. Alamo is walking fast and nearly bypasses the Luján place. Suddenly Alamo turns his head and sees Danny Lyon, who has just finished filming Ramón castrating some sheep. Alamo turns back in mid-stride and walks over to the Luján farm. We could meaningfully ask: Is Sanchez brought back to see his neighbor of many years, or is he intrigued by Lyon and his camera? Maintaining the gaze of the observational filmmaker, Lyon does not reveal—indeed, he too may be unaware of—why Alamo decides to stop by. Nonetheless, Lyon seizes the opportunity to film the interactions of these two "ancestral neighbors" as they greet one another. The pair engages in friendly handshakes and banter. "Mr. Alamo," Ramón begins and, employing the grammatical embrace of the *nosotros*, the first-person plural Spanish verb form, he asks "¿Cómo estamos, bueno?" (How are we?). A prankster and joker, Ramón then inquires, "How is the ranchito? How are the muchachas [the gals]?" rib-bing Alamo with this innuendo. "Everything is fine," he answers. The two continue in conversation, code-switching from English to Spanish as they talk about sheep, rabbits, goats, and so on. Then Lyon cuts to Ramón and Alamo as they survey Luján's planting in a nearby field. They point to the new sprouts of *rábanos* (radishes) and *alverjón* (green peas in New Mexican Spanish) as the conversation turns to the method of farming itself. Alamo insists that the mexicanos have a different method of irrigation. "Mira," he says, pointing to the furrows, "de los indios así y la gente no siembra asina." "¿Por qué?" asks Ramón. "No más el agua asina." Alamo is attempting to explain the puddle method of irrigation, a customary method employed in Indian gardens. Ramón touts the benefits of acequias and sangrías (lateral ditches to distribute water) and *bordos* (furrows) laid out in straight rows to take up the rivulets. Alamo continues, acknowledging that the mexica-nos *now* have all this apparatus of acequias, bordos, and *melgas* (a Spanish term Alamo brings up, referencing a Spanish colonial unit of measure), and speaking in contrast to the Pueblos' older memory of agriculture on the very lands that in fact may have been lost to the mexicanos. The scene is not exactly about neighborly concern for how the planting is going, since on another level it is a not-too-hidden allusion to land adjustments and losses among Hispanos and Indians, one where old grievances surface among these neighbors of long standing. Spotty though it may be, it is also a rare exchange based on the residual narrative of a world systems encounter that leads back to Ramón Luján's foundational narrative of the 1540 Coronado *entrada*. It is not a small matter that these two neighbors are haggling over the most efficient use of water in an arid environment. Alamo and Ramón leave the field, heading back toward the dirt road to the village. They go on talking about the Indian men who come to sit and drink wine under the nearby trees, men known to both of them. They have let the ancient feud rest for the time being and re-center their conversation on matters in the present. Pointing to the sprouts, Ramón asks, "You know that Manchego? Not Manchego his brother?" Alamo answers, "You mean Tiger, Tony?" *Llanito* ends as it begins, with the sound of a train whistle looming nearby.

Danny Lyon has said that he turned to filmmaking to pursue "pure cinema," principally "to take real people and use them as actors." Today, cinéma vérité of this sort has become commonplace, having been appropriated by Hollywood and commercial cinema in wholesale fashion. Documentary and ethnographic filmmaking yields countless examples of researchers putting ordinary people in front of the camera to act out and narrate their stories. When Lyon began to experiment with the idea of "pure cinema" as he understood it, he was breaking ground, more so as I have said because of his aversion to sanitizing his subjects, something he could have easily done by cutting out the less appealing aspects of their personas, what today would be called politically incorrect language and encounters, from his films.

Plebe Atroz / Vatos Locos: Time as a Trashing Machine

Above all else, Danny Lyon is certain of the documentary purpose of his filmmaking and the ontological reach that such documentation will have in future years: "No matter what I'm doing there's a moment in time that's being preserved, and you know time is relentless. It's just like this trashing machine gobbling up everything" (Lyon interview). Six years after *Llanito*, Lyon would make *Little Boy* (1978), a film that maintains Lyon's fascination with Bernalillo's traviesos. Lyon's next film, *Willie* (1983), would eventually fill out the portrait of Willie Jaramillo. On one of Lyon's return trips to Bernalillo, he and his wife, Nancy, caught sight of a group of young men and women hanging out near a gas station. Lyon recognized Willie Jaramillo as part of the group and quickly got in touch with him.

Lyon would reconnect and focus his next film on Willie and his circle of friends. In following this strand of Bernalillo residents, Lyon's attention would be directed away from other groups of people he had filmed earlier. Most noticeably absent are Bernalillo's *gente madura*. But in this way, *Willie* establishes a space of intra-generational interaction, becoming in effect a longitudinal film study of *los traviesos*. The kids who first appeared in *Llanito* have aged and the group has both lost and added members. The harmless antics of childhood have given way to the consistency of the rough life, *la vida dura*, and the traviesos have become a band of street-living, *plebe atroz*. Draw the terminology out of its rural connotations and these traviesos are now best described by the grittier, more ominous designation of being an urban pack of *vatos locos,* young men often associated with a gang and distinguished by their dress and appearance.

Filmed in color and with a storyboard that tightly centers on Willie, the film also changes the proxemics between filmmaker and subject. In *Willie*, Lyon is in continual dialogue and exchange with his subjects. *Willie* marks Lyon's full embrace of "participatory cinema" (MacDougall 1995) as a method. Lyon is everywhere in the film asking questions and probing the details of the interactions among this group of at-risk barrio youth. One critic uncomfortable with the process noted, "Lyon's work displays an utter disregard for the presumed adulteration of filmmaker intervention. Lyon as a shaping presence can never be forgotten; he frequently carries on full blown conversations from behind the camera" (Revon, qtd. in Horak 1997). In one scene, Lyon is visiting Willie Jaramillo at the county lockup and Willie turns to his cellmates and introduces him as if they were at a party: "This is my friend Danny from New York."

When Willie reencounters Lyon, he and his friends are coming off the loss of a close associate. A week or two earlier, twenty-one-year-old Johnnie Sanchez, a young man with a job and some aspirations to settle down, had been killed in a car accident. Johnnie's story runs like a dark ballad through the film. His close friends retell the fateful hours before Johnnie's death, how he was knifed at a party and then chased down the highway until he lost control of his car, crashed, and was killed. Lyon's clips now become time capsules, (re)screenings of a life cut short. Earlier footage of Johnnie in good times effects a powerful resurrection of the young man. Johnnie is placed before the viewers, they witness him and find that he was likeable, and they mentally measure the waste that results from losing him to la vida dura.

Willie's group now includes younger brothers David, Fernie, and Randy and a Spartan nephew, Jamie, who is active in a local boxing club and aspires to be an athlete. The younger kids are still wet-behind-the-ears traviesos, but the influence of the older boys is accelerating them toward the harrowing and seductive pull of street life. The film begins in summer. Lyon follows the vatos as they load themselves onto the back of an old pickup truck and head out to the irrigation canals to swim and pass the time. The scene gives viewers the chance to consider how even older veterans of the hard life revel in these carefree afternoons that remind them of childhood. Beer flows freely: the camera pans Budweiser cans held tight-fisted in the hands of the young men or chugged empty and strewn on the ground. It's the younger kids, Fernie, Randy, and Jamie, who do the most to update Lyon about Willie in recent times. They say he is often argumenta-tive, he rambles, and he presses forward with harangues as if no one else were present. They recall Willie's frequent absences from town and his long stints in the county jail. Younger brother Randy confides that, because Willie has been locked up in the penitentiary for five years, from when Randy was twelve years old, he is really only getting to know Willie now.

In another scene, the county sheriff, Gennaro Ferrara, goes over Wil-lie's record while Lyon films. Willie's defiant behavior with local county officers is legend. His record lists repeated acts of disorderly conduct, resisting arrest, assault on a police officer, and aggravated battery. We learn that Willie's troubles are nearly always local and his rifts have been with town cops or neighbors. He has been especially quarrelsome with Mexican nationals who he calls mojados.

Lyon includes lots of footage of Jaramillo serving time in county and state lockups. Lyon talks to Willie through the bars of jail cells and films him singing hymns with a group of Christian missionaries who hold prayer services for the inmates. In the course of the filming, Jaramillo is sent to the state penitentiary in Santa Fe. Before leaving Bernalillo, Willie senses that Santa Fe is going to be his next stint. The reason for his sudden trans-fer is never fully explained by police, by Jaramillo, or by Lyon. As the day of transfer nears, Willie becomes increasingly paranoid. He becomes con-vinced that once he's in Santa Fe his enemies, "cowards, homosexuals, bisexuals," as he calls them, will find a way to kill him. His fear of returning to Santa Fe is warranted. Lyon notes,

> While fighting to protect his brother David, Willie broke a police-man's right leg with a two-by-four, for which they sent him to the penitentiary. That was where they started to give him Thorazine. He was in prison for years, unfortunately including the year the con-victs took over the penitentiary at Santa Fe and murdered over forty inmates. It was one of the worst prison uprisings in United States history, with inmates burning other inmates alive in their cells. Wil-lie was right in the middle of it. He survived by hiding. (1999, 96)

Lyon catches up to Willie while he is held at the Sandoval County Jail and later at the New Mexico State Penitentiary in Santa Fe, and he inter-sperses these moments with footage of Willie from *Llanito.* In Santa Fe,

Jaramillo is sullen and withdrawn. He tells Lyon he wants to get out of there, that he can't take it. For Lyon the Santa Fe visits become more than a reencounter with Willie: while walking on the cellblock he encounters other inmates who hail from Bernalillo. One young man whom Lyon knew from the neighborhood tells of getting busted for selling pot and about the mysterious theft of some marijuana plants he was to tend for another friend serving time in jail. Most disturbing is Lyon's unplanned reencounter with Willie's cell neighbor, Michael Guzmán, a twenty-one-year-old convicted murderer.

Even in the depths of lockup in the state penitentiary, a moment to "seize the opportunity" comes to Lyon in the person of Guzmán and Lyon seizes it. The aside becomes an exceptional instance of "opportunistic sampling." Lyon interviews Guzmán, who spends a fair amount of the time rekindling connections. "Did you know Johnnie Sanchez?" Lyon asks. "Yeah, I knew him. I mostly know Willie and his brother Danny, used to hang around with his brothers, 'cause I went to school with Fernie, and I knew Willie when he got in trouble . . . out there. . . . I'm just as old as Fernie, Willie's little brother, I'm twenty-one the youngest one out of us. . . . Yeah, I used to sniff with him at school. I used to sniff with all of them for a while. Willie is good people, it's just that people don't understand him . . . but who's going to be able to understand someone who has been beaten so much?" (*Willie*, 1983). Lyon says, "Well, what I don't understand is that you are here and Willie is next to you and all Willie did was break some windows." Guzmán responds, "That's justice man, that's what they call justice."

Lyon is fully involved in the exchange and interrogates Guzmán, becoming especially pointed on the matter of the murder he committed in 1980: "Well, look at what you did. How can you talk about a beating? You murdered a helpless girl." Guzmán admits that his acts were horrible. He explains that he was high on drugs and booze and that he was just a kid. He tells Lyon that he has no memory, "no picture in my mind," of the attacks. His memory of the ensuing violence was jarred only by the words of the surviving victim when testifying; as she was being stabbed she cried out, "Oh God, let me die in peace!" Guzmán ends the interview by saying that he carries the pain of knowing that he took an innocent person out of this world. At the time Guzmán was the youngest Hispanic ever sentenced to death in New Mexico.

FIG. 13. Danny and Nancy Lyon filming *Willie* inside the New Mexico State Prison, 1985. Used by permission of Danny Lyon, courtesy Magnum Photos, Dektol.wordpress.com.

Willie closes in two ways. In the first ending Lyon films one of the many times Jaramillo is being locked up and returned to the Sandoval County Jail. In Bernalillo, Willie is led into the interior of the facility. A commotion occurs out of sight of the camera. Viewers deduce that Willie has become disorderly and, perhaps, is refusing to enter his cell. Nancy Lyon, who was taking the audio, catches Willie's voice as he shouts, "Danny, help me. They are killing me."

As he has done earlier, Lyon cuts away from these last shots and sounds of Willie and splices vintage footage of *los traviesos* taken on a Fourth of July in the early 1970s. Willie and his friends are lighting M-80 firecrackers, squealing gleefully at their own audacity and generally being traviesos. Willie is happy. His face opens in a wide smile and his body is bouncy with midsummer adrenaline. Standing next to him is an equally carefree Michael Guzmán, age fourteen or fifteen, a mere three years before he would find himself drugged out of his mind in Tijeras Canyon committing one of the most heinous crimes a teenager ever committed in the state. Guzmán is pointing a .22 rifle while other kids stuff firecrackers into the barrel. One travieso lights the charge, the others scatter into the darkness. Michael Guzmán levels the rifle, aims, and waits for the firecracker to explode.

Murderers

The terms traditional nuevomexicano culture reserved for its most incorrigible members, those I listed earlier, are really insufficient when it comes to labeling those who commit the kind of crimes that Michael Guzmán and others of his generation ended up carrying out. It is as if the customary typology of a rural, agrarian people is unprepared and unable to catch up with the progression of brutal deeds that have been playing themselves out in their communities with ever-greater frequency and intensity at least since the 1970s. Those *sinvergüenzas* (shameless) or *locos* (crazed) of earlier times don't match up with the more contemporary legions of violent offenders that prey on rural and urban communities. Lyon's typology for these offenders is clear, direct, even biblical, and it gives the title to his 2002 film, *Murderers*. It's an easy matter to translate the moniker into Spanish and render it as *Los asesinos*, but it is another matter entirely to find an equivalent in the folk culture of New Mexico's rural past to fit the intensified level of depravity in the referent. It is not that homicides and murderers were unknown in quaint New Mexico, and Guzmán's story of molestation by an older relative puts an end to edenic gestures in the agrarian setting I have been describing. On the other hand, it is also true that ferocious, violent crime was not common and so did not engender a behavioral profile or commonplace term in the typology of deviance.

Lyon came to learn that Willie Jaramillo died in the years just before making *Murderers*. Lyon writes, "In 1992 Willie was locked up, this time in the new Sandoval County jail they had built out by the dairy. He told his jailers he was ill. He had a fever. No one did anything for him. Ten days after Willie first complained they decided to take him to a hospital. He died the same day. Willie was buried in the graveyard in Bernalillo, by the interstate beneath Sandia Peak" (1999, 96). For all his faults and his late diagnosis as a bipolar, manic-depressive, Willie died an *atroz,* never graduating to more truculent behavior.

Lyon's investment, and our own as viewers, in the end is not misspent; while uncouth and incorrigible, Willie did not cross the line to permanently injure or kill another human being. Lyon paid for Willie's headstone after learning of his death, and he keeps in touch with some of the family members who live in Bernalillo (Lyon interview). A gentle undertow in the film sweeps us toward an understanding of Willie and the problems that beset him. As viewers we pocket these *recuerdos*, these third-eye moments of Willie and of his bare, raw, and painful life. The film gives Jaramillo a few filmic moments to state his case, despite what others may think. Somewhere he summons up the resistance to affirm "I'm truthful." His *a capella* rendition of "The Old Rugged Cross" and "When the Roll Is Called Up Yonder" (hymns he learned from the missionaries), which he sung under the bridge over the Rio Grande, cause us to consider that while his mind is fogged by *pisto* (beer) and other substances, there was in him the glimmer of conscience and hope. But it is the *Llanito* footage of the bright-eyed, wide-smiling brown kid, the *traviesito* he once was, that has the most powerful and lasting effect on the psyche of the viewer.

The Michael Guzmán Story

Murderers is a kind of epilogue to Tim Robbins's 1995 feature film *Dead Man Walking*, a film that tells the story of how a Catholic nun, Sister Helen Prejean, becomes a spriritual advisor to Matthew Poncelet, a death row inmate awaiting execution at the Lousiana State Penintentiary. *Murderers* was filmed at three locations: New York's East River, inside the Tucker Unit of the Arkansas State Prison, and inside New Mexico prisons. Technically and stylistically, the film represents a significant change from Lyon's earlier works. For one thing, it is shot with high-definition digital cameras. Lyon heightens the aesthetic quality of the work by adding various outdoor scenes and shots of the environment (the East River, woodland scenes in Arkansas, and high desert and mesa landscapes in New Mexico). The film also makes use of a rhapsodic music track (from Glenn Gould to Doc Watson to Lightnin' Hopkins), one carefully choreographed to the visual track—a tactical counterpoint to the painful revelations from the death row subjects that populate the film. It is a short film, some thirty minutes in length.

Murderers opens with Lyon interviewing Michael Guzmán, nearly twenty years after he encountered him at the New Mexico State Penitentiary in the early 1980s. Guzmán, clad in prison-issued, pea-green shirt and pants, tells Lyon that he is the first person he has shared his story with and the first to whom he has expressed his remorse. The film segues to two other parcels of stories on the lives of convicted murderers. One segment presents the story of Jesse Ruíz, a Puerto Rican New Yorker convicted of beating his sister's boyfriend to death with a bat. Ruiz is the only subject in the film who is not incarcerated at the time of the filming. A second installment of the film deals with three convicted murderers ("Pinky" Sheridan, "Mojo" Rhoads, and Harold David "Dinker" Cassell) housed at the Tucker Unit of the Arkansas State Prison.

The film extends Lyon's interest in death row inmates, a subject he first took up in his book *Like a Thief's Dream*, published in 2007. *Dream* is a nonfictional account of the life of James Ray Renton, a convicted bank thief charged with the murder of an Arkansas policeman in 1976. "Dinker" Cassell, an associate of Renton, was still on death row when *Murderers* was being filmed. The other two residents of the Tucker Unit featured in the film are cellmates of Cassell. James Ray Renton had died by the time *Murderers* was shot.

My particular interest is with Bernalillo-born Michael Guzmán, whose presence in the film, as I have shown, is linked to Lyon's Bernalillo films. The extended exchange between Lyon and Guzmán is placed midway into *Murderers*. The segment includes footage of Michael Guzmán from *Willie* and *Llanito,* creating an intertextual node between the films. The spliced, nearly split-screen segments of Guzmán at twenty-one and of him nearing his forties is as jarring as it is revelatory. Here again, Lyon's longitudinal viewfinder plows along the ground of linear time to heave up and redistribute assemblages of human drama in new and sometimes confrontational ways. In front of the camera, Guzmán is a changed man, forced to live with himself and to deal with the trauma of the sexual abuse that he experienced in his own childhood. The interview moves forward with Guzmán describing the events leading up to his violent attack on two women he had never met. Lyon edits down the story to some scant details. Guzmán hints at having had a bitter argument with his pregnant girlfriend and with another friend, Debbie. His erratic and threatening behavior unnerved the girls, who feared he was about to harm them. A seething Guzmán reacted by swallowing a large number of pills, drowning them with bottles of beer, and driving madly away. It appears that by the time he reached Tijeras Canyon and happened upon his victims he was totally out of control. He remembers nothing of what ensued some ten miles away save for a snippet of memory of him driving up on a curb, flinging a car door open, and vomiting.

Guzmán goes on to talk about when his parents would take him as a child to visit his grandparents in Jémez. He remembers that while the adults visited, an uncle would take him to an outhouse and sexually violate him. Still affected by the trauma, Guzmán says, "It took having to go to prison to realize what had happened was not my fault." The pattern of Guzmán's childhood mirrors the early life of poet Jimmy Santiago Baca. As teenagers, both men went through a succession of bitter abandonment. The script of their lives runs parallel as they spent their teenage years in and out of foster homes and being bounced around between relatives who couldn't supply them with any kind of security or love.[2] Guzmán recalls the times when he ran away from foster care and headed for his family home in Bernalillo, only to find an empty house there.

In 2010 Lyon received a letter from Guzmán, who by then had served thirty years and was eligible for parole, but instead another thirty-five years were added to his sentence. Lyon was shocked by the new verdict. Viewers of the Bernalillo films can empathize with his outrage, not because Guzmán should not have been locked up for his crimes, but because it is beyond comprehension that we as viewers know more about Michael Guzmán than the very people charged by the institutions of the state to make determinations about his rehabilitation and suitability for reentering society. Michael Guzmán committed the crimes he was charged with. He has been locked up for thirty years, but these too are facts: he is no longer the *vato loco* hopped up on pills and out of control that attacked two women unknown to him. It is important to come back to Lyon's point that "time is a trashing machine." He adds, "No matter what I'm doing there's a moment in time that's being preserved." Beyond preserving moments, Lyon's films also provide information (something Lyon might be apt to see as an infringement on "pure cinema"). The most relevant information here, as is obvious to anyone who has a chance to see *Llanito, Willie,* and *Murderers,* is that the letter-writing Michael Guzmán is not the travieso of his boyhood, nor the *atroz* teenager, not even the depraved murderer he was in 1975.

Traditional nuevomexicano agrarian culture did reserve a name for the damned and unrepentant. Those lost for all time were called *malditos,* still in contradistinction to our own society; the traditional society I speak of did not pass judgment on who was to be damned for all time. Rather, nuevomexicanos lived by the rule that even the most wicked among them could hope for final deliverance in both this life and the next one. There is a moment in *Willie* where Lyon asks Willie Jaramillo to explain a drawing that he has taped to the wall of his cell and which Lyon mistakes for three anonymous gravestones. Willie explains that the three crosses stand for Christ in the middle of the two criminals who were crucified with him on Good Friday. The one disbelieving thief taunts Christ to use his power to take them down from the cross, while the other repents and asks Christ to remember him in his kingdom. It is not surprising to learn that the story of Dysmas, "the good or repentant thief," resonates with inmates and felons. It also had appeal with New Mexican villagers, even while the norms of their pastoral life, as I have said before, made such incorrigibility rare.

Despite that fact that they were unaccustomed to the heinous behavior of the kind Michael Guzmán exhibited one day in 1975, New Mexican villagers knew the word for mercy and understood repentance and remorse. Given the epilogue to Guzmán's story, it appears that our own judicial institutions simply forgo the reassessment and mercy that are part of our Judeo-Christian legal framework. Danny Lyon is much more direct in responding to the absolutism of the penal institution. He writes simply, "We have all been trained to not give a shit about each other, especially the Michael Guzmáns of the world" (Lyon correspondence, February 25, 2010).

Perhaps the most convincing thing about Danny Lyon's viewpoint comes from his resolute belief that his work is about cutting away particular matter from the whole cloth of the existential possibilities open to artists and writers. He has made it his aim to zero in on a subset of subjects. Ultimately this is Lyon's way of "giving a shit" for those seen in our society as peripheral and unimportant. On this point Lyon is philosophical: "Hear me out for a minute. There's a vast world out there, it's infinite, it's so huge that we aren't even like specks of sand in the sea, but you can say, here are ten specks of sand. I'm going to drag them over here and that's where I'm going to make my film, so there's some really critical decisions that narrows down this world to very, very small places. So you say OK it's Willie, it's Mr. Luján." I agree, just as there is no doubt that it is also Michael Guzmán and it is also Bernalillo and paradoxically it is also us as insiders and outsiders and about where the "ten specks of sand" fit in the sea of our institutions and how they are subject to the very times in which we live and the society we preside over.

8

Toward a New Proxemics

Historical, Mythopoetic, and Autoethnographic Works

The commitment to record the group experience of Chicanos from an insider vantage point and in the service of a documentary impulse represents a decided turn in the cinematic representation of Mexican Americans, a move which also makes it appropriate to speak of a number of documentary and independent film projects ushered in by the Chicano movement as filmic autoethnographic works.

Autoethnographic Documentaries and Docu-Dramas

The volume of such films produced in the last thirty years makes it nearly impossible to cover in a single chapter the gamut of self-representational impulses, so I seek to give space to but a small number of projects. Moctezuma Esparza's *The Ballad of Gregorio Cortez* (1982) is based on Américo Paredes's brilliant study of the epic border ballad about a young *vaquero*, Gregorio Cortez, and his run-in with Texas lawmen. Although *Ballad* deals with a historical event on the Texas-Mexico border in 1901, both the ballad and the film are a synecdoche of post-1848 Anglo-mexicano conflict in the Southwest. In this regard, the film's symbolic content reads the same for all Chicanos, a point that allowed Esparza the freedom to film *Ballad* in New Mexico and not in south Texas where it takes place. He made the decision both for symbolic and practical reasons—a major one being that the location reinforces the film's documentary feel:

Because that movie, as you know, *Gregorio Cortez* has this neo-realistic quality to it and you feel like you are there, the way the camera moves, . . . the naturalistic performance of the actors. You know, things are not quite choreographed; they are more staged, if the distinction makes sense to you. People are allowed, put into a set and allowed to play out their roles in a naturalistic way and Bob [Robert Young] covered it, and that's why the movie feels a little bit like a documentary. (Esparza interview)

In 1981 Jack Parson (cinematographer) and Michael Earney (director) produced *Luisa Torres*, a documentary funded by the New Mexico Arts Division and the National Endowment for the Arts. Like its close predecessor, *Agueda Martínez*, the Parson-Earney film follows the life of an elderly woman from northern New Mexico as a means to document a way of life deeply connected to the earth and to the traditions of her forebears. The film, which also had the sponsorship of the Anthropology Film Center based in Santa Fe, is the attempt of a new generation of post-Chicano movement filmmakers to document traditional Hispano/Chicano lifeways. Whereas Esparza's *Agueda Martínez* resounded with social meaning as implied by land tenancy, livelihood, and the economy of self-sufficiency, the Luisa Torres documentary aims to better understand the worldview of an older woman, giving greater attention to documenting the religio-philosophical tenets exposed by a nuevomexicana elder and matriarch.

The documentary becomes an example of autoethnography largely because narrator-translator and participant-observer Gioia Tama spent an extended period of time living next to the Torres family, thus establishing a personal relationship with Doña Luisa well in advance of any filming. In some ways the film is also about Tama and this time of her life. Tama, a native speaker of Spanish but not a native New Mexican, manages to have meaningful and extended conversations with Luisa Torres and her husband, Eduardo, many of which mark the forty-three-minute film. In introducing the subject of the film, Tama is clear about announcing her own part in the making of the documentary:

This is Luisa Torres. I call her mamá. She has been like a mother to me ever since I first came to this valley. We are neighbors now, *veci-nas*. Because I have known mamá and her husband Eduardo now for

many years, I was asked by my friends to help make this film about
her and her life here in Guadalupita.

The bond of friendship between Luisa and Tama has grown deep over
the years and rests on mutual respect. Tama is so deeply identified with the
family that she has been given permission to call Luisa "mamá" and her
husband, Eduardo, "papá." These familiar exchanges and courtesies suggest that the filmmakers have dispensed with the objectifying proxemics
of the kind that is so commonplace in classic ethnographic encounters
between researchers and informants. In doing so they have inverted the
subject-object position in an effort to dismantle the imperializing anthropological gaze so often associated with the ethnographic encounter.

Submitting herself to an apprenticeship in nuevomexicano village life,
Tama participates directly in Luisa's daily activities. She helps with food
preparation, accompanies Luisa into the nearby fields to hunt for medici-
nal plants, and helps care for the animals. Throughout, Luisa is aware that
she is being filmed and that her role is to explicate a set of cultural habits
and mores mostly ignored by mainstream society. A notable directorial
choice was to encourage Luisa to speak directly to the camera. The decision breaks with what Fregoso sees as "the didactive narrative style of documentary that uses the authoritative convention of the voice-over" (1993,
13). In her direct address in Spanish, Luisa Torres, the would-be subject of
the film, becomes its narrator. Here, Luisa explains the origins of the small
strawberry patch that she still tends:

> Voy a decirles a ustedes queridos visitantes . . . cuando mi mamá y
> papá todavía estaban jóvenes. Mi mamá tomó tres matas de fresas
> y las comenzaron a cultivar. Mi papá no tenía buena vista, miraba
> muy poco y iba con mi papá, yo muy chiquita no más a enseñarle
> las plantas que estaban marcadas con una rueda de metal y él les
> pegaba con el pie y sabía que hay estaba la mata.
>
> [My dear visitors, I am going to tell you . . . when my mother and
> father were still young. My mother [went to my grandmother's house
> and] took three strawberry plants and began to cultivate them. My
> father did not have good eyesight. He could only see poorly and I,
> when I was very little, would go with my father just to show him the

plants which mother marked with a metal ring around the plants and he would hit the ring with his foot and know that the plant was there.]

The film follows Luisa Torres as she makes her own cheese, attends to household chores, and shares her knowledge and understanding of the wild and domesticated plants that grow on her farm. Each film segment provides important lessons on self-sufficiency and living in balance and harmony with the earth. The film also includes an extended parenthetical moment when Luisa tells of a pilgrimage she made in 1976 to the Basilica of Our Lady of Guadalupe in Mexico City. Recalling the trip, Luisa fondly recalls the powerful effect that visiting the shrine of Our Lady had on her. Equally vivid is her recollection of the stopover she made in Chihuahua to visit the home and museum of the famous insurrectionist Pancho Villa.

Uncharacteristic of the participant-observer, Tama is permitted to join the family in prayer before and after meals, an action that further substantiates the closeness that Tama is able to establish with Doña Luisa. This direct entrance into the religious life of the Torres family also gives Tama access to the most remarkable aspect of Luisa Torres's worldview. A long segment of the video explains how Doña Luisa has instructed her husband and son, the operators of a small sawmill, to manufacture the coffin in which she wishes to be buried. The coffin, a simple pine box painted with dark brown enamel and embellished with a large rosary, sits in a back room of the house. Luisa Torres explains her reasons for taking the unusual step of making her own funeral arrangements:

> Yo deseo ser sepultada muy humildemente como fueron mis ante-pasados . . . que siempre en la casa se fabricó el ataúd y vecinos y parientes venían con sus serruches y martillos y hacían el ataúd para el que se moría y todos venían a ayudar, unos aforrando y otros ayud-aban en la comida. Vivíamos una vida muy humilde pero muy feliz. Y al mismo tiempo yo pensé, mi famila no es rica, mi famila es pobre, y yo no quiero que tengan una cuenta por años y años, sino que, me parece que es más fácil asina para nosotros que somos pobrecitos.

> [I want to be buried very humbly as were my ancestors. . . . It was always the case that the coffin was made at home and neighbors

and relatives would come with their saws and hammers and make the coffin for the one who was dying and everyone helped out, some lining the coffin and others preparing the food. We lived a very humble, but very happy life. And at the same time I thought, "My family is not rich, my family is poor," and I don't want to leave an expense that they would go on paying year after year, but rather, it seems to me, that this is easier for us who are the poor.]

As with *Agueda Martínez*, this film seeks to deepen our understanding of what living *la vida buena y sana* means in terms of a traditional Mexican American village life.

In 1992 a group of Denver-based filmmakers released an investigative documentary that took "tierra o muerte," words made famous by the Mexican revolutionary leader Emiliano Zapata, for its title. *Tierra o Muerte: Land or Death*, produced by Carolyn Hales, is narrated by Luis Valdez and includes the participation of long-time Chicano filmmaker Hector Galán, best known for his 1996 series *Chicano: The Mexican American Civil Rights Story*. Galán lends his talents to the film as a production advisor, and Hales's credentials in the Chicano documentary field include collaboration with noted Chicano filmmaker Paul Espinosa on the classic film adaptation of Tomás Rivera's novel *And the Earth Did Not Swallow Him*, a docu-drama released in 1996. *Tierra o Muerte* is a long overdue update to the story of land grant activism in northern New Mexico. Coming twenty-seven years after *The Most Hated Man in New Mexico*, the film adds factual detail on persistent grievances still present in the rural north. On one level the documentary aims to give an account of northern New Mexico in the years following Tijerina's courthouse raid. Viewers are informed that following the raid came ten years of federal aid programs designed to curb poverty and ameliorate the persistent under-education and under-employment in rural northern New Mexico. Despite the War on Poverty programs, the land grant question remains a smoldering issue that signals the deep philosophical chasm that divides native land use and tenure from market-driven concerns.

Tierra o Muerte recounts the history of the land grant struggle going back to 1848. In particular the documentary traces the history of the Tierra Amarilla land grant back to the time when 594,000 acres of common lands were confirmed as a private grant to Francisco Martínez in 1860. The matter of the common lands becoming designated as a personal grant caused great turmoil in the history of the grant. Hales covers this history up to the development of community-based initiatives of the 1970s, such as the agricultural cooperative, "la cooperative agrícola," that led to the development of today's Tierra Wools/Ganados del Valle, a livestock cooperative built from a community shareholding base. Using sociological reasoning that *And Now Miguel* patently avoided, *Tierra o Muerte* documents the importance of sheep agriculture by including footage of lambing and lamb-shearing provided by Tierra Wools itself and by including the history of how lambing as an industry in the hands of nuevomexicano villagers was strangled by land policies imposed on the villagers.

The last third of the documentary follows the case of Amador Flores and his claim to 200 acres of land first held by the New Mexico Bureau of Land Management and later slated for private development. Flores and other land activists set up an armed camp on the contested land, flew the U.S. and Mexican flags, and challenged state officials to physically remove them from the parcel. At the same time, they take their claim to court to fight eviction through legal means. The Flores case is representative of all the unresolved issues relating to land tenure in northern New Mexico. A handful of *alianzistas* from the Tijerina movement join this struggle; the most vocal and eloquent among them is Pedro Archuleta, who had been a very young man at the time of the Tijerina uprising. *Tierra o Muerte* is attentive to inserting the now well-documented story of the rise of the Tijerina movement, District Attorney Alfonso Sánchez's plans to quell it, and the dramatic courthouse raid (see chapter 6). Historical photos and news footage, including portions of *The Most Hated Man*, bring the events to life in such a powerful way that Héctor Galán ended up using most of the section in part 1 of his *Chicano* series. In short, *Tierra o Muerte* presents a number of historical and sociological issues that go unaddressed in commercial films like *The Milagro Beanfield War.*

A second, lesser known work on the Tierra Amarilla land grant controversy also appeared in 1992. *Una lucha por mi pueblo* (A Struggle for My People),[1] a twenty-five-minute short by emerging filmmaker Federico Reade, takes a decidedly more subjective approach to documenting the history of land grant fraud and deception. Reade filmed *Una Lucha* alongside the

Denver-based film crew that produced *Tierra o Muerte*, at times assisting and contributing footage to the Hayes-Galán group and at other times moving his own project toward completion. The impasse produced by Amador Flores's claim to land held by the New Mexico Bureau of Land Management was eventually broken in August 1989 when counter-claimant Brazos del Chama Land Development Company arrived at an out-of-court settlement that awarded Flores $117,000 in damages and the 200 acres of land in dispute. News of the ruling sparked regional concern that a new round of land grant activism was sweeping the Southwest. The specter was raised that the Flores decision would ignite a movement bent on the return of the Tierra Amarilla land grant to claimants. *Tierra o Muerte* and Reade's *Una Lucha* emerge out of the context of this renewed activism. Reade, then a master's degree candidate at the University of New Mexico, opted to give the Tierra Amarilla land struggle an epistemological dimension by suturing performances of the border ballads or *corridos* into his account of the matter. Recalling this aspect of the documentary, Reade says, "I have been collecting and interviewing land grant activists since the 1980s. Many of the Alianza's core members were not willing to talk to me initially; however, the poets and corridistas were. I soon realized that one could follow the anatomy of the land grant movement by looking at the corridos" (Reade correspondence).

Una Lucha opens with a rendition of a popular ballad from the Mexican Revolution performed by Jesús "Chuy" Martínez and closes with a rendition of "El corrido de Amador Flores" performed by Roberto Martínez and his group, Los Reyes de Albuquerque. Influenced by Paulo Freire's book *Pedagogy of the Oppressed*, Reade saw in the corrido tradition an emancipatory ideology that allowed nativo nuevomexicanos to define themselves. *Una Lucha* is not without merit, and in 1998 *Aztlán: A Journal of Chicano Studies* recognized it as one of the top twenty-five new works by emerging Chicano filmmakers. Subsequent to its release, the documentary was added to the *De Colores* series on popular New Mexico subjects sponsored by the local PBS affiliate KNME.

In contrast to *Tierra o Muerte*, Reade's footage deals exclusively with the Amador Flores case, choosing not to explore other community-based initiatives that in one way or another owe their start to the Tierra Amarilla courthouse raid. Reade intersperses interviews with land grant scholars

Clark Knowlton and Francis León Quintana and utilizes historical footage and photos from the 1967 courthouse raid to round out his telling of the Flores standoff. Interviews with land claimants and scholars are spliced in with the performance of *corridos* dedicated to Amador Flores. Up to this point the Hayes and Reade documentaries differ only in degree and not in substance. However, Reade's close participation in the Flores case makes for a key difference, since he unabashedly embraces an *engagé* positionality: "Being a Nativo Nuevomexicano, I felt a responsibility to do my best in accurately portraying land grant activists as a noble group" (Reade correspondence). His views on social justice, allied as they were with those of the land activists, angle *Una Lucha* toward the activist camp.

A telling example of a third-eye moment comes as Reade is filming a victory celebration at the Flores compound set to coincide with Mexican Independence Day on September 16, 1989. As friends, family, and supporters of Amador Flores gather to celebrate the recent court decision granting Flores ownership of his parcel of land, the epidermis of the documentary is peeled back with the arrival of an unexpected guest, local realtor George Gee. Reade recalls the moment: "The Denver crew broke down early, ate, and left as they had little in common with the people whose story they were telling." A short time later Gee arrived. Reade noticed he was walking up to the tables where folks where eating. "Pedro [Archuleta] told me: 'Get the camera and start shooting.'" With Reade filming, Gee and Archuleta began to exchange pointed, verbal digs. Under the pretense of neighborly conversation, the exchange seethes with animosity and distrust. Addressing Pedro Archuleta, Gee begins, "What are you doing monkeying around with this 200-acre piece?" Archuleta responds, "Are you going to help me?" Gee becomes testy: "Hey, I have my own property. I guarantee you one thing. You come after my property and it's not going to turn out like this." Other celebrants counter by imputing the legality of Gee's claims to properties that were once part of the original Tierra Amarilla grant. Gee chafes at the accusation: "You prove it. Hey man, you prove it. I got title insurance if you can prove it you'll get paid, you'll get paid off." The banter simmers until Gee crosses a line of propriety with an off-color remark about the static population of the nearby town of Chama: "Let me tell you something. That's why the population stays the same in Chama. Every time a baby is born, some guy leaves town." The activists offended by the comment ask Gee if the high fences, high-powered lighting, dogs, and rifles stationed at the windows of his ranch are signs that he lives in fear of his neighbors. Gee responses with bravado: "Hell no, I am not afraid of anybody up here." The crest pecking continues and Gee explains that the rifles are there because he likes to shoot prairie dogs, while the dogs and fences are there "to keep the skunks out." Archuleta digs back: "Or to keep the skunks in." The conversation ends abruptly when Archuleta's son confronts the realtor with harsh language: "If you are here to congratulate these people, you congratulate them, if not you keep your mouth shut." Gee responds: "No man, I . . . just cool it." It is at this point that Gee is asked and then required to leave the gathering.

Like the third-eye experiences residing in other films in this study, the conversation at the Flores camp is brief (just under three minutes), and despite this it derives its power from the inversion of the customary and expected interplay of the subject and filmmaker that is the standard performative choreography of classic documentaries. Here, irony grows out of happenstance, and equally important, from the unexpected turn of the camera and the new set of proxemics that is established when it is wielded by an activist documentarian. Things get interesting when the scene, a mundane one, becomes a tense intercultural encounter, seemingly without cause. It should now be clear that the degree to which the camera has been turned, sometimes doubling back on itself, whether by design or arbitrarily, is of special interest to me. It is similar to Helen Blumenschein's narration of events shot long ago in *Adventures in Kit Carson Land* or the moment when Willie Jaramillo peers through the camera veil stretched over Danny Lyon's exploration of Bernalillo and innocently asks the filmmaker, "And what is it exactly that you are doing by filming us?" In this vein, the footage highlighted above from *Una Lucha* evinces a near instantaneous breach in the assumptions of what kinds of things should be "documented" by the documentary film. These three examples share the common element of providing some visual substantiation that causes us to rethink our assumptions about how cultural encounters are irrevocably changed at the moment that the camera appears on site to preserve or record the event. In this segment, *Una Lucha* provides a reverse moment of opportunistic sampling such that the off-camera story, the backdrop of fear and suspicion seeding generations of struggle for land rights in northern New Mexico, comes to light before the eyes of the audience.

What is uncanny about this moment is how the backdrop becomes a part of the film story itself. Earlier in *Una Lucha*, sociologist Clark Knowlton comments, "As I said, Tierra Amarilla has always been the center of land grant agitation in New Mexico. And the only way this question will be resolved is when the people see that justice has been done or that the common lands of the grants have been restored to them. And then the land grant agitation will cease." Knowlton's comments confirm the long-standing social forces that in part give rise to a number of the Chicano-centered documentaries on northern New Mexico since NBC aired *The Most Hated Man*; and yet the off-screen encounters between largely poor and destitute nuevomexicano land grant claimants and incoming Anglo American investors and speculators have rarely been documented. The Gee–Archuelta clash in *Una Lucha* provides a rare glimpse into the sociological dynamics of intra-group mistrust that might simply be misconstrued as unneighborly, raucous behavior and nothing more. However, in the context of this study, it is a moment in which the bitter offscreen encounters rooted in questions of the political economy of the region make their on-camera debut and thus provide testimony of the long intergenerational struggle over language, culture, religion, and land, continuing to play itself out on- and off-camera. That the footage is largely the result of the good fortune of Reade to set up his camera at an opportune moment is less important to me than the fact that he and his generation of Chicano documentarians have had the presence of mind to aim cameras right into the eye of the sociopolitical and cultural encounters that swirl around them into the present era.

Chicano/a Mythopoetics: "Mother Malinche/Father Cortes"

The Miles-García group (Marc Miles, producer, and José García, director) deserves credit for initiating the work of turning the Malinali Tenepal story into a film. The story of Malinali Tenepal, better known as La Malinche, provides the foundational archetype of Indo-Hispano experiences in the Americas. Indeed, the absence of the La Malinche story from any substantial film treatment is a curious lacuna in Chicano filmmaking. This becomes especially apparent in view of Emma Pérez's estimation that, "just as Oedipus is everywhere, always, reinscribing sociosexual and cultural relations, for Indias/mestizas/Chicanas, La Malinche is always everywhere reinscribing woman's agency. In Chicano/a myths, histories, tropes, taxon-omies, and so on, La Malinche cannot be avoided. La Malinche encodes all sociosexual relations and there is no way out" (1999, 122). In recent years a number of revisions and reversals of the La Malinche myth have been brought forth by Mexican and Chicana writers, an operation that owes its start to the work of Mexican novelist and poet Rosario Castellanos, who began a serious reconsideration of La Malinche and other iconic figures in her seminal work "Once Again, Sor Juana," first published in 1963.[2]

Given the central place of La Malinche in Mexican and Chicana cultural studies, it is surprising that the only sustained treatment to date of her would come to be found in a very modest docu-drama shot in 1991 by Marc Miles. Titled *La Llorona*, the film casts the story of La Malinche as a New Mexico leg-end. Completed in the early 1990s, the film benefits from the trends released through Chicano film poetics in the prior decade. Chon Noriega argues that an overriding concern for "first wave" Chicano filmmakers was to deal with the "ambiguous genealogy" resulting from the historical process in the Américas known as *mestizaje*. On one hand, early Chicano/a film projects represented *mestizaje* as a fixed set of representations pressed through a mythopoetic sieve where notions of indigeneity emerge exclusively from pre-contact motifs and idealizations of the Mesoamerican past. As Noriega explains, it became of paramount concern to put forth a Chicano story of *mestizaje* that was heroic in its resistance to the European invader. This version required that the messy business of racial and cultural mixing be strained away so as to only deploy symbolism of the kind that connected Chicanos and Chicanas to an edenic notion of group and self-identity. Noriega asserts:

> For Chicanos, then, it is a simple story, really, even if *mestizaje* blurs the racial boundaries between the social actors, oppressor and oppressed, thereby making history into family melodrama. There is the period of myth, the prehistory of the Americas, the source of our redemption, followed by conquest and *mestizaje* (the racial mix-ture between Spaniard and Indian), until the *hijos de la chingada* (the sons of the violated mother) won their independence from Spain. (2000, xxv–xxvi)

Move the focus from before the fall of las Américas to the time fol-lowing the arrival of Europeans in Mexico, or even to the very moment of encounter between Indians and Spaniards, and the story is anything but simple. Indeed, keeping track of the messy business of mestizaje becomes a huge and vastly complicated undertaking as Noriega rightly observes: "In any case, the Chicano body politic partakes of a particularly ambivalent genealogy. Drawing from Mexican nationalism, Chicanos become the product of violence, between male and female, Spaniard and Indian, conqueror and conquered, resulting in a 'cosmic race' both national and universal" (2000, xxvi).

A tall order indeed, and one that makes it remarkable that Miles and García, in remote, faraway, and unconsidered *la Nueva México,* would be naturally drawn to the story of La Llorona/La Malinche and by association "to the moment of the fall, that is the time of the encounter of 'Mother, Malinche,' and 'Father, Cortez.'" Chicano mythopoetics in these early film representations, as Noriega points out, was largely about filmmakers wanting to portray the redemptive qualities of a time said to exist prior to the fall, that is, to the era when Chicanos were not properly Chicanos at all, but untainted members of indigenous tribes native to the American continent. One might speculate that stories of unredeemed ancestors were simply too painful, too gendered, too complex to pat down neatly into myth, symbol, and image, even when such matter could be passed under the filmmakers' wand—and emerge as newly minted Chicano cinematic imaginary. Noriega writes, "If the story is simple, starting it has been a problem, since few are familiar with the context of the telling. And nothing hampers a good story—not to mention its social function—like having to stop and provide context" (2000, xxvi).

The novelty of taking up La Malinche/La Llorona as subject should not be underestimated. Not since *Captain of Castile*, the 1947 Hollywood epic of Cortez's conquest of the Aztecs, had the legendary moment of the Aztec fall received any kind of attention in narrative filmmaking. In Darryl F. Zanuck's 1947 epic, La Malinche appears onscreen a handful of times. In each instance, she occupies a subservient role, attending to Cortez (Cesar Romero) as the interpreter in his encounters with Aztec chiefs and emissaries. The great Chicano family "melodrama," the one that explains La Malinche and Cortez's relationship as one of sexual desire, lust, consummation, and the betrayal of "Mother, Malinche" by "Father Cortez," is not, of course, explored in *Captain,* as the film predates the theoretical postulations associated with Chicano mythopoetics and rests only on Hollywood formulas. Thus the film is most ostensibly about Spanish swashbuckling and high adventure in the Americas, and in this way it more closely resembles DreamWorks' animated film *The Road to El Dorado* (2000).

Hollywood in the 1950s required a romantic subplot no matter how contrived and sutured into historical narrative it might be. Chicano mythopoetics would quite naturally have gendered or sexed the Cortez–La Malinche liaison as a way to explain the symbolic birth of the mestizo, a kind of new personhood representing the mixed raced origins of mexicanos and Chicanos. Zanuck sidestepped La Malinche and Hernán Cortez, the obvious pair of lovers, in order to construct the romantic subplot between Captain Pedro de Vargas (Tyrone Power) and Catana Pérez (Jean Peters), a Spanish gypsy girl. De Vargas and Pérez are completely gratuitous add-ons to the conquest of Mexico story, who by pure happenstance manage to attach themselves to Cortez's march on Tenochtitlán. The story of Captain de Vargas, which gives the film its title, parasitically latches onto the story of the conquest of Mexico and has the curious effect of making the major historical figures in the drama of conquest (Cortez and La Malinche) secondary figures in the film. The decision to avoid the whole sexual and racial history of Cortez and Malinche may have been carefully determined to provide censor-conscious Zanuck a way to avoid exposing postwar audiences to the story of an illicit love affair. Only a studio that feared being censored by the Production Code could confabulate a storyline in which the two key figures become sidebars to their own epic. The immediate benefit for Zanuck was to sidestep the socially vexed question of how to deal with racial miscegenation that would come from depicting the birth of a mestizo son to Malinche. As I have noted in an earlier chapter, the first cinematic challenge to racial phobias regarding the depiction of mixed-race mestizo children onscreen would come with *Giant*'s bold confrontation of racial politics in Texas. Here, the decision to substitute one tale of desire with one acceptable to postwar censors runs in the opposite direction of Emma Pérez's recent admonition that studying history should included the matter of "sexing the colonial imaginary."[3] By marginalizing Cortez and Malinche's story of sex and romance and replacing it with the captain and gypsy pairing, the film is driven down parallel story tracks, neither of which reaches the dramatic power that resides in the narrative of Malinche and Cortez. Curiously, one astute critic in 1948 incisively read the gender-racial convention at work in this retrofit of the Spanish invasion:

> Tyrone Powers as the sorely beleaguered Pedro de Vargas falls in love, runs afoul of his apparently indestructible enemy, one Diego de Silva (John Sutton), and acquits himself gallantly as a gentleman, swordsman, and lover. He also has a baby (legitimate) by a onetime servant (Jean Peters) who came along for the trip, and looks better and better as time lags on the road to the halls of Montezuma. (*Newsweek*, January 5, 1948, 68)

There are only vague allusions in *Captain* to a romance between Cortez and Malinche (referred to in the film as Doña Marina). Upon landing on Mexican shores and at a first encounter with Moctezuma's emissaries who gift La Malinche to the Spaniards, Cortez remarks: "Yucatan presents me with treasure beyond belief. This lovely creature [*taking Malinche's chin in hand*] that is the voice of these people and then this [*pointing to the gifts of gold and silver Moctezuma has sent him*]." On the trek inland, we see Malinche ceremoniously carried on a platform, a conceit of her lover to elevate her station among that of other Indian vassals and accomplices. On two occasions Cortez bedecks his woman with necklaces taken in tribute. As Cortez places the silver necklace on his mistress he says, "My dear, this seems to have been made just to fit your lovely neck." By this act the conqueror makes the subaltern complicit in the assault on Mexico. Finally, there is the encounter with Cacamatzin, a nephew and counselor to Moctezuma. Cortez calls for Doña Marina: "Come here, incomparable *amiga*. Once more we have need of your precious voice."

It is no accident that by contrast Miles and García, students of Chicano mythopoetics, center their telling of the La Malinche/La Llorona story on the very question of how power and carnal desire intersect in the story of Mexico lost to the invaders. The prefatory scene of *La Llorona* is a shot of La Malinche (Jill Scott Momaday) in the embrace of Hernán Cortez (Clark Sánchez).[4] The shot functions as a mise-en-scène that draws on popular Mexican calendar depictions of the legend of Ixtacihuatl and Popocatepetl. Once popular fixtures in every barrio bakery and eatery, the image on these giveaway calendars is of an Aztec warrior holding a swooning Aztec princess in his embrace. By substituting Cortez for the more commonplace rendering of the warrior, the shot functions, as Emma Pérez notes, as a way to unmask "power relations established through sexualities that remain unspoken, unsaid, even avoided, yet always present" (1999, 125). The shot causes the viewer to question the very nature of the intimate relationship between father Cortez and mother Malinche and brings forth a question unthinkable in Chicano mythopoetic school: did "Father Cortez" and "Mother Malinche" really love each other deeply and honestly? Or is it, as Pérez suggests, a case where "desire for power overwhelms and polices the power of desire" (125)?

La Llorona employs a classic storytelling motif provided by the figure of a kindly grandmother who is retelling the story of La Llorona to her two grandchildren. The retelling is a framing device that brings past events (history) into relationship with the present (a new generation of listeners), an encounter not often seen in the current age of Nintendo, Game Boy, and X-Box. As the film opens, two children, a brother and sister, venture about their small town, peeking in and out of storefronts. Curious by nature, they are also testing the rules imposed on them by the adult world. When a store owner catches them lighting up a cigarette, he issues the ever-ominous warning meted out to generations of children in New Mexican towns and villages: "Hey you kids, the Llorona is going to get you." Fearing they will be punished for their misdeed, brother and sister panic and run to the river that cuts through their town—precisely to the place reputed to be the haunt of La Llorona. An ominous and threatening storm builds. The sky darkens as the children race through the scariest section of their neighborhood. In their fright they are sure they can hear the shrill call of La Llorona: "Ay, mis hijos, ¿dónde están mis hijos?" Scared out of their wits, the children burst through the doorway of their house, where they are met by their kindly grandmother who is miffed by their unruly entrance, but she ushers them in all the same. Once safely nestled in warm blankets and having had a chance to warm up with some freshly brewed tea, they turn to their grandmother and ask: "Abuela, who's La Llorona?" As the abuelita begins her story the camera pans to a shot of a hand against the windowpane and the specter of La Llorona backing away into the darkness of night.

The film shifts back to 1519 as the Spanish, under the leadership of Hernán Cortez, cut a bloody swath across the Yucatán on their march to

Tenochtitlán. Malinali Tenepal, La Malinche, is party to the Spanish invasion; we see her acting as interpreter and, as some scholars have argued,
as a mediator between the Spanish and the Tlaxcalans, their Indian allies.
The Miles-García version cuts out much of the historical record, retaining
only enough elements of the siege of Tenochtitlán to install La Malinche
symbolically as the mother of all mestizos, "a new people" unknown before
in world history.

The birth of La Malinche's child, Martín, is a climactic moment in the
film. The birth of Martín takes on elements of the fantastic when Malinche
is attended by her servant (the Branded Woman). Entering the scene from
another world in a way reminiscent of Guillermo del Toro's 2006 film *El
Laberinto de Fausto* (released in the United States as *Pan's Labyrinth*), the
mythical figure of Coatlicue performs a ritual dance around the birthing
mother. The intensity of the dance is heightened by a troop of Aztec *dan-
zantes* who circle Malinche as she labors to bring forth the child, a symbol
now of the violent and painful birth of the mestizo.

Following the birth of Martín, the narrator informs the audience that
a new adventure, the search for the Isle of the Amazons, has taken Cortez
south of Mexico to the jungle regions of Honduras. When he returns to
Tenochtitlán two years later, he is met with an order from the Council
of the Indies ordering him to return to Spain to face charges of mutiny
and reckless adventurism. Cortez's spiritual counselor is one Padre Rivera,
played by José García. Rivera is a manipulative, self-interested cleric who
counsels Cortez to take the child Martín with him to Spain. The padre reasons that since the child is a Christianized mestizo and the son of a daring conquistador and a noble Mayan princess, Cortez will be seen with
favor in Spain. Padre Rivera counsels that the child will offer proof to the
Spanish court that the Indians of Mexico can be Christianized and become
worthy servants of the crown. A meeting between Malinche, Cortez, and
Father Rivera follows in which Malinche is told that Martín is to be taken
to Spain. A distraught Malinche returns to her abode and cries out to a
figure of Christ on the cross, only to be set upon by the horrific presence of
Coatlicue, a vengeful and jealous goddess who requires Malinche to bring
her the heart of Martín as an offering, lest her son be made a slave to
the ways of the Spaniards. The following day Malinche, Martín, and the
Branded Woman flee to avoid Cortez, but the Spaniards catch up to them

along the escape route. Before Cortez manages to have Malinche turn over Martín to him, the Branded Woman, knee-deep in a bog, is set to follow her prearranged instructions. She pushes Martín's head below the waters and drowns the boy. An enraged Padre Rivera attacks the servant and plunges a dagger into her chest. With his hands and face bloodied by the murderous act, the priest lashes out against the apparent intransigence of the Indians. Cortez, for his part, exacts punishment on Malinche. She in turn, having lost Martín, is transformed into the grieving La Llorona and is required to now live in total submission to the conqueror.

The film shifts to the present as the grandmother concludes her telling of the tale. She ends her narration with the ominous invocation: "La Llorona no tiene nombre, no tiene cara, no tiene amor. La triste Llorona es la somber que nos recuerda que tan preciosos nuestros niños son. [La Llorona has no name, no face, and no love. Wretched La Llorona is the shadow that reminds us just how precious our children are.]" At its end the folktale of La Llorona picks up a political motif, for contained in the words of the grandmother is a warning that present-day folk, Chicanos and non-Chicanos, must struggle for cultural integrity and dignity in the face of cultural dominance and imperialism that would strip children of their culture and their history.

It is lamentable that the Miles-García *La Llorona* never managed to get any appreciable distribution and was never presented to any sizeable audiences. The project simply came to an unceremonious close after receiving only one brief mention in the local press. The news article "N.M. Crew Films Hispanic Legend" in the *Albuquerque Journal* was meant to recognize the ongoing work but had some unintended effects. According to co-producer José García, the article led to entanglements with some members of the local Screen Actors Guild who objected to the project because it employed local union actors who were working on a non-union film. It appears, however, that by the time this issue came forth, there was little camaraderie among the producers and no one sallied forth against post-production obstacles. Prior to this the Miles-García group had laid some plans for the film that included various forms of distribution and outreach. The *Albuquerque Journal* noted that Eduardo García Kraul, executive producer of the film, was hoping for national Hispanic organizations to help distribute videocassettes of the production and was even predicting spin-off Llorona products (coloring books, jewelry, and T-shirts) to follow the film's premiere (*Albuquerque Journal*, August 18, 1991).

In the end, only a handful of videocassette copies of *La Llorona* were ever produced, and they were only made available to a few participants on the project. Still, that the idea of this project had merit can be seen in the fact that efforts to tell the Malinche story through film continue. In 2006, Monique Salazar and Bernadine Santistevan, two emerging film-makers, decided to take up the La Llorona myth as a film subject. A news-paper article describes the project: "Shot in Taos and New York City, [it] is a modern-day thriller about a woman from New Mexico, a New York detective and others terrorized by a crying ghost. It was originally to be shot completely in New Mexico, but the producers ran out of financing here and had to move the production from Taos to New York. Salazar and Santistevan hope to take advantage of the current climate in vogue in the state to nurture film projects in New Mexico and at last report had a bill in legislation to the New Mexico State Senate asking for $600,000 in funding to help market and distribute the film."[5] This latest movie gives rise to the hope that, indeed, in some not-too-future day the story of La Llorona will become part of U.S. popular culture.

The Proxemic Value of Critical Regionalism in the Borderlands Documentaries

Since the mid-1990s the Center for Regional Studies (CRS) at the University of New Mexico has had a pivotal role in supporting independent, documentary filmmakers through its community documentation program. CRS, according to its mission statement, "promotes the quest for knowledge about New Mexico and the Southwest" (CRS pamphlet). Dr. Tobías Durán, the founding director of CRS, refined the statement further when, after twenty years of teaching Chicano Studies at UNM, he asserted:

> It always seemed to me that we didn't have any written material or information in any other form about the communities in this area [Albuquerque] and New Mexico. You can't rely on written survey histories of New Mexico. These are too general, and, frankly, not very exciting because they are too removed from the majority of

the people who made the history and often reflect a scholar's narrow interpretation. Very quickly you realize you can't know a more complete history about these communities unless you go out and get it. (Martínez 1991, 9)

The first part of Durán's argument underscores the importance of community oral history as a methodology that offers an antidote to the longstanding erasure of a people's history in the Borderlands. Seeing the utility of such work turned into media projects, CRS would quickly move into funding documentary films that aimed to unearth the Southwest's hidden or unremarked categories of cultural and historic consequence. While generally endorsing the "documentary impulse" Chicano and Chicana filmmakers subscribe to, Durán's statement is also concerned with the matter of proxemics. He asks how best to judge the epistemological space in which outsiders and insiders aim to assess the social inner workings of historically marginalized communities. Durán's concern with the unreliability of written surveys stems from the proliferation of the master narratives of Southwest Borderlands history. Most often these accounts have been predicated on Manifest Destiny, and occlude the history of peoples that formed the social fabric of the region before the arrival of the United States. Chicano scholars tend to emphasize that such histories have been "too removed from the majority of people who made the history." A second concern arises from the occlusion of New Mexico and nuevomexicanos from film, media, and written texts authored by Chicanos and Chicanas who tend to focus their scholarship on Mexican Americans in Texas or California. Thus, Durán inserts critical regionalism into this quandary over the epistemological proxemics that come into play even as autoethnographic filmmaking finds a space within which to operate.

The latter concern is best seen in the intervention CRS has made in assisting emerging filmmakers with the creation of critical regional documentary projects. In 1994 CRS provided a team of UNM professors, headed by anthropologist Sylvia Rodríguez, with start-up funds to complete a documentary on the 1994 mayoral race in Santa Fe. The resulting film, *This Town Is Not for Sale*, had two objectives. The first was to witness the charismatic appeal of councilwoman Debbie Jaramillo in her bid to become mayor of Santa Fe. Jaramillo, the first Chicana to seek the office, ran on an anti-establishment, anti-development platform, and her dissident views were decidedly at odds with the official line that Santa Fe was a model of growth, prosperity, and cultural harmony. Indeed, Rodríguez's stated aim was to track the "class and ethnic conflict [that] had been brewing in northern New Mexico, including the sociocultural impacts of the resort industry'" (qtd. in Burroughs 1996, 19).

In addition to Rodríguez, the faculty team included sociologist Phillip Gonzales, photojournalist Miguel Gandert, and political scientist Chris Sierra. Most observers and certainly the researchers involved in *This Town* attributed Jaramillo's win to the groundswell of public discontent that followed the police shooting of a young man named Pancho Ortega on Santa Fe's predominantly nuevomexicano Westside. The Ortega shooting was the catalyst that pushed social discontent among nuevomexicanos in the city to a breaking point. When an angry crowd of barrio residents arrived en masse at one city council meeting following the shooting, Jaramillo, alone among the council members, was able to steady the situation. It is telling that when Jaramillo emerged the victor on Election Day, March 1, 1994, it was the CRS research team that had the only camera on site to cover the culmination of what had been a bitter campaign. In this and other ways, *This Town*, with its attention to racialized social fractures that belie the tourist image of Santa Fe, partakes in Durán's call to "go out and get the history."

Wholly committed to the idea of fueling the "documentary impulse," CRS next moved to fund emerging filmmaker Paige Martínez, commissioning her to do an hour-long documentary on the legendary Mexican American politician Dionisio "Dennis" Chávez, who served in the U.S. Senate from 1936 to 1964. Best characterized as a bio-documentary, *"El Senador"* employs the familiar logic of the classic documentary format, even down to the detail of employing a celebrated figure with name recognition to carry off the "voice of God" narration. In this case, Henry Cisneros, the former mayor of San Antonio and a person widely regarded as presidential material, was enlisted to narrate Chávez's life—in many ways, he was Cisneros's mentor in politics. *"El Senador"* follows a predictable, linear presentation of Chávez's life story, one that is sequentially punctuated by summary sections on the Great Depression and New Deal era, World War II, the Cold War, and the civil rights era, to establish how Chávez responded to the tenor of the times. Then, too, there is the *de rigueur* appearance on camera of members of the Chávez family, Chávez scholars, and other experts who offer their viewpoints on the impact of the senator's career. *"El Senador"* is buoyed by an impressive amount of historical and archival investigation presented in an even-toned narration.

In 2002 CRS premiered a second feature-length installment on New Mexico history called *Colors of Courage: Sons of New Mexico, Prisoners of Japan.* It tells the story of the fall of the Philippine Islands to Japanese forces on April 9, 1942. The fall of Manila still remains the single largest surrender of American troops to a hostile enemy. Prior to the Japanese victory, the defense of the Philippines had fallen to recently federalized state national guard units, the main contingent of which had been formed out of New Mexico's 200th and 515th Coast Artillery. The story of these units and their fate in the Pacific theater treads a fault line of local, regional, national, and international importance.

Employing the standard documentary formula, *Colors* raises the celebrity coefficient, with two-time Academy Award winner Gene Hackman as narrator. The documentary is also exceptional in regard to its length, close to two hours. The first ten minutes retrace the complexity that characterizes New Mexico history, using scholars and writers to outline its four recognized periods: the pre-Columbian period, the Spanish and Mexican periods (1598 to 1821), the American territorial period (1848 to 1912), and the statehood period (1912 to 1941). The next ten minutes focus on New Mexico's multiracial groups, particularly its mexicano and Native American population segments. Appearing on camera, film consultant and writer Hampton Sides estimates that no more ethnically diverse a unit could be found in the United States on the eve of World War II. He notes that the 200th was composed of members of groups who had been bitter enemies just half a century before. The film stresses diversity for two reasons: first, to account for the racial makeup of the 200th and 515th Coast Artillery, stemming as it does from New Mexico's uncharacteristic history of mestizaje and conquest, and second, to evidence the racial segmentation that prevailed in the United States as it entered into this global conflict.

The remaining segments of *Colors* deal with the rise of Japanese military power in Asia and the Pacific, the prelude to the attack on Pearl Harbor in December 1941, and the strategic defense of the Philippines.

The last third of the documentary examines the infamous Bataan Death March endured by members of the 200th and 515th when they became prisoners of war. Some time is given to examining military strategy, even to the degree of finding and recording interviews with Japanese commanders and soldiers, but the film returns to the Bataan survivors themselves who relay memories of their capture, torture, and internment on the Japanese mainland.

In 2007, following the PBS broadcast of Ken Burns's seven-part series *The War*, Latino media advocacy groups voiced outrage at Burns's failure to include the history of the half million Latinos who served in the U.S. armed forces during the Second World War. Critics charged that *The War*, which did not include a single interview with a Latino veteran, was not the first time Burns had "inexplicably erased or minimized Latino contributions to American society" (*New York Daily News*, May 11, 2007). The Burns flap and its contingent meaning as social and epistemological proxemics come into clear view when *The War* is set aside *Colors of Courage*. Media activists have long expressed concern that Burns's documentaries play out the erasure of Latinos on a national scale, pointing to the dearth of attention to Latino athletes in Burns's 1994 documentary *Baseball* and the near total absence of Latin musical influences in his highly acclaimed PBS series *Jazz* from 2001. Erasure on a national level also operates at every other possible category of social distance (international, regional, and local) and, whether uninformed or willful, returns audiences to the realm of intercultural encounter. The earliest films on the Southwest exploited mexicano exotica and in doing so heightened distrust in the initial encounter of one group with another. In contrast, the Burns case is riddled with the complexities of representation in a post-multicultural United States. Historical erasure is not the only sticking point here; the case raises questions about the support that public funding agencies conferred on Burns. Thus, while Burns gave a nod to diversity in his 2004 grant proposal for the series to the National Endowment for the Humanities (NEH), it now seems clear that he excluded Latinos from the outset. As Latino media advocate Gus Chávez charged, "Ken Burns and PBS . . . play[ed] recklessly with our history, both as Latinos and Americans." Chávez's comment takes the matter beyond Burns's disposition to a redefinition of American multiculturalism, and he indicts the NEH as well for giving Burns carte blanche to redirect

the nation's history ("'War' against Ken Burns"). Here social and epistemological proxemics that are as critical to representation as any are voiced
in the concerns of Latino advocates who point out that the documentary
will shape the collective imaginary on World War II. Neglecting Latino
military service only reinforces the widespread ignorance of how Latinos
have contributed to the building of the United States. Following weeks of
complaints from Latino organizations, Burns agreed to amend *The War* to
address the omission of Latinos. Burns also agreed to hire Hector Galán,
a director best known for his own PBS series, *Chicano: The History of the
Mexican American Civil Rights Movement,* to produce the Latino segments.
These weak efforts, however, did little to improve the flawed epistemological proxemics that had already been built into Burns's camera.

In the wake of the controversy, PBS did manage to find *Colors of Courage* through its New Mexico PBS affiliate KNME and to broadcast *Colors* in
some markets as a rejoinder to *The War,* thus strategically defusing further
embarrassment by offering viewers content that the Burns project lacked.
The whole affair confirmed Tobías Durán's view that "you can't know a
more complete history about these communities unless you go out and get
it," an admonition that applies to Chicano and non-Chicano filmmakers
with equal force.

Insider Proxemics and the Borderlands Documentary

With a career spanning the last three decades, writer, producer, and director
Paul Espinosa is widely recognized as being among the foremost Chicano
border documentary filmmakers, a distinction that rests on his extensive
filmography of Borderlands subjects. Espinosa's academic training as a
Stanford Ph.D. in anthropology and his decision to do his ethnographic
fieldwork at a Hollywood studio brings into view the operations of what
I term the critical proxemics in Borderlands documentary filmmaking. In
this light, Espinosa, like others of his generation, participates directly in
the filmic turn I have addressed in an earlier chapter.

In a recent interview, film scholar Daniel Bernardi perceptively asks
Espinosa, "What is a film anthropologist like you doing in a space like the
documentary?" Espinosa expounds on his decision to turn away from work
resembling ethnographic film in the service of salvage anthropology. He

recalls, "I came into anthropology at a reflexive moment for the discipline. When I began my graduate studies at Stanford, nearly 25 percent of the entering students in the Department of Anthropology were Chicano. As students from a community that had often been studied by anthropologists in ways that were often seen as uninformed, we were particularly critical of anthropology" (qtd. in Bernardi 2007, 45). Espinosa eschews questions of genre, preferring to make audience reception the defining criterion for his filmic choices. Situating audience at the center of his filmmaking has had a twofold effect, since his documentaries are in the tradition of applied anthropology but made in a way that is proportional to the need to populate the media with the untold stories of Latinos in the Borderlands. In this regard, Espinosa employs an interdisciplinary studies lens that provides him the flexibility to present stories that are at once historical, anthropological, and sociological, as well as forms of incisive investigative journalism.

Among his first films, *The Trail North* (1983) addresses the migration story of a particular California family. It grew out of a collaboration with Robert Alvárez Jr., a fellow graduate student at Stanford who was engaged in a study of the migration history of his extended family, the Mesa-Smiths, as they moved north from Baja California and eventually came to reside in San Diego. Espinosa was able to get actor Martin Sheen to narrate the piece, which heightened interest in the film, but it is the inclusion of Alvárez in the film that gives the work its autoethnographic quality. Alvárez and his young son, Luis, cross the border at Tecate to retrace the 800-mile trek north their ancestors made from Las Parras, Baja California. Alvárez and his son try to visualize the journey their forebears made as they visit mining camps and towns where the ancestors once resided. Since the path his ancestors took is a matter of both personal and sociohistorical import, Alvárez's presence, specifically his quest to "feel the experience, to sense what it was like to be a migrant" (Espinosa 2010, 16), collapses the space surrounding this film document; on the surface, it is about one of the largest and most sustained mass migrations in the Americas, and at a deeper level about the formation of Chicano identity. The collaboration of two "native" scholars—the one wielding a camera, the other providing personal disclosure—evinces a new proxemics at work in Borderlands cinema.

In 1998 Espinosa used the 150th anniversary of the U.S. war with Mexico to produce a four-hour series for PBS that he titled *The U.S. Mexican War: 1846–1848.* Told in classic documentary fashion, the series gave Espinosa the opportunity to explore the question of why this historical event remains absent in the popular imagination of both countries. Using a binational advisory board of respected historians, the series remains the most informative and comprehensive documentary on "an event which both countries wished to forget" (Espinosa 2010, 14). Espinosa's steadfast efforts to confirm the historical record in this series suggests that the "documentary impulse," so highly invoked at the outset of Chicano and Chicana filmmaking, had reached the capacity to deal with the contradictory and adversarial contests over the historical record. It also signaled the abiding interest of Chicanos and Chicanas in the formative questions of their Borderlands history and identity.

As a producer and director, Espinosa has guided some thirty border films to completion, each of which merits additional analysis; however, I wish to conclude this chapter by selecting a moment from two of Espinosa's films to further illustrate how the new proxemics work in his films.

The Lemon Grove Incident (1986) is a continuation of Espinosa's collaboration with Alvárez, who wrote his dissertation on the little-studied court challenge brought by the Mexican residents of Lemon Grove, California, against the school board that in 1931 barred students of Mexican descent from attending the local grammar school. The case resulted in the school board's decision being overturned in what was the first legal challenge to school segregation in the nation. Using dramatized scenes, archival footage, and on-camera testimony of Lemon Grove residents who were children at the time of the case, *The Lemon Grove Incident* evinces moments in which the distance between residents and filmmakers narrows and sharpens to reveal not just a precedent-setting legal case, but something about how the act of standing up for oneself transcends the moment and announces itself in the present of the film production. Robert Alvárez Sr., in whose name the suit was filed and who was called upon to testify as a boy of ten, offers the most eloquent on-camera *testimonio* of his day in court in 1931. Agile and clear, he speaks English with confidence but does not deny his working-class roots. His comments are intelligent and lucid as if he were a professor and not the father of a Stanford Ph.D. This, too, supplies a kind of intimate knowledge, an inkling of how he inculcated the importance of education in his son and how his own struggle for the right to an education did not end in Lemon Grove but extended forward to the moment of filming.

Los Mineros (1991) brings forth a comparable moment. It tells the story of how Mexican and Mexican American miners in the Clifton-Morenci area of southeastern Arizona struggled over several decades, beginning in 1900, to create a union and win key concessions from the mining giant Phelps-Dodge, which controlled all aspects of these mining communities. Narrated by Luis Valdez and directed by Hector Galán, *Los Mineros* extends the story of labor organizing that *Salt of the Earth* raised in 1954. As in *The Lemon Grove Incident*, however, there is another moment when the racial social contract that had set the conditions for how social groups interacted in the Borderlands is revealed and personal experience flows out of the interview. The moment comes almost as an aside, a seemingly off-topic issue that by some circumlocution creates a punctum, a third-eye experience. That moment comes halfway into *Los Mineros* following a recap of how Chicano World War II veterans returned to the mining towns of Arizona with new skills and an assertiveness to change the racial status quo of the prewar years. But the punctum to the outward history of veterans claiming their civil rights is found in the deeply personal anecdote rendered by Ed Montoya, an Arizona veteran who saw some of the deadliest fighting in Okinawa. He recalls how his company of 186 men, after a day of fighting the Japanese, was reduced to 24 survivors by five o'clock on the evening of April 13, 1945. In war he sees what he had never seen back home in Morenci: a white man crying in despair. He remembers processing the revelation in terms of how social norms played out back home: "I said, hey, hey, what's going on around here? You guys are supposed to be Superman, you're Batman, you're Roy Rogers, you're super, you're not supposed to be crying!" In the days that followed, Montoya remembers a couple of Anglo soldiers trying to back out of going on a reconnaissance patrol, and he recalls the anger that welled up inside him. A tearful Montoya recalls, "Because back in the States I had been discriminated and I should refuse to go right now, but no, I'm ready—come on, bastard, let's go. See, those things are inside of me!"

Conclusion

It has come time to ask what might be profitably learned from stringing together a comparison of a handful of difficult-to-locate films and proceeding to analyze them on account of two elements: first, they happened to be filmed in the Southwest Borderlands, and second, they present and in some instances re-present mexicano/Chicano/Hispanic stories. In some instances, these are stories we know a great deal about, while others are relatively unknown. My initial supposition about the films and documentaries I have looked at here is that all point to a set of offscreen stories about intercultural encounters. It holds true that films generally say something about the period in which they were made and about the people represented in them, but what I did not anticipate finding when I began this work was the sheer ironic power that emerges from comparing the filmic drama of these works to the social drama that shapes their appearance in the first place. In a real sense, here is a set of film representations that spring from the particularly complex contact zone that is the Southwest Borderlands. These films share a common denominator, since to one degree or another they are infused with the historical, cultural, racial, gender, socioeconomic, religious, and ethnic complexity of the Borderlands. When Governor David Cargo established the first New Mexico Film Commission in 1970, he pushed to bring Southwestern and New Mexico–themed film projects to the state. By the summer of 1970 such prospects were on the horizon:

In a news release in late June, Cargo said a 20th Century Fox special, "Everyday is a Special War," will use the Santa Fe Fiesta as background, as will a Walt Disney feature. A Western by Jack Warner will be filmed in northern New Mexico, and a Metro-Goldwyn-Mayer production in Albuquerque, Roswell, or Las Cruces. "Red Sky at Morning" is definitely scheduled for the state this summer, said Gov. Cargo, "the filming to be done at Santa Fe, Taos and Truchas." (*Las Cruces Citizen-Sun,* July 3, 1970)

New Mexico's culture and history were already being offered up for popular consumption. Where better than the Southwest Borderlands to film gunfights, fiestas, TV episodes of *Lassie, Gunsmoke, The Virginian,* and the antics of a present-day paranoid cowboy chased by Apaches?[1] Where else could you find real Indians, real Indian reservations, real Mexicans, and real Mexican American villages to serve as on-location film lots? In addition to *Red Sky at Morning,* New Mexico did get *Easy Rider* (1969),[2] *The Hired Hand* (1971), and several Billy Jack movies, along with a host of lesser-known westerns.

New Mexico's current film industry boom was led by former governor Bill Richardson. His new film commission did little of the old romancing of the Southwest that characterized Cargo's tenure. The present situation is cut and dried. It makes no overtures to culture, history, or even western landscape. Film commission representatives in fact crow about the fact that Albuquerque (the site of most of the current filmmaking in the region) can double for Phoenix, Los Angeles, Montreal, and other urban locales. There is simply not much call for filming against the backdrop of the Santa Fe Fiestas, Chaco Canyon, or the high-low ranching country of eastern New Mexico, not that (as I have tried to demonstrate here) Southwest exotica and landscape was ever a panacea. The new film commission's agenda is about providing tax incentives to film companies, enticing film executives to take advantage of New Mexico's lower production costs, and accommodating production teams and movie executives when and wherever they wish to set up filming in the state.

Consequently, it is difficult to know whether the current spate of filmmaking will or will not do anything positive or negative in the matter of representing Chicanos, Indo-Hispanos, or Borderlands culture in cinema. We know that it played almost no role in supporting independent and documentary filmmakers. This work is in some ways detachable from film production needs. Still, it is important to ask what is to become of the entire matter of cultural encounters. Have the old Borderlands themes and antagonisms been surpassed? Are we in a post-Chicano era? Is the contact zone no longer relevant? Where have all the Indians and Mexicans gone?

In 1989, the independent specialty film *The Penitent*, starring the late Raul Julia coming off his starring role in *Kiss of the Spider Woman*, flickered briefly in limited theatrical distribution before being consigned to video distribution. The film is interesting on two counts, first because it resurrects the once commonplace trope of "My Penitente Land," as writer Fray Angélico Chávez was given to calling New Mexico, and second because this revival of an old theme did not bring back to the screen the Penitente vengeance narrative of old. In fact, *The Penitent* is much closer to what I imagine D. W. Griffith's 1915 *The Penitentes* would have been. Like its silent film counterpart, *The Penitent* is a romantic melodrama in which a couple's love is tested and then made demonstrable through the kind of self-sacrifice emblematic in retellings of the passion of Christ. The film is interesting because, while set in northern Mexico, it employs the ritual trappings (processions, religious iconography, sacred songs, and sites) that anthropologists, ethnomusicologists, and members of the Brotherhood know to have originated in the New Mexico context. This effects a curious transfer of extant cultural material from one Spanish-speaking locale (New Mexico villages) to another (rural northern Mexico). The film avoids the sensationalism and the voyeurism of the old film narratives where outsiders ogled the foreign and the curious by winding its dramatic power around the spring of internal tensions. Since the film seeks to dramatize notions of sacrifice, propriety in friendship, and romance, *The Penitent* is not about an Anglo-Mexican standoff, and thus ogling and vengeance are absent as themes here. The film's internal dynamics, however, still require it to build anticipation by heightening the dramatic import of the much-mythologized idea of staging a yearly penitential crucifixion. The opening intertitle purports to convince viewers that there is a factual basis for this happening: "In the remote villages of New Mexico, Colorado, and northern Mexico, a group known as the PENITENTE continue to this day a 200 year old tradition. Every year before Easter, one of the Penitente is chosen to hang on a cross—to be crucified. Whether he lives or dies depends on his strength and courage or as the

PENITENTE say 'God's will.'" At the conclusion to this book and after a careful look at earlier claims of Penitente crucifixions, it is remarkable to find a contemporary movie regurgitating the old myth and displaying it as fact in the service of a melodrama. While it would be unimaginable to expect that commercial filmmakers would shield their eyes from sensationalism of this sort given its potential to entertain and draw in the curious, it bears asking once again: What effect does film have when it represents the Other? Film retreads like *The Penitent* attest to the continuing impact of the celluloid curriculum Carlos Cortes has written about. It is for those who study film to find the "teachable moments" that these encounters provide. Once found, it is important to strip them of their power to misinform uninitiated audiences and to make a space in our understanding for those who have known "the experience of the third eye," precisely by inscribing "a third voice" in film scholarship: a voice that as much as possible accounts for the magnitude of the film encounter on and off the screen.

Commercial filmmaking aside, it is the new proxemics established in, for example, Espinosa's investment in Borderland experiences that allow those "things inside," things long unvoiced, to become the film moments I have discussed here. These "things inside" are still a very real part of the Borderlands experience and thus will continue to shape film encounters into the future. I would add that this new way of getting close to film subjects has the potential to reverse older filmic practices, the very formula of otherness that filmmakers once traced out in the business of encounters on and off the screen. Given the long history of filmmaking in the Borderlands, riddled and vexed as it is by strained social and cultural encounters, it is expected that most often this kind of intimate disclosure would appear in the work of Chicano documentarians who are themselves members of the historical subordinate group. But lest I be misunderstood, I insist that being an insider is not the prerequisite for this manner of proximate filmmaking. Far more significant to this aesthetic is locating the source of Borderlands concerns and the stories these concerns have engendered, just as it is equally important that the new proxemics rest on mutually edifying collaborations irrespective of insider or outsider status. The best of these are collaborations where everyone involved knows who and why they are participating in the film project and all are aware of the position of the camera and of those holding it.

NOTES

CHAPTER 1 BORDERLANDS CINEMA AND THE PROXEMICS OF HIDDEN AND MANIFEST FILM ENCOUNTERS

1. My reliance on Fatimah Tobing Rony's *The Third Eye* (1996) stems from the fact that her work provides an exhaustive and detailed discussion of links between Western tourism, the travelogue, and race and cinema. A second valuable study is Ellen Strain's article in *Wide Angle*, "Exotic Bodies, Distant Landscapes: Touristic Viewing and Popularized Anthropology in the Nineteenth Century" (1996).

2. See Flores (2002) for more on how *Martyrs* misaligns history and popular belief. Among Flores's chief concerns is that *Martyrs* flattens out the complexities of the Texas War of Independence to render a film depiction based on partial truths: "Partial projections treated as wholes obscure and omit critical features that serve as important counterpoints. When these visualizations are those of the past, what remains absent is history itself, that is history as a condition that warrants these projections in the first place" (99).

3. Charles Montgomery writes, "In 1926, to provide close up views of actual Indian villages, the company initiated its Indian Detours. Although Indian settlements like San Idelfonso and Santo Domingo were always the outfit's principal destinations, the so-called Harvey cars also made occasional stops in Hispano villages such as Chimayó and Truchas. Soon the paisano, no less than the Pueblo, was a figure on display. As drivers positioned their Packards so as to afford tourists the most picturesque views of the village, well-versed tour guides interpreted what they saw" (2002, 162).

4. For a complete discussion of the history of the Taos Art Colony and its interactions with local residents, see Sylvia Rodríguez's article, "Art, Tourism, and Race Relations in Taos: Toward a Sociology of the Art Colony" (1989). Concerning the image of Native Americans cultivated by Taos artists, Rodríguez writes, "It is important to note that the Indian paintings were not realistic portraits of individuals as they actually appeared in everyday life, but rather romantic compositions for which the subjects dressed in prototypical costume. Indians tended to be portrayed as ideal types in harmony with Nature, caught at some pristine, eternal moment" (83).

5. Rodríguez's article lists the full name of each of the artists in Helen Blumenschein's narrative. They are Victor Higgins, E. Irving Couse, and Walter Ufer.

The other individuals she names are Taos merchants and other non-native elites.

6. In "Ig/noble Savages of New Mexico: The Naturalization of 'El Norte' into the Great Southwest," Lamadrid writes, "Fielding's portrayal of the Mexican as 'Depraved Other' is consistent with other 'greaser' films of its time. The 1992 audience is shocked, but not necessarily surprised to see a rather complete set of overt negative stereotypes depicted through the character of Happy Tony. Mexicans are (naturally) lazy, oversexed, filthy, vicious, thieving, violent, and cowardly, with a tendency to carry knives" (1992, 13).

7. This term comes from historian Daniel Boorstin by way of Carlos Cortes.

8. The most extensive treatment of conquest fiction published after the Mexican War (1846–1848) can be found in Arthur Pettit's *Images of the Mexican American in Film and Fiction*. Pettit's exhaustive analysis shows how the foundation for the cinematic degradation of the Mexican in early film was laid out in characterizations found in the conquest fiction that preceded the advent of film.

CHAPTER 2   ILL WILL HUNTING (PENITENTES)

1. While Lummis was convalescing in New Mexico, he made it a habit to write the entries in his diary in Spanish. Taken as a whole, his diaries for 1888 and 1889 show him to be quite proficient in his adopted language, even correctly expressing local New Mexican idioms and lexicon. It also was customary for Lummis to render information from his diary entries in a translated, typed, and reorganized format that he took to calling his journals. His secretary assisted him with this work once he was back at El Alisal in Los Angeles.

CHAPTER 3   A LIE HALFWAY AROUND THE WORLD

1. For more on Miguel Archibeque and the organization of brotherhood councils in New Mexico, see Steele and Rivera 1985. Marta Weigle includes Archibeque's obituary among the appended materials of her dissertation. For the item as published in the *Santa Fe New Mexican* on June 19, 1979, see Weigle 1971, 518–519.

2. Information on Taylor is drawn from a biographical sketch found in Raines 1935, 70–71.

3. In addition to his mother and father, the people who visited Modesto in his early months of incarceration were mostly family members. The New Mexico Penitentiary Visitor's Register lists the following individuals, all residents of Cedar Crest, New Mexico, visiting Modesto Trujillo on July 7, 1936: José León Trujillo, María L. Trujillo, Jesusita Gutiérrez, Mónica Baca, Benita Gutiérrez, Julia Grego [sic], Lorenzo Grego [sic], Elia Gutiérrez, and José Salinas. On October 24, 1936, Modesto was visited by José León Trujillo, María L. Trujillo, Merced Trujillo, Mariana Trujillo, Antonio Garcías [sic], and Ermelinda García.

4. Governor's Inmate Notebooks, Serial #17163, New Mexico State Records Center and Archives.

CHAPTER 4   LIVES AND FACES PLYING THROUGH EXOTICA

1. To appreciate this difference, one need only consider a couple of films done in Native American communities by both professional and amateur anthropologists. Jeff Spitz's documentary *The Return of Navajo Boy* (2000) is compelling testimony of the impact of filmic and photographic intrusions into Navajo life. It tells the story of the making of *Navajo Boy*, a short ethnographic film shot in Monument Valley, Arizona, in 1952 by Robert J. Kennedy. *Navajo Boy* is without a sound track and follows the life of the Cly family. Some forty years later, Kennedy's son Bill would return to Arizona intent on finding the Clys and returning the film and its memories to them. The film unearths from the present-day Clys their feelings about being the subject of a nearly endless stream of photographers who made it their work to film real Navajos at work in Navajo country. Another powerful example of the effect of the gaze of anthropologists and filmmakers is Victor Masayesva's 1993 film, *Imagining Indians*. Both films investigate the impact of several generations of ethnographic incursions on Native people.

2. William Wroth reports that Roy Stryker, Lee's boss and head of the historical unit of FSA, fostered professional association between Russell Lee and George I. Sánchez. William Wroth draws on the correspondence between Stryker and Lee to set forth the details of Lee's interactions with Sánchez prior to the Taos County survey. Wroth writes: "In early April 1940, Stryker suggested to Lee that he make contact with Dr. George Sanchez, a native-born sociologist, since known for his pioneering work on Hispanic New Mexicans. Al Hurt of the Amarillo Land Coordinator's Office had visited Stryker. Hurt brought him 'the manuscript of Sanchez's new book on the Spanish Americans. He says it is the finest thing that has ever been done.' Stryker told Lee to try to find Sanchez in Albuquerque and 'tell him that you . . . would like to have a chance to see the manuscript and talk with him about the whole Spanish American situation.'"

   Lee's meeting with George Sánchez proved to be very productive, for through Sánchez he was able to gain a real understanding of the rural Hispanic culture of northern New Mexico. Lee was impressed by Sánchez's grasp of the situation and wrote to Stryker: "He certainly knows the problems of the Spanish Americans." Stryker suggested to Lee that "concentrated work on *one* of the isolated Spanish American villages would be representative of them all."

   By June, thanks to Sánchez's advice, Lee had determined that the Taos County communities of Chamisal and Peñasco would be ideal for an in-depth documentation of Spanish-American culture (Wroth 1985, 134).

3. For a complete discussion of this point see Krupat's chapter "Native American Autobiography and the Synecdochic Self," in *Ethnocriticism* (1992).

4. There are two filmed versions of *And Now, Miguel*. The story was made into a Hollywood feature film by Universal Pictures in 1966. The Universal production, shot in Technicolor, is much more of an entertainment film. It was directed by James B. Clark and featured Michael Anasara in a lead role as Miguel's father, Blas. Anasara, a second-tier actor of Lebanese extraction, was often called on to portray Latinos in the 1950s. Hollywood's version of *Miguel* most obviously falls into the commonly accepted practice of using non-Latinos in major speaking and acting roles, while relegating Latinos to bit parts and extras. This aspect of filmmaking also impacts Indo-Hispano representation, although here I am more concerned with the Krumgold version of *Miguel* as it is one of a very small number of films that uses an ethnographic vantage point to portray the lives of Indo-Hispano New Mexicans in rural communities. For its careful inclusion of village celebrations, dances, and religious and other cultural practices associated with rural New Mexicans, *Miguel* remains the best in-situ film ethnography of villages like Los Córdovas, New Mexico.

5. Both a disclaimer and a list of film credits, the intertitle reads: "The events that follow were made into a motion picture by Joseph Krumgold with the help of Kenneth Marthey, cameraman and his assistant Richard Kent, George Feldsler, production manager, Helen Krumgold, continuity, Jack Sheindlin, musical director and Louis Applebaum, the composer, as well as with the cordial cooperation of the people of Los Córdovas, NM."

6. As one would expect in a rural agricultural area like the Taos Valley, a cooperative and beneficial relationship existed between the Chávez family and the Agricultural Extension Service agent for Taos County. It is worth noting how decisive that relationship would become in the case of Gabriel Chávez, who in the interview credits County Agent Ernesto Gutiérrez with helping him make the decision to enroll at New Mexico State University. It is also telling that through its various efforts, the Department of Agriculture stood out for George I. Sánchez as the kind of public institution that had not completely failed the rural poor of New Mexico. For Sánchez, it was the one beacon of hope assailing the deep poverty and need of Taos County residents. Citing the need for more such interventions, Sánchez observes: "The Activities of the Agricultural Extension Service, of the Agricultural Adjustment Administration, of Farm Security, and the Soil Conservation Service have tended to lessen the economic decline of the region and have been both of material and educational assistance to the *taoseños*. Through farmers meetings, agricultural compensation, 4-H clubs, and future farmers organizations, these agencies have been reaching into a vital aspect of the Taos situation. It must be pointed out, however, that there is great need for an expansion of this type of service. One county agent, alone, cannot cope with the complexity of rural problems in so large an area. Here the work of the county agent, of the soil conservation office, and of the other agricultural and land use agencies cannot be limited to

the usual type of remedial service. It is important that this work be extended along educational lines and that new procedures be instituted that will permit these agencies to reach deeper into the life of the people" ([1940] 1996, 81). It is also a key point that Gabriel Chávez names his friend and mentor, giving in some way credit to work that otherwise would have gone unacknowledged. Gabriel Chávez's personal appreciation of Ernesto Gutiérrez comes up at a couple of points in his interviews, as when I asked him if the agricultural agent had been instrumental in bringing Joseph Krumgold to the Chávez farm. Chávez responded: "I would think so because he was a very, very well known and well respected county agent here. He was very well liked and he knew everybody and he helped everybody and I'm sure he had something to do with it. He was a very good friend of the family, a very good friend of mine who just passed away about a year ago in Florida" (Chávez interview).

CHAPTER 5   *RED SKY AT MORNING,* A BORDERLANDS INTERLUDE

1. The distribution rights to *Red Sky at Morning* are currently held by MCA/Universal Pictures, and while the film has appeared at one or another time on cable channels, it is unavailable in video distribution.
2. Orson Welles's film noir classic *Touch of Evil* (1958) is by far the best, though quite regrettably it is one of only a few major films of the 1950s to accomplish a complete role reversal in the standard Hollywood formula that called for Mexicans to play the foil to the Anglo American. In *Touch of Evil* Miguel Ramón "Mike" Vargas, played by Charlton Heston, is the forthright honest cop who triumphs over the machinations of Hank Quinlan (played by Welles), a vengeful, racist xenophobe. For a careful analysis of the film see Nericcio 1992.
3. Charles Ramírez Berg (2002) has identified nine films made between 1930 and 1960 that he considers to constitute the whole of the Chicano social problem genre: *Bordertown* (1935), *A Medal for Benny* (1945), *Right Cross* (1950), *My Man and I* (1952), *The Ring* (1952), *Salt of the Earth* (1954), *The Lawless* (1954), *Trial* (1955), and *Giant* (1956).
4. Charles Montgomery's template for marking off the distinctive history of the region includes the following: "In the sixteenth century, when the Spaniards first made their way up the Rio Grande's floodplain, they came to a point where the river's progressively steepening banks gave way to canyon walls. Lying near the Pueblo village of Cochiti, the site came to be known as the divide between New Mexico's upriver and downriver zones, two adjacent sub-regions that were administered separately by Spanish authorities and to this day remain a part of New Mexico's cultural geography. Roughly speaking, the upriver area, the Rio Arriba, comprises the state's north-central mountains and river valleys on both sides of the Rio Grande between Cochiti and Colorado's San Luis Valley. The Rio Arriba was the earliest and most densely settled area of Spanish colonization, and with its numerous picturesque villages, set among pine forests and snow-capped peaks, it remained during the twentieth century a much-loved wellspring of colonial imagery" (2002, 5).

5. In a recent op-ed piece, the syndicated columnists Roberto Rodríguez and Patricia Rodríguez make the following points about the portrayal of Latinos in the media: "Anything but brown. That's not the name of a book, but an assessment of the Hollywood entertainment industry. Prior to the 'George Lopez' show, we had this theory: The entertainment industry so despises Mexicans that you'll rarely, if ever, see one on television or in the movies. You will not see a Mexican on the screen unless in an undignified, subservient and heavily accented or criminal role . . . or unless they are not Mexican or are de-Mexicanized or de-Indianized, or unless they're chasing after a white/Caucasian hero/heroine. . . . Percentage-wise, today, there are fewer Mexican or Hispanic/Latino actors on television than there were in the 'I Love Lucy' (Ricky buffoon Ricardo) generation (3 percent). Keeping in mind that there are now 40 million people from this demographic, this percentage represents a dramatic decrease" (2003).

6. Keller argues that when it was adopted in 1934, the Production Code only formalized Hollywood's longstanding penchant for happy endings and good-versus-evil plot lines: "The code expresses in pontifical and hypocritical fashion the moral value system behind the Hollywood formula, decrying criminal violence and intimate sexuality, upholding the sanctity of marriage and the home and other traditions that had already become heartily compromised in the movies." To prove his point, Keller cites the Code as follows: "Among the specific dos and don'ts of this document were:

   'Illegal drug traffic must never be presented.'

   'Seduction or rape should never be more than suggested.'

   'Miscegenation (sexual relations between the white and black races) is forbidden.'

   'Sex hygiene and venereal diseases are not subjects for motion pictures.'"
   (1994, 115)

7. For an in-depth discussion of this movement see Charles Montgomery's chapter "Regionalism and the Literature of the Soil, 1928–1938" (2002).

8. Enrique Lamadrid notes, "For his revival of *Los Comanches*, Dr. Roberto Vialpando had to recruit actors with superb equestrian skills. When Richard Bradford's novel *Red Sky at Morning* was made into a 1971 Universal movie starring Richard Thomas, the Sánchez brothers, Juan, Leo and Tomás, along with the rest of the Comanches cast, were engaged to stage a traditional *corrida de gallo*, or 'rooster pull,' in one of the scenes" (1992, 242n11).

CHAPTER 6   THE KING TIGER AWAKENS
THE SLEEPING GIANT OF THE SOUTHWEST

1. Reies López Tijerina is singularly responsible for bringing to light the legal implications of the Treaty of Guadalupe-Hidalgo that ended the U.S.-Mexican War of 1846–1848. He reminded all who would listen that international treaties entered into by the United States were, in his words, the "supreme law of the land." In the treaty, Mexico recognized the U.S. claim to Texas and ceded the

land that now makes up parts of New Mexico, Arizona, Colorado, Wyoming, Nevada, and California. The treaty also provided guarantees to protect the land, language, culture, and religion of the former citizens of Mexico who remained in the Southwest after the United States assumed political control of the region. Tijerina's insistence that the federal government needed to abide by and live up to the terms of the Treaty of Guadalupe-Hidalgo is now more fully appreciated. After four years of study by the GAO, the investigative arm of the U.S. Congress only recently validated the treaty as a legal and binding document. In June 2004 the *Albuquerque Journal* reported: "The Federal government on Friday issued a landmark study of New Mexico land grant claims concluding that the Treaty of Guadalupe-Hidalgo—the basis for many of the claims—was implemented legally" (June 5, 2004).

2. For more on the work of "La Academia de la Nueva Raza," see Montiel 2009.

3. In an interview Esparza said of Carmen Zapata: "Well, she's a wonderful actress who has a theater company here in L.A. that she's had for over thirty years called the Bilingual Foundation for the Arts and I had worked with her once before in my thesis film *Cinco Vidas*, she had, Ernestina Evans was the lady that I had profiled there, a Los Angeles version of Agueda but without the land, aside from that they are parallel figures and I had used Carmen to do the voiceover in English for that as well, so then I called Carmen again to do this one."

4. Not only were members of a growing antiwar counterculture drawn to New Mexico for the expressed ways that Nichols cites, but other previously unin-terested sectors of society were finding new reasons to reconsider the region's markers of cultural difference. Alyosha Goldstein has recently exposed the little-studied motives that gave rise to the placement of Peace Corps field training schools in New Mexico in the 1960s. He reveals how the University of New Mexico obtained a major grant from the federal government to site a Peace Corps training center on its campus and to provide participants with field-training experiences in impoverished areas of northern New Mexico. As Goldstein notes, the proposal rested on the logic that the New Mexican con-text provided a close parallel for volunteers being deployed to Latin America: "It was precisely this belief that it was possible to replicate in poor and cultur-ally unfamiliar contexts in the United States the situations and experiences volunteers would encounter abroad that underwrote the logic of Peace Corps field training" (2012, 97). For more on this see "Between the Foreign and Famil-iar" (in Goldstein 2012).

5. Texas-born Richard Bradford, who has been described as a character actor with snow-white hair, is not to be confused with Richard Bradford, the author of *Red Sky at Morning*.

6. Goldstein includes a photo from the University of New Mexico Peace Corps Col-lections showing a volunteer working alongside a northern New Mexico vil-lager. The original caption reads, "Part of the training program by the University of New Mexico consists of community development work. Here a Columbia

trainee helps a farmer near Taos build another room on his house out of adobe brick" (2012, 101). The photo illustrates that encounters between Peace Corps volunteers and members of counterculture movements were commonplace in northern New Mexico in these years.

CHAPTER 7   FILMING BERNALILLO

1. Marez finds that the *partidario* or "shared" system of herding New Mexico's millons of head of sheep always benefited the larger landowner over the village hand or shepherd who had few options once he signed on to do this work. According to Marez, "The resulting form of livestock 'sharecropping' effectively bound shepherds in debt to leasing companies. In 1935, for example, after thirty-five years under a sharecropping contract with the appropriately named 'Bond Company,' Amarante Serna remained in debt and therefore tied to the company" (2004, 117).
2. For a complete look at Jimmy Santiago Baca's early life see Meléndez 1991.

CHAPTER 8   TOWARD A NEW PROXEMICS

1. The title of the Reade documentary is borrowed from Reies López Tijerina's memoir published in Mexico in 1978.
2. For more on La Malinche as icon, see Rosario Castellanos's incisive analysis of Mexican female archetypes in her essay "Once Again, Sor Juana" (in Ahern 1988).
3. For a complete discussion of this concept see Pérez 1999.
4. Some two-thirds of *La Llorona* was filmed on location in Peña Blanca, New Mexico, a village astride the Rio Grande thirty miles south of Santa Fe. For the remaining segments Marc Miles and José García, perhaps intuitively, returned to Las Vegas, New Mexico, the site of early silent films, to shoot the framing story that opens and closes *La Llorona*. The production values of *La Llorona* are clearly those one associates with a nascent community theater group. The producers employed a cast of local, mostly first-time actors, and the film, some forty-five minutes in length, exhibits the limitations of low-budget, self-made projects (makeshift sets and improvised shooting, self-designed wardrobe, uneven acting skills, miscast roles, etc.). Still, the film's uneven filmic quality should not deter students of film from taking a closer look at the project.
5. The original project is more fully described in "Legislation Would Help Finance La Llorona Film," *Albuquerque Journal*, January 28, 2006. Bernadine Santistevan completed the film project in 2007 under the title *The Cry: La Llorona*, her debut as a feature film director. Billed as a supernatural thriller, *The Cry* stages the story of La Llorona in New York City and brings into play terrified, modern-day urban dwellers and police detectives as they work to solve a set of mysterious child drownings in and around Central Park. Santistevan's webpage describes a number of harrowing events that beset the production of *The Cry*. In addition, she lists several well-known infanticides she researched for the film, including the capital murder case of Andrea Yates in Texas for the drowning of her own

children. This mix of the real and the uncanny is summed up in Santistevan's last item on her webpage: "After many years of searching for La Llorona, Bernadine is convinced that she is real" (http://www.laLlorona.com/1legend.html). Santistevan also notes that negotiations are under way to distribute and market the film.

CONCLUSION

1. This last reference is to Walt Disney's *Scandalous John*, filmed in the Silver City area in 1970. Disney officials told the press that the movie was the story of a confused old man who "thinks the Apaches are still on the warpath and who takes matters into his own hands in getting his herd on the trail and to market" ("Moviedom," *Las Cruces-Citizen Sun*, July 5, 1970).

2. In the course of writing this book, several friends and colleagues asked if I was planning to include a section on the cult classic *Easy Rider*. I toyed with the idea and then discarded it, largely because the presence of Chicanos in the film is so minimal and so oblique. But there is a cultural encounter story that connects to the making of this film in Taos, one that revolves around the antics of the film's star, Dennis Hopper, and of his antagonizing of local residents. Hopper had a long-running enmity with taoseños in the years that he resided in Taos after completing the film. The *Albuquerque Journal* reported in July 1970 that his hard feelings culminated in "some kind of fracas with some kids north of Taos." Hopper, the report continues, was released from jail on bond after some taoseños brought charges of assault with a deadly weapon; he had pulled a gun on them in a bar in Arroyo Seco, New Mexico. Jason Silverman writes that Hopper was viewed as an icon and representative of incoming hippies and counterculture generally. "In the early 1970s he found himself at the center of Taos's escalating, sometimes violent tensions, old-timers vs newcomers, free love and drug experimentation versus staunchly traditional Catholic beliefs" (2006, 79).

BIBLIOGRAPHY

INTERVIEWS

Chávez, Gabriel. 2003. Interview with the author. Los Córdovas, New Mexico, January 19.

Durán, Rosa Tijerina. 2000. "Interview of Rosa Tijerina Durán with Dr. José Angel Gutiérrez, July 3, 2000." Center for Southwest Research, University of New Mexico.

Esparza, Moctesuma. 2002. Interview with the author. Glendale, California, February 19.

Krumgold, Joseph. 1971. *Profiles in Literature*, hosted by Jacquelyn Schachter. Temple University, Office of Television Services and the Department of Educational Media, Philadelphia.

Lyon, Danny. 2010. Interview with the author. Bernalillo, New Mexico, January 28.

———. 2010. E-mail correspondence with the author, February 25.

Reade, Federico. 2011. E-mail correspondence with author, July 27.

UNPUBLISHED MATERIALS

"Adventures in Kit Carson Land." N.d. Typescript. New Mexico State Library Southwest Collections, Santa Fe.

"Amado Chaves Letter to Son Win." 1929. Amado Chaves Papers, New Mexico State Records Center and Archives, Santa Fe, October 28.

Campa, Arthur L. N.d. "Back to Barbarism." Typescript. Dorothy Woodward Penitente Materials, New Mexico State Records Center and Archives, Santa Fe.

"The Clod" (release bulletin). 1913. Theater Collection, The Free Library of Philadelphia.

Lummis, Charles Fletcher. 1917. Letter to Amado Chaves. Los Angeles, May 6. Amado Chaves Papers, New Mexico State Records Center and Archives, Santa Fe.

———. N.d. "Personal Diaries and Journals: 1888 and 1889." Lummis Collection, Autry National Center's Southwest Museum of the American Indian, Los Angeles.

———. N.d. "Lummis Journals: 1888–1921." Lummis Collection, Autry National Center's Southwest Museum of the American Indian, Los Angeles.

Meléndez, M. Santos. N.d. Personal papers in possession of the author.

Miles, John E. N.d. Inmate Notebooks. Serial #17163, New Mexico State Records Center and Archives, Santa Fe.

Nichols, John Treadwell. 2000a. "University of New Mexico Honorary Degree Speech." Typescript. Office of the Secretary, University of New Mexico. May 13.

Pearce, Thomas M. 1936. "T. M. Pearce Diary, February 9, 1936." Manuscript. T. M. Pearce Collection, Center for Southwest Research, Zimmerman Library, University of New Mexico, Albuquerque.

"Response to Laurence Lee's Letter of Queries, September 25–27 [no year given]." Amado Chaves Papers, New Mexico State Records Center and Archives, Santa Fe.

St. George Cooke, P. 1970. "Romaine Fielding and the Lubin Motion Picture Company." Newspaper accounts compiled by the New Mexico State Center and Archives, Santa Fe. March.

PUBLISHED MATERIALS

"Actor Dennis Hopper to Get Hearing Soon." 1970. *Albuquerque Tribune,* July 6.

Ahern, Maureen, ed. 1988. *A Rosario Castellanos Reader.* Austin: University of Texas Press.

Bachman, Gregg, and Thomas J. Slatter, eds. 2002. *American Silent Film: Discovering Marginalized Voices.* Carbondale: Southern Illinois University Press.

Baker, Ellen. 2007. *On Strike and On Film: Mexican American Families and Blacklisted Filmmakers in Cold War America.* Chapel Hill: University of North Carolina Press.

Barthes, Roland. 1980. *Camera Lucida: Reflections on Photography.* New York: Hill and Wang.

Bernardi, Daniel. 1996. *The Birth of Whiteness: Race and the Emergence of U.S. Cinema.* New Brunswick, N.J.: Rutgers University Press.

———. 2007. "Traversing Cinematic Borders: An Interview with Paul Espinosa." *Journal of Film and Video* 59, no. 2 (Summer): 41–54.

Biella, Peter. 2001–2002. "The Legacy of John Collier, Jr." *Visual Anthropology Review* 17, no. 2 (Fall-Winter): 50–60.

Bogart, Leo. 1976. *Premises for Propaganda: The United States Information Agency's Operating Assumptions in the Cold War.* New York: Free Press.

"Boy, 15, Faces Death for Murdering Taylor." 1936. *Albuquerque Journal,* February 6, pp. 1, 2.

"Boy Goes to Prison." 1936. *Albuquerque Journal,* February 19, p. 1.

"Boy Tells of Witnessing the Shooting." 1936. *Albuquerque Journal,* February 6, p. 1.

Bradford, Richard. (1968) 1999. *Red Sky at Morning.* New York: HarperCollins.

Burroughs, Chris. 1996. " Researchers Use One Campaign as a Lens to Examine Grassroots Activism in Santa Fe." *Quantum: A Journal of Research Scholarship at the University of New Mexico* 13, no. 1 (Spring): 19–21.

Caldwell, Genoa, ed. 1977. *The Man Who Photographed the World: Burton Holmes Travelogues, 1886–1938.* New York: Harry N. Abrams.

"Carl Taylor Is Mysteriously Slain, Writer Found Shot in Mountain Cabin, Suspect Penitentes." 1936. *Albuquerque Journal,* February 6, pp. 1, 2.

Carroll, Michael. 2002. *The Penitente Brotherhood: Patriarchy and Hispano-Catholicism in New Mexico*. Baltimore: Johns Hopkins University Press.

Collier, John Jr. 1995. "Photography and Visual Anthropology." In *Principles of Visual Anthropology*, edited by Paul Hockings, 235–254. Berlin: Mouton de Gruyter.

Collier, Malcolm. 1993. "John Collier, Jr.: Cultural Diversity and the Camera." In *Treads of Culture*, exhibit catalog, 11–21. Santa Fe: Museum of New Mexico.

Colson, J. B. 1993. "The Art of Human Document: Russell Lee in New Mexico." In *Treads of Culture*, exhibit catalog, 3–9. Santa Fe: Museum of New Mexico.

Cortes, Carlos. 1992. "Who Is María? What Is Juan? Dilemmas of Analyzing the Chicano Image in U.S. Feature Films." In *Chicanos and Film*, edited by Chon Noriega. Minneapolis: University of Minnesota Press.

"Cries in Cell after Sentence, Modesto Trujillo Slayer of Writer, Breaks First Time." 1936. *Albuquerque Journal*, February 18, pp. 1, 2.

"Death Is Penalty for Taking These Pictures of Secret Cult." 1936. *Cleveland News*, February 8, 9.

Eckhardt, Joseph P. 1997. *The King of the Movies: Film Pioneer Siegmund Lubin*. London: Associated University Presses.

Elder, Robert E. 1968. *The Information Machine: The United States Information Agency and American Foreign* Policy. Syracuse: Syracuse University Press.

Espinosa, Paul. 2010. "Transnational Explorations of a Chicano Filmmaker: Views from the U.S.–Mexico Border." *Camino Real, Estudios de Hispanidades Norteamericanas* 1, no. 2: 11–26.

"Feds: 1848 Land Treaty Legal." 2004. *Albuquerque Journal*, June 5, E3.

Flores, Richard R. 2002. *Remembering the Alamo: Memory, Modernity, and Master Symbol*. Austin: University of Texas Press.

Forrest, Suzanne. 1989. *The Preservation of the Village: New Mexico's Hispanics and the New Deal*. Albuquerque: University of New Mexico Press.

Fregoso, Rosa Linda. 1993. *The Bronze Screen: Chicano and Chicana Film Culture*. Minneapolis: University of Minnesota Press.

———. 1999. "Recycling Colonialist Fantasies on the Texas Borderlands." In *Home, Exile, Homeland, Film, Media, and the Politics of Place*, edited by Hamid Nacify, 169–192. New York: Routledge.

———. 2003. *MeXicana Encounters: The Making of Social Identities on the Borderlands*. Berkeley: University of California Press.

García Berumen, Frank J. 1995. *Chicano/Hispanic Image in American Film*. New York: Vantage Press.

Goldstein, Alyosha. 2012. *Poverty in Common: The Politics of Community Action during the American Century*. Durham, N.C.: Duke University Press.

Grimshaw, Anna. 2001. *The Ethnographer's Eye: Ways of Seeing in Modern Anthropology*. Cambridge: Cambridge University Press.

Guerrero, Dan. 1988. "The Milagro Beanfield War." *Vista* 3, no. 7 (March 6): 14–18.

Hanson, Patricia King, and Alan Gevinson, eds. 1998. *The American Film Institute Catalog of Motion Pictures Produced in the United States, 1911–1920*. Berkeley: University of California Press.

Holmes, Burton. 1953. *The World Is Mine.* Culver City, Calif.: Murray and Gee.

Horak, Jan-Christopher. 1997. *Making Images Move: Photographers and Avant-Garde Cinema.* Washington, D.C.: Smithsonian Institute Press.

Keller, Gary. 1994. *Hispanics and United States Film.* Tempe, Ariz.: Bilingual Review Press.

Kibbe, Delia, E. 1924. *Burton Holmes Travel Stories: Egypt, Teaching Suggestions.* Chicago: Wheeler Publishing.

Krupat, Arnold. 1992. *Ethnocriticism.* Berkeley: University of California Press.

Lamadrid, Enrique. 1992. "Ig/noble Savages of New Mexico: The Naturalization of 'El Norte' into the Great Southwest." SHRI Working Paper #121. Albuquerque: University of New Mexico.

Limón, José. 1994. *Dancing with the Devil: Society and Cultural Poetics in Mexican American South Texas.* Madison: University of Wisconsin Press.

———. 1998. *American Encounters: Greater Mexico, the United States, and the Erotics of Culture.* New York: Beacon Press.

López-Pulido, Alberto. 2000. *The Sacred World of the Penitentes.* Washington, D.C.: Smithsonian Institute Press.

Lorence, James J. 1999. *The Suppression of Salt of the Earth: How Hollywood, Big Labor, and Politicians Blacklisted a Movie in Cold War America.* Albuquerque: University of New Mexico Press.

Lummis, Charles F. 1889. "The Penitente Brothers." *Cosmopolitan: An Illustrated Monthly Magazine* 7, no. 1 (May): 41–51.

———. (1893) 1952. *The Land of Poco Tiempo.* Albuquerque: University of New Mexico Press.

Lyon, Danny. 1999. *Knave of Hearts.* Santa Fe: Twin Palms Publishers.

———. 2007. *Like a Thief's Dream.* Brooklyn: Powerhouse Books.

MacDougall, David. 1995. "Beyond Observational Cinema." In *Principles of Visual Anthropology,* edited by Paul Hockings, 116–131. Berlin: Mouton de Gruyter.

Marez, Curtis. 2004. *Drug Wars: The Political Economy of Narcotics.* Minneapolis: University of Minnesota Press.

Martínez, Frank. D. 1991. "Barelas y Los Padillas: Preserving Oral History." *Quantum: A Journal of Research Scholarship at the University of New Mexico* 7, no. 2 (Fall): 8–11.

Meléndez, A. Gabriel. 1991. "Carrying the Magic of His Peoples' Heart: An Interview with Jimmy Santiago Baca." *America's Review* 19: 64–86.

Moneta, Daniela P., ed. 1985. *Charles F. Lummis, The Centennial Exhibition.* Los Angeles: Southwest Museum.

Montejano, David. 1987. *Anglos and Mexicans in the Making of Texas, 1836–1996.* Austin: University of Texas Press.

Montgomery, Charles. 2002. *The Spanish Redemption: Heritage, Power and Loss on New Mexico's Upper Rio Grande.* Berkeley: University of California Press.

Montiel, Miguel, et al. 2009. *Resolana: Emerging Chicano Dialogues on Community and Globalization.* Tucson: University of Arizona Press.

"Moviedom Moves in on New Mexico." 1970. *Las Cruces Citizen-Sun,* July 5.

"The NBC Program." 1969. *El Grito del Norte* (Española, New Mexico), May 19.

Nericcio, William Anthony. 1992. "Of Mestizos and Half-Breeds: Orson Welles' *Touch of Evil*." In *Chicanos and Film: Representations and Resistance*, edited by Chon Noriega, 47–58. Minneapolis: University of Minnesota Press.

"N.M. Crew Films Hispanic Legend." 1991. *Albuquerque Journal*, August 18.

Nichols, John Treadwell. 1971. "Reies Lopez Tijerina: A Man Like the Northern Weather." *New Mexico Review and Legislative Journal* 3, no. 11 (November): 12–13.

———. 1974. *The Milagro Beanfield War*. New York: Ballantine Books.

———. 2000b. "Night of the Living Beanfield: How an Unsuccessful Cult Novel Became an Unsuccessful Cult Film in Only Fourteen Years, Eleven Nervous Breakdowns, and $20 Million." In *Dancing on Stone: Selected Essays*, 133–153. Albuquerque: University of New Mexico Press.

———. 2000c. *Armageddon and New Mexico: Writing for Fun and Profit in the Poorest State in the Nation*. Santa Fe: Rydal Press.

Noriega, Chon. 1992. *Chicanos and Film: Representations and Resistance*. Minneapolis: University of Minnesota Press.

———. 2000. *Shot in America: Television, the State, and the Rise of Chicano Cinema*. Minneapolis: University of Minnesota Press.

"100 Years of Filmmaking in New Mexico, 1898–1998." 1998. *New Mexico Magazine*. Santa Fe: New Mexico Department of Tourism and New Mexico Film Office.

"The Penitentes" (film review). 1915. *Variety*, December 3, p. 21.

"Penitentes' Vengeance for Exposé Blamed in Taylor's Death." 1936. *Los Angeles Examiner*, February 8, pp. 1, 3.

"'Penitent' Americans Torture Themselves: The Murder of a Writer Who Was Spying on Them Brings to Public Attention the Activities of New Mexico's Tribes." 1936. *Cleveland Plain Dealer* (magazine section), March 15, p. 1.

Penn, Michael. 2002. "Con Nombre." *On Wisconsin* 103, no. 2 (Summer): 20–27 and 54.

Pérez, Emma. 1999. *The Decolonial Imaginary: Writing Chicanas into History*. Bloomington: Indiana University Press.

Pettit, Arthur. 1980. *Image of the Mexican American in Film and Fiction*. College Station: Texas A&M University Press.

Raines, Lester. 1935. *More New Mexico Artists and Writers*. Las Vegas, N.M.: Department of English and Speech, New Mexico Normal University.

Ramírez Berg, Charles. 2002. *Latino Images in Film: Stereotypes, Subversion, Resistance*. Austin: University of Texas Press.

Rivera, José A. 1998. *Acequia Culture: Water, Land, and Community in the Southwest*. Albuquerque: University of New Mexico Press.

Rodriguez, Roberto, and Patricia Gonzales. 2003. "Any Thing but Brown." *The Americas*, November 28.

Rodríguez, Sylvia. 1989. "Art, Tourism, and Race Relations in Taos: Toward a Sociology of the Art Colony." *Journal of Anthropological Research* 45 (Spring): 77–99.

Rony, Fatimah Tobing. 1996. *The Third Eye: Race, Cinema, and Ethnographic Spectacle*. Durham, N.C.: Duke University Press.

Rosenfelt, Deborah, and Michael Wilson. 1972. *Salt of the Earth*. Old Westbury, N.Y.: Feminist Press.

Ruby, Jay. 1991. "Speaking for, Speaking about, Speaking with or Speaking along-side—An Anthropological and Documentary Dilemma." *Visual Anthropology Review* 7, no. 2 (Fall): 50–67.

Sánchez, George I. (1940) 1996. *Forgotten People: A Study of New Mexicans*. Albuquerque: University of New Mexico.

Scacheri, Mabel DelaMater. 1936. "The Penitentes, Murderous or Misguided?" *Family Circle*, March 20, pp. 14–16.

Silverman, Jason. 2006. *Untold New Mexico: Stories from a Hidden Past*. Santa Fe: Sunstone Press, 2006.

Sorenson, Richard E., and Allison Jablonko. 1995. "Research Filming of Naturally Occurring Phenomena: Basic Strategies." In *Principles of Visual Anthropology*, edited by Paul Hockings, 151–163. Berlin: Mouton de Gruyter.

Sothern, Robert. 1936. "The Strange Murder in the Penitente Hills." *Famous Detective Cases*, July, pp. 34–39, 65–66.

Steele, Thomas J., and Rowena A. Rivera. 1985. *Penitente Self Government: Brotherhoods and Councils, 1797–1947*. Santa Fe: Ancient City Press.

Strain, Ellen. 1996. "Exotic Bodies, Distant Landscapes: Touristic Viewing and Popularized Anthropology in the Nineteenth Century." *Wide Angle* 18, no. 2 (April): 70–100.

Taylor, Carl N. 1936a. *Odyssey of the Islands*. New York: Charles Scribner's Sons.

———. 1936b. "Agony in New Mexico." *Today*, February 15, pp. 2–4, 20–21.

"Taylor Manuscript, 'Agony in New Mexico,' Described Ceremonies of the Penitentes." 1936. *Albuquerque Journal*, February 7, p. 2.

Thompson, Mark. 2001. *American Character: The Curious Life of Charles Fletcher Lummis and the Rediscovery of the Southwest*. New York: Arcade Publishing.

Threads of Culture: Photography in New Mexico, 1939–1943. 1993. Exhibit catalog for the Pinewood Collection of FSA Photography. Santa Fe: Museum of Fine Arts.

Tijerina, Reies López. 2000. *They Call Me "King Tiger": My Struggle for the Land and Our Rights*. Translated and edited by José Angel Gutiérrez. Houston: Arte Público Press.

"Trujillo to Face Juvenile Court Today." 1936. *Santa Fe New Mexican*, February 7, pp. 1, 2.

Turner, Graeme. 1988. *Film as Social Practice*. New York: Routledge.

Vélez-Ibañez, Carlos. 1997. *Border Visions: Mexican Cultures of the Southwestern United States*. Tucson: University of Arizona Press.

Villanueva, Tino. 1993. *Scene from the Movie Giant*. East Haven, Conn.: Curbstone Press.

Wallace, Irving. 1977. "Everybody's Rover Boy." In *The Man Who Photographed the World: Burton Holmes Travelogues, 1886–1938*, edited by Genoa Caldwell, 11–26. New York: Harry N. Abrams.

"The 'War' against Ken Burns/PBS' 'The War' Is Not Over: Why the Latino Community Can't Let This Matter Rest." 2007. PR Newswire, August 20. www.prnewswire.com/news-releases/the-war-against-ken-burnspbs-the-war-is-not-over-58309882.html.

Weigle, Marta. 1971. "Los Hermanos Penitentes: Historical and Ritual Aspects of Folk Religion." Ph.D. diss., University of Pennsylvania.

———. 1976. *Brothers of Light, Brothers of Blood: The Penitentes of the Southwest.* Albuquerque: University of New Mexico Press.

———. 1982. *Santa Fe and Taos: The Writers' Era.* Santa Fe: Ancient City Press.

Woal, Linda Kowall. 1995. "Romaine Fielding: The West's Touring Auteur." *Film History* 7, no. 4: 401–425.

Woal, Linda Kowall, and Michael Woal. 1995. "The Golden God: Romaine Fielding's Allegorical Realism." *Journal of Popular Film and Television* 23, no. 1: 28–35.

———. 1995. "Romaine Fielding's Real Westerns." *Journal of Film and Video* 47, nos. 1–3 (Spring-Fall): 7–25.

Wroth, William, ed. 1985. *Russell Lee's FSA Photographs of Chamisal and Peñasco, New Mexico.* Santa Fe: Ancient City Press.

Young, Colin. 1995. "Observational Cinema." In *Principles of Visual Anthropology,* edited by Paul Hockings, 99–113. Berlin: Mouton de Gruyter.

"Youth Admits Slaying Carl Taylor, Trujillo Relates Gruesome Details; Robbery Is Motive." 1936. *Santa Fe New Mexican,* February 6, pp. 1, 2.

"Youth Confesses Killing, Absolving 'Torture' Cult." 1936. *New Haven Evening Register,* February 6, pp. 1, 2.

FILMOGRAPHY

Adventures in Kit Carson Land. 1917. El Toro Film Company. New Mexico State Library Collection.

Agueda Martínez. 1978. Directed by Esperanza Vasquez. Produced by Moctezuma Esparza.

And Now, Miguel. 1953. Directed by Joseph Krumgold. United States Information Service, Washington, D.C.

Chicano: History of the Mexican American Civil Rights Movement. Volume 1, "Quest for a Homeland." 1996. Series Producer, Héctor Galán. Produced by Sylvia Morales, Susan Racho, Myléne Moreno, and Robert Cozens.

Colors of Courage: Sons of New Mexico, Prisoners of Japan. 2002. Center for Regional Studies, University of New Mexico.

El Senador. 2001. Written and produced by Paige Martínez. Center for Regional Studies, University of New Mexico.

La Llorona: A New Mexico Legend. 1991. Marc Miles Group, Santa Fe.

The Lash of the Penitentes. 1936. Directed by Mark J. Levinson (abridged version). Hollywood Attic, Burbank, Calif.

The Lemon Grove Incident. 1986. Written and produced by Paul Espinosa. Espinosa Productions.

Little Boy. 1978. Directed and produced by Danny Lyon. Bleak Beauty Films.

Llanito. 1972. Directed and produced by Danny Lyon. Bleak Beauty Films.

Los Mineros. 1991. Written and produced by Paul Espinosa. Espinosa Productions.

Luisa Torres. 1981. Directed by Michael Earney. Cinematography by Jack Parsons. Anthropology Center.

The Milagro Beanfield War. 1988. Directed by Robert Redford. Produced by Moctezuma Esparza. Universal Studios.

Murderers. 2002. Directed and produced by Danny Lyon. Bleak Beauty Films.

The Penitent. 1989. Written and directed by Cliff Osmond. Produced by Michael Fitzgerald. International Video Entertainment.

The Rattlesnake, A Psychical Species. 1913. Directed by Romaine Fielding. Lubin Film Company. New Mexico State Library Collection.

Red Sky at Morning. 1971. Directed by James Goldstone. Produced by Hal Wallis. Universal-MCA Pictures.

Reies Tijerina: The Most Hated Man in New Mexico. 1969. NBC *First Tuesday White Paper,* NBC.

Salt of the Earth. 1954. Directed by Herbert Biberman. Written by Michael Wilson. Produced by Paul Jarrico. Independent Production Company.

This Town Is Not for Sale: The 1994 Mayoral Election. 1997. Senior Producer, Silvia Rodrí- guez, Center for Regional Studies, University of New Mexico.

Tierra o Muerte. 1992. Produced by Carolyn Hayes. KBDI (PBS), Denver.

Tijerina. 1969. Produced by Moctezuma Esparza. Department of Chicano Studies, UCLA.

The Trail North. 1983. Produced and written by Paul Espinosa. Espinosa Productions.

Una Lucha Por Mi Pueblo. 1993. Directed and produced by Federico Reade. KNME, *De Colores Series.*

The U.S. Mexican War: 1846–1848. 1998. Series Producer, Paul Espinosa. Espinosa Productions.

Willie. 1983. Directed and produced by Danny Lyon. Bleak Beauty Films.

INDEX

ABOUT THE AUTHOR

A. GABRIEL MELÉNDEZ is a professor of American Studies at the University of New Mexico and was the department chair from 1999 to 2008 and again from 2010 to 2013. Meléndez's teaching and research interests include Borderlands cinema and critical regionalism. He has authored a number of books and scholarly articles on Mexican Americans and Borderlands expressive culture. *Hidden Chicano Cinema* combines his interest in film studies, Chicano culture, Borderlands history, and critical regionalism regarding the Southwest.

CPSIA information can be obtained at www.ICGtesting.com
Printed in the USA
BVOW070504080713

325054BV00002B/2/P

9 780813 561066